D0931370

K. ZELINSKY

SOVIET LITERATURE.

PROBLEMS AND PEOPLE

PROGRESS PUBLISHERS
MOSCOW

Translated from the Russian by *Olga Shartse*
Edited by **Bryan Bean**
Designed by V. Ilyushchenko

К. ЗЕЛИНСКИЙ

СОВЕТСКАЯ ЛИТЕРАТУРА.
ПРОБЛЕМЫ И ЛЮДИ

На английском языке

First printing 1970

Printed in the Union of Soviet Socialist Republics

CONTENTS

AUTHOR'S PREFACE

In this book I have tried to present Soviet literature to the reader in its three main aspects. First, the stages of its development, and the general laws and factors governing this development. Second, the problems posed by the development of Soviet literature. For instance, the problem of inherited traditions and their influence on Soviet literature; the problem of socialist realism, and partisanship in literature; the role of the Communist Party in the development of Soviet literature; and problems of content, form and method. Third, the outstanding personalities in Soviet literature. As I go along I shall also examine those books which for one reason or another had aroused the interest of critics and stirred public opinion.

This book is not a history of Soviet literature in the true sense of the word, nor did I make it my aim to set out the material systematically, the way it is done in text-books or historical reviews of an academic nature. Nevertheless, I did try to give a sufficiently comprehensive account of modern Soviet literature and its historical background from its genesis to the present time.

Two reasons prompted me to make a survey of Soviet literature intended not just for specialists but for the general reader. The first is a personal reason. As a literary scholar and critic, I grew up together with Soviet literature. My youth coincided with the first years of the Soviet state. On graduating from the philosophical section of the department of history and philology at Moscow University in the spring of 1918, I plunged straight into public activity, and throughout most of the Civil War and foreign intervention, I worked as a war correspondent, travelling all over the country. When I finally returned to Moscow in 1922, I devoted myself wholly to literature. I wrote for the first literary magazines to come out after the Revolution, took part in the first literary battles, joined the constructivist group, attended all the congresses of Soviet writers as a delegate, and so on and so forth.

I saw and heard Mayakovsky, Yesenin, Selvinsky, Fedin, Paustovsky, Leonov, Ehrenburg, Fadeyev, Alexei Tolstoi, Serafimovich, Ostrovsky, Makarenko, Pasternak and many other writers, who were either my literary colleagues or opponents. I was one of the

5

first readers of their first works about people of the revolutionary Soviet epoch. It was not only from their books that I formed my impressions of most of these Soviet writers. I also knew them personally, meeting them at conferences and in editorial offices.

I have pondered over my own past and that of my literary friends. I feel that anyone who has lived for almost fifty years in the thick of revolutionary events, anyone who has not merely witnessed but taken part in the social reconstruction of Russia, has a right to cast a retrospective glance over the road he himself and his literary contemporaries have travelled in the light of history. To look at oneself from outside, so to speak. And that is what I have attempted to do in my book.

When the Socialist Revolution took place in October 1917, Marxism meant little to me. By virtue of my upbringing and education I was far removed from politics and took no part in the revolutionary struggle. But after the Revolution, everyone in our country, each in his own way, began to join the struggle for the new life. The same thing happened in literature. We were parting with old illusions and assimilating new ideas and views. It did not come easily. But I am not going to dwell on my personal emotions here. They are beside the point. The theme of this book is the ideological course of Soviet literature.

I cannot say that acceptance of the new truths came easily, without any inner struggle at all, to someone like me who in the 1920s belonged to the literary group of the constructivists. But once I had understood these new truths, I became a convert of socialist realism, and have been one ever since the early 1930s. And for some time now I have felt an urge to sum up my own experience and, as far as I am able, that of Soviet literature as a whole, in which I have been working now for close on fifty years.

I am afraid I have not been able to avoid a subjective approach to my literary colleagues and their works. But then, a literary critic reserves the right to give his own evaluation of writers and writings.

So, the first reason which prompted me to write this book was the desire to sum up my recollections and impressions of Soviet literature which has constituted the essence of my life.

My second reason is a polemical one. I felt the urge to write this book after reading some of those works on Soviet literature published in the West, mainly in the United States, then in England, and to a lesser extent in France and Italy. Most of them came out at a time when many were blinded by the whitish neon glare of the cold war.

In one American book about Soviet literature, entitled *The Cult of Optimism*, published in 1963 by the University of Indiana Press, I came upon a very sensible line of reasoning. The author writes that people in the West love to play a sort of intellectual parlour game where the idea is to search Soviet literature for all kinds of "evils and vices" in the "Soviet system". They use the word "system" as if they were speaking of a rare make of car. But these people, the author goes on to say, are forgetting that the shortcomings and vices exposed by Soviet writers are by no means a monopoly of Soviet society, and it is therefore absurd to state, as some anti-Soviet Western authors do, that the capitalist way of life is superior in every way to the Soviet.

It is true that people in the West, who feel hostile to the Soviet Union, read our writers from a peculiar angle, hunting for facts, characters and situations that might cast aspersions on the U.S.S.R. But indulging in this pastime is no better proof of the players' intellectual powers than doing the crossword in the Sunday paper.

There are also authors who strive to denigrate Soviet literature in a different way. They "pity" the Soviet writers because, they say, they are forced to balance on a tight rope, like circus acrobats. A Soviet writer must not show reality in a rosy light, nor dare he paint it black. He must not gloss over the difficulties, nor can he brood too much on the gloomy sides of life. At one time, he was obliged to sing praises to Stalin, and although he has now been relieved of this duty, he still feels constrained to sound optimistic whatever the circumstances.

I am not going to set about refuting this nonsense, nor am I going to enumerate the other incongruities and mistakes in all those tendentious books about Soviet literature published in the West. By and large, I have no intention of devoting this book to the refutation of all sorts of mistakes and misconstructions, for this would only involve me in an endless examination of particular instances.

My book is devoted to something else—to reflections on Soviet literature based on my personal experience and the experience of my fellow writers. I should like my book to guide the reader to that main source which gives Soviet literature its inner power, and to explain why it is that Soviet writers have no wish to denigrate the life they describe, and why this life needs no embellishing. I also want to give an answer to the question why we really are so full of optimism, why we have such faith in our future, and why we believe in the cause served by the whole country with such enormous dedication. Why indeed? Does it never occur to those people who feel hostile to the Soviet Union that writers like Mayakovsky, Alexei Tolstoi and Sholokhov are hardly the sort of men who would think and write only as the Party leadership ordered them, as second fiddles obeying the wave of the conductor's baton? Let us take a closer look at Soviet writers and try to understand their books, bearing in mind the ideological and artistic aims they themselves had chosen to pursue. Let us try to understand what they have tried to tell the world, and how they have gone about it. These are the questions I set out to answer in my book.

The main subject of this book is Soviet Russian literature. I regret to have been unable to give a wider and more detailed account of the other Soviet national literatures. After all, the multinational character of Soviet literature is certainly one of its main features. It is a law of socialism that the national cultures and literatures of all the peoples inhabiting the country should come to flourish. Even of those peoples who fell badly behind in their historical development and were cruelly oppressed by tsarist colonialism. Even of those who had only a rudimentary written language or none at all.

Soviet multinational literature makes an extremely interesting object of study. One will find in it all the known kinds and genres of writing. From the simplest to the most modern forms. From the unpretentious little song or the recitative of a folk bard—like the Armenian and Azerbaijan *ashug,* or the Kazakh and Kirghiz *akyn*—to the sophisticated and complex socio-psychological novel. All this lives thrives and interacts because the Revolution rallied to the task of creating a socialist culture involving not only the large and culturally developed nations, who had already gone through the stage of industrial capitalism, but also the small national groups and tribes living in the deserts of Central Asia and in the Far Eastern taiga.

I felt it would be impossible to embrace all this in one small book. But I do realise that by keeping to Russian literature alone, I am narrowing down my field of vision and failing to do full justice to all the aspects of Soviet literature.

Nevertheless, the concluding chapters of this book are wholly devoted to the theoretical side of this question which, I am convinced, is of tremendous importance to many nations in the world. Especially in this age of national liberation struggle and the consequent establishment of new independent states in Africa, Asia and America.

The young writers of many of the newly independent states are confronted by problems of fundamental importance: the ideological aims of young literatures, political freedom, artistic means and forms, the role of national tradition, identification with the people, and many others. The experience of Soviet Russian literature, which is one of the most prominent literatures in the world, may be found useful and, I sincerely hope, of interest to the reading public in general.

Moscow, 1970

Chapter 1
The Revolution and Literature

What exactly do we mean when we speak of the literature of a particular country or people?

As a rule we mean two things: all the works of literature produced by the country or people in question, and—more frequently—the literary life, the discussions important new books trigger off, and the conditions in which literature develops there.

Multinational Soviet literature is too vast a subject for one man to review. In the more than fifty years since the Revolution of 1917, Soviet authors, Russian and non-Russian, have written an enormous number of books. Fiction is published in more than seventy languages spoken in the U.S.S.R., and over a million titles have come out to date.

In order to study and critically evaluate the literary merits of this profusion of books, special institutes have been set up in Moscow, Leningrad and twenty-odd towns in the non-Russian republics and regions. Our literature is also studied in many institutions abroad (though not always with equally good intentions). In the U.S.A., for instance, there are two institutes engaged in the study of Soviet and, mainly, Russian Soviet literature. Libraries in all the large cities of the world devote whole sections in their catalogues to translations of Soviet literature.

A profound study of numerous books made over the course of years is not how the ordinary reader usually forms his opinion of a national literature. More often than not his judgements are based on the impressions he gains from reading its most outstanding authors. Maxim Gorky used to say that Lev Tolstoi was in himself a whole world, and that to know Russia one had to read Tolstoi. Readers today also tend to judge Soviet literature—and quite rightly—from the works of such outstanding and strikingly individual authors as Mayakovsky, Alexei Tolstoi, Sholokhov, Fadeyev, Fedin and Leonov. And this is only natural. For literature is not statistics. As in all other forms of art, it is talent and not numbers that counts.

Readers are also influenced in their judgements by literary critics whose articles provide a survey of a country's literature and, more especially, an analysis of the various schools of thought, the individual writers' artistic methods, and their aesthetic quests.

In speaking of Soviet Russian literature I shall do both: I shall make a general critical survey and describe the most representative writers.

Every national literature has its own distinctive character according to the range of ideas and images it embraces and the artistic method it has adopted for its own. Literature mirrors the life of a country, its creeds and customs, the character of the people and their ideals and aspirations. Just as we can speak of a people's national character, so we can speak of a literature having its own distinctive character, in the sense that the works of different authors share certain features.

Soviet literature was born of the Socialist Revolution of 1917, and its roots are in the victory of the workers and peasants and the victory of Lenin's ideas about the building of a communist society. The Revolution gave it voice, ideas, images and songs, and therefore if we are to begin to appreciate Soviet literature, we must first understand just what the October Revolution did for the development of Russian and, for that matter, of world progressive literature in general. In the first place, this means understanding the ideas of the Revolution: and not just the ideas alone, but the process by which the new society was established as well.

The entire history of Soviet society has found its reflection in Soviet literature: the overthrow of the bourgeois government by the workers and peasants in 1917, the Civil War and the defeat of the foreign intervention, the creation of new industry and agriculture under the first five-year plans, the Great Patriotic War against nazi Germany, and post-war construction. Literature has reflected the life of all strata of society, the life of the Party, the Armed Forces, and the Komsomol. Last but not least, it has reflected that which most of all promoted its development—the establishment and consolidation of the new state, and the guidance and influence of the Party and Government.

Alexander Fadeyev, addressing an audience of scholars, writers and students in Paris in 1949, said: "How did Soviet literature begin? It was started by people like us. When, after the Civil War, we began to converge from all over our vast country—young Party members, and even more non-Party people—we were amazed to find how similar our life stories were, although each one of us had travelled his individual road. It was so with Furmanov, the author of *Chapayev*, the screen version of which was even more famous than the book. It was so with Mikhail Sholokhov, the youngest and probably the most gifted among us. And it was so with Nikolai Ostrovsky, whose life was nothing short of heroism. Blind and totally paralysed as a result of the wounds he had received in the war, he wrote an immortal book about our generation–How the Steel Was Tempered. We came into literature wave upon wave, there were many of us then. Each brought with him his own personal experience, his own individuality. We were united by a sense of belonging to the new world and by our love for it."

The generation preceding Fadeyev's, brilliantly represented by Alexei Tolstoi, and the next, war-time generation which produced Konstantin Simonov and Alexander Tvardovsky, and the post-war one, and the younger writers like Yevgeny Yevtushenko and Vasily Aksyonov who entered the literary scene in the 1950s, and the writers who have appeared just recently–all of them, each new wave added its own new experience to Soviet literature. Personal experience–ideological and artistic–was derived from the historical experience of the whole people fighting for communism. Because the internal life of the country–what with the class struggle, the consolidation of the state, the economic development and social reorganisation–was so dynamic and wrought such a change in the mentality of the people, Soviet writers were faced with philosophical tasks of the first magnitude. It can be said without exaggeration that Russian literature had never had to face anything like the demands of those first decades following the Revolution. The Soviet epoch is one of the most exciting in world history for the scale and drama of its events in which passions ran so high. The power of renovation had probably never been so all-enveloping. Literature's judge and guide at the decisive revolutionary turning-point was the Leninist Party and Marxist-Leninist ideology.

Not all the Russian writers were able to keep their balance at this sharp turning-point in history. Some refused to accept the Revolution and emigrated (physically or emotionally). Others bore up and manfully faced the storms of the new times. Not all found it easy to readjust themselves either ideologically or aesthetically. They had to overcome delusions and mistakes. But perhaps never before did life hold such an irresistible attraction for literature as it did at this "sharpest of sharp turning-points in history" (Lenin).

In everything that the Communist Party of the Soviet Union says today about literature and the arts we recognise a further development of those ideas which Lenin expounded at the time of the Revolution. Our revolutionary yesterday and communist today are linked by the same Party line, which is the guiding principle in all our undertakings and achievements.

Owing to the revolutionary development of the country and by force of circumstances, Soviet literature was obliged to embark on a road of constant and indefatigable search. History imposed on it the task of telling the world "with its yet childish lips" (Fadeyev) about events, people and plans of a magnitude unknown in old Russian literature, for all the greatness of its classics. Soviet writers were called upon to express the new communist truth of the 20th century, the Atomic Age, the age of communism. I recall Gorky's words pronounced long before the Revolution. They were aimed against art that was shallow or too individualistic, against circumscribed truths that disunited men: "People become wholly absorbed in the truth of the day, and they cannot see the great truth which is crystallised from the blood and brain of living men and is immortal!"

I should say that Soviet literature as a whole is characterised by a struggle to break free of the cramping confines of the circumscribed truth of the day and express the great truth of our age by presenting real, living people who have grasped this truth and are heroically building a new world.

Such is the essence of Soviet literature. Its new ideological content is a result of the new revolutionary essence of life itself, for all its contradictions, difficulties and negative sides. But while the literature of socialist realism is called upon to detect and generalise in artistic images all that is new in the creative endeavour of the people building communism, this does not at all mean that Soviet literature is renouncing its national heritage. Just as the Russian people in building communism today draw on progressive national traditions and display such traits of the national character as Russian revolutionary enthusiasm, so does Soviet literature follow the progressive traditions of Russian realism which gave us the great 19th-century novels, and the traditions of universal humanism inherited from Tolstoi, Dostoyevsky, Pushkin and Chekhov.

Chapter 2

Problems of Inherited Traditions

Russian classical literature was formed mainly in the 19th century, in other words under the tsars. What ideas fed it, and whence did it draw its remarkable strength and humanism?

No one would dispute the tremendous contribution of Tolstoi and Dostoyevsky to world culture. Wherein does their greatness lie? The answer to this question must be sought in the particularities of Russian history.

It is, of course, wrong to think that any one nation, endowed with élite biological qualities, is capable of producing geniuses from its midst, while other nations of "inferior" blood (the nazis in Germany pointed to the Jews in particular, and the reactionaries in the U.S.A. to the Negroes) are incapable of higher spiritual activity. No one would deny that different national characters do exist. Only the difference between them is not biological; it is conditioned by their history, geography and climate, and, especially, by social struggle and the development of the productive forces.

For centuries Russian history seemed to hold out a sort of challenge to every Russian and to the nation as a whole. Russian history always mobilised the population of the vast Russian land and demanded the utmost effort from the people. Chaadayev, a friend of Pushkin and Herzen, once wrote that Russia, unlike the vale of Kashmir, was constantly hardening and not softening man.

If I dwell on this question for a while, it is because I believe it to be of help in understanding the Soviet period.

What gave the Russians strength on the one hand, and caused Russia's economic backwardness on the other?

In his book *History of Russia* (1863-1864), the famous Russian historian S. M. Solovyov gave a general outline of the course of ancient Russian history, and in the chapter entitled "Russia Before the Age of Great Reforms" spoke as follows of the difference between Western and Eastern Europe:

"Looking at the map of Europe we are amazed first of all by the dissimilarity of its two uneven halves—the western and the eastern. Geographically and climatically, Europe has the advantage over other parts of the world, and these beneficial conditions are given as the reason for the brilliant development of the European nations and their domination of other peoples. When speaking of these beneficial conditions, however, one must have only Western Europe in mind, for Eastern Europe has not been endowed with them. Nature has been a loving mother to Western Europe, and a mean stepmother to the nations fated to live in Eastern Europe. Thus we observe European civilisation gradually spreading from the West to the East as decreed by Nature, since it was in the West that the most favourable conditions for its early successes were created, growing less and less favourable as one moved East. In this connection, it is interesting to note the limits of the invasion of the wild Asiatic hordes in Europe, the point where it was stopped. . . . How many centuries separated Attila's defeat at Chalons and Catherine the Great's conquest of the Crimea which was finally to put an end to Asiatic domination on European soil! Think of the advantage, measured in centuries, which history gave Western Europe over Eastern Europe!"

I have quoted this long paragraph from a mid-19th-century Russian historian in order to show that Russia had long been aware of the need to catch up with the capitalist states in science and culture—a task which the Soviet Union is successfully tackling today. These words of Solovyov are also repeated, without mention of his name, in Pierre Paté's book *Phénomène soviétique*. The author points out how the inequality of Western and Eastern Europe's potential was fully appreciated by Russian statesmen several centuries ago. After the overthrow of the Tatar yoke, which lasted for more than two centuries and was the main reason why Russia fell behind Western Europe in her development, two of Russia's tsars made Herculean efforts to give Russian history a great thrust forward. The first was Ivan the Terrible who united the Russian state and extended its boundaries, and the second was Peter the Great who, to use the words of Lenin, attempted to put an end to Russian barbarity by barbarous means. But it took another two centuries, the book goes on to say, for historical conditions to ripen to the point at which Lenin, backed by Russia's progressive working class, tackled anew the problem of overcoming Russia's backwardness by introducing a socialist system of planning and socialist principles of labour organisation.

There are two points I want to make quite clear here. The first is that both Sergei Solovyov in his view of Russia's historical development and those historians and publicists in the West who (like Pierre Paté) a hundred years later, turn to the same view again, completely overlook the main factor—the development of production and the class struggle. In this respect the same laws of development apply to East and West. But the "East is East, and West is West" idea is the favourite argument of bourgeois historians, and it is on this aphorism that Hans Kohn, author of *Basic History of Modern Russia. Political, Cultural and Social Trends*, bases his "scientific" reasoning. Actually, neither the climatic and geographical contrasts nor even the tragedy of being dominated by the Tatars for more than two centuries, set Russia outside the general laws governing the world's cultural development. These laws, which were discovered and elaborated by Karl Marx, apply to all nations and historical formations without exception.

The second point concerns national and historical traditions and their role in shaping national character. This is also frequently misinterpreted in the West (by the same Hans Kohn, for one), and we find the following line of reasoning. Say what you will, but you Russians, even in your new shell, are exactly like you were a hundred years ago. No revolution can break the hold of the past. In saying this they sometimes refer to Marx's famous work *The Eighteenth Brumaire of Louis Bonaparte* in which he says: "The tradition of all the dead generations weighs like a nightmare on the brain of the living."[1] But Marx was referring to bourgeois revolutions. Of the proletarian revolution he said that in order to arrive at its own content it "must let the dead bury their dead".[2] This content is the building of a new society where there will be no exploitation of man by man and where production forces will develop to the full.

It is rather amusing to find Western apologists of capitalism and critics of Soviet Russia's new, socialist system going so far as to call in the ghost of Guizot and say: "You may fly to the stars in your spaceships, but you'll never shake off your Oblomov. Our Western civilisation is anyway ahead of yours. As Kipling has said: 'East is East, and West is West, and ne'er the twain shall meet.'"

François Guizot in his *History of the English Revolution* (1854-1856) was trying to prove that revolution, no matter how bold and powerful, is incapable of destroying old national traditions. Thus Guizot, who was the first bourgeois historian to advance and develop the idea of class struggle (actually borrowed by him from Saint-Simon), ascribed the greatest importance to the role of national and historical traditions.

These traditions, certainly are important in shaping a people's character and its literature. But in the West people often make the mistake, when discussing Russia and the character of the Russian people, of overestimating the importance of those old national tradi-

---

[1] Marx and Engels, *Selected Works*, Vol. I, Moscow, 1958, p. 247.
[2] Ibid., p. 250.

tions which grew up under tsarism, and of carrying forward the past into the present. What was true in Guizot's time, and the age of the bourgeois revolutions, no longer applies in the conditions of the proletarian socialist revolution. The Russian Revolution of October 1917 did not simply sweep away the vestiges of feudal relations, thereby finishing what the February bourgeois revolution had not accomplished: it actually went much further.

In solving the problem of Russia's backwardness and of "catching up with the West and overtaking it", the Soviet people have left their past far behind them. In the process of building socialism, Russian people are determinedly shedding those negative traits in their character produced by their country's historical backwardness.

I always remember what Ivan Pavlov said about the Russian character in one of his scientific works, *Reflexes of Aim* (1916).

"Whenever I am depressed by such negative traits of the Russian character as laziness, lack of initiative, and an indifferent or perhaps even a careless attitude to every kind of work, I always tell myself: no, these are not our native traits, it's just dross, a cursed legacy of serfdom. It turned the serf-owner into a drone, relieving him of the need to exercise such normal human desires as a striving to provide himself and his dear ones with their daily bread, or to win himself a place in life, and leaving his reflex of aim with nothing to do on life's main lines. It turned the serf into an utterly passive creature with nothing to look forward to, since his most natural desires were always thwarted by the insurmountable obstacle presented by the absolute power of his master or mistress's will and pleasure. My thoughts run further. A ruined appetite and undernourishment can be cured by careful nursing and special hygiene. The same can and must be done for the reflex of aim which has been downtrodden by history on the Russian soil. If each one of us will cherish this reflex in himself as a most precious part of his being, if parents and teachers of all ranks will set themselves the task of fostering and developing this reflex in their charges, and if our public organisations will provide generous opportunities for exercising this reflex, then we shall become what we must and can become, judging from many episodes in our history and from some of our bursts of creative strength."

We Russians, and all the other peoples of the U.S.S.R., have now become what we must and can become. By carrying out the Great October Socialist Revolution and by adopting Lenin's aim of collectively building communism, our people have opened, as it were, a vast historical school for the cultivation of a taste for aim in every person, a school for re-education. Look at the main characters in Soviet literature—Furmanov's Chapayev, Fadeyev's Levinson, Ostrovsky's Korchagin, Fedin's Izvekov, Polevoi's Meresyev, and

16

Tvardovsky's Vassily Tyorkin–personal and social aims merge into one for all these men whose characters were shaped by the reflex of aim.

In his novel *Mother* (1907), Gorky showed how a "taste" for a revolutionary aim ennobled people. Looking back over the last fifty years in the history and the development of literature both of Western Europe and the U.S.S.R., one is forced to reject the idea that the way to freedom lies through anarchy, through "throwing off the fetters" of civilisation. The way to freedom and "natural man" lies through the cultivation of noble, humane aims and the setting up of a society–a communist society–where people will not feel stifled by exploitation and where their creative powers will unfold to the full. Such is the logic of history.

The fact that tsarist Russia, both technically and economically, was about a hundred years behind Germany, France, Britain and the U.S.A. was a challenge to Lenin's Russia. Hence the urgent appeal of the slogan "to catch up and surpass", which was reflected both in the speed of socialist construction and also in the country's cultural life. As for the reasons for Russia's backwardness they were best explained by Lenin in 1913, in his article "How Can Per Capita Consumption in Russia Be Increased". He asked: "Why is the development of capitalism and culture proceeding at a snail's pace? Why are we falling farther and farther behind? Why does this increasing backwardness make exceptional speed and 'strikes' necessary?" His answer was: "Our industrial satraps are afraid to answer this question, which is quite clear to any politically conscious worker, because they are satraps. They are not the representatives of capital that is free and strong, like that of America; they are a handful of monopolists protected by state aid and by thousands of intrigues and deals with the very Black-Hundred landowners whose medieval land tenure (about 70 million dessiatines of the best land) and oppression condemn five-sixths of the population to poverty, and the entire country to stagnation and decay."[1]

Such then were the historical conditions which, compounded of acute class struggle, geographical and climatic factors, and contrasts in the whole pattern of Russian life, had influenced the shaping of the Russian national character. How were they reflected in classical literature?

Like a lake that mirrors the sky, the Russian spirit mirrors the endlessness of the rolling Russian plains, and the severe climate. The very conditions of their existence conspired to produce in the Russians a strong sense of duty towards their fellow men and an elementary human decency. In their life of hard toil which required

---

[1] V. I. Lenin, *Collected Works*, Vol. 19, p. 293.

unspectacular, everyday heroism, they were constantly reminded of the importance of a helping hand. Forever warding off the attacks of their bellicose neighbours, they lived patiently tilling the soil and building their log houses which in winter were buried so deep in snow that often only the plume of smoke trailing from the chimney identified them as human habitations.

Bismarck was fond of repeating that "the Russian takes a long time to harness his horse, but he drives quickly". And this applies both to Russian history and to the Russian character.

How then was this "everyday heroism" of the Russians, their inherent humaneness and their sober appraisal of their harsh existence with its sharp turns from cruelty to kindness and back, portrayed in literature? In the first place these features were reflected in the profound realism of Russian literature, in its honest, unvarnished depiction of life.

Georg Brandes, who visited Russia at the end of the last century and wrote numerous articles about it, observed that "intellectually the Russians often amaze foreigners by that realism, that sense of reality which made them a great nation and proved so victorious in their life's struggle". I think this is one of the most accurate remarks about Russia and Russian literature made by a foreign observer. A keen interest in life's truth was always a basic feature of Russian literature. This was why even trends like decadence which led literature away from social interests acquired a rather different character in Russia from that they had in the West. Awareness of social contradictions and the imminence of a revolutionary crisis was always pronounced in Russian literature, even in the work of the symbolists. This insistence with which life forced its way into literature, giving it no chance to indulge in purely aesthetic problems and interests, was also a feature of literature in the Ukraine, Georgia, Armenia and Azerbaijan, where the national liberation movement left its imprint on such fashionable pre-revolutionary trends as decadence and modernism, imported from France and Russia. This is why the Armenian and Georgian symbolists (for example, Vaan Teryan and Galaktion Tabidze) little resembled their West European counterparts and why, after the establishment of Soviet power in the Caucasus, they entered the mainstream of the country's multinational literary world with its new themes and moods easily and naturally enough.

Thus realism, a strong sense of reality, was always the main feature of classical Russian literature. It was this realistic approach to the portrayal of Russian life and people which gave Russian literature its particular position and influence in world culture. The Russian 19th-century classics—the poetry of Pushkin, the novels of Turgenev, Herzen, Tolstoi and Dostoyevsky, the stories of Chekhov, and later the writings of Gorky—won recognition and popularity in many countries of the world. Hundreds of works in different languages have been devoted to the influence of the Russian novel on the development of the European and American novel.

Russian literature began to play this important role around the turn of the century when translations became widespread in Europe. Gradually 19th-century Russian literature came to be used as a sort of yardstick of the literary merits of books everywhere.

In the West, Russian literature is far from always acclaimed for its realism. What critics and readers tend to look for mainly in it (especially in Dostoyevsky) is an explanation of the now legendary "enigmatic Russian soul".

For many people in the West "the Russian soul" has come to mean a penchant for mysticism, violent action, anarchism and melancholy songs. According to some philosophers, like Jules Leger, a professor at the Sorbonne who wrote a book on this subject before the war, the "Russian soul" is something dark, with the most unexpected things lurking in its depths. It is a tangle of contradictions, and its natural elements is vast Russian spaces, log houses, snowdrifts, bears and vodka. This myth, which attributes to the Russians all sorts of barbaric habits and irrational behaviour, is centuries old. Foreigners who visited Muscovy in the 15th-17th centuries (mainly Germans like Olearius, Herberstein, and others who came later, like de Custine in the 19th century), tried to present Russia to the Western rulers as a backward country which was just waiting to be colonised. And although the mysterious "Russian soul" had actually very little to do with the real Russian national character, and although Russia's history and way of life gave no reason to place it in a class of its own as a barbarous and exotic land radically differing from countries in the West, the legend nevertheless struck firm root and was invariably to be found in the various philosophical and historical Baedekers published in Europe. It was a convenient myth because it obviated the need to study facts and added exotic glamour to the whole subject.

This myth has been played up greatly by the enemies of the new Soviet system as a useful "confirmation" of the irrelevance of the Russian experience for Europe. Besides, this allegation of the exclusiveness and psychological barbarity of the Russians fitted into racialist theories splendidly. No wonder nazi "philosophers" (like Rosenberg, for instance) seized upon the myth of the "enigmatic Russian soul" to prove the necessity of exterminating a few dozen million of the said souls.

A large number of Western propagandists of anti-communism are at present engaged in elaborating this colonialist myth about Russia and the traits of "the Russian soul" which, they allege, is barbarous and inclined to totalitarianism. Among these scholars, Professor Hans Kohn, whom we have already had occasion to mention, surely occupies the place of honour. Professor Kohn is the author of over a dozen books in which he investigates "the national spirit" of different peoples.[1] In 1960, he was elected president of the International Society for History of Ideas, founded in the U.S.A. In his books about Russia and the Russians (one of them called *The Mind of Modern Russia* which gives excerpts from Chaadayev to Berdyaev and from Tyutchev to Lenin, and the other entitled *Basic History of Modern Russia*) Professor Kohn advances the thesis that there is not much difference between tsarist and Soviet Russia. Both are barbarous and totalitarian. There was hope, he says, that the Russians would join the liberal and humane West. There was a glimmer of this hope in the reign of Nicholas II, when the bourgeois-landowner party, the Constitutional Democrats, entered the scene. But everything collapsed in 1917. Lenin came to power, and once again he faced Russia round to the East, tearing up by the root the tender shoots of liberty and western civilisation.

I do not propose to make a detailed analysis of Hans Kohn's mythopoetic activity. It is based on garbled quotations, an arbitrary interpretation of facts and, of course, a complete disregard for the class approach. The unscientific nature of his method could be easily and convincingly proved. The aim of a bourgeois ideologist is clear from the whole pattern of his reasoning, which is that of a typical Western propagandist of anti-communism.

This aim is to discredit Russia and the Russians for taking the road to communism. The idea of presenting Lenin as a successor to Nicholas II! Yet this is what Professor Kohn tries to do. Both, he says, opposed "the freedom of the individual" and were for "a totalitarian state"!

I have quoted this example for its curiosity value rather than anything else, as an instance of the lengths to which anti-communist propaganda in the West can go in its blind frenzy.

Naturally, nations differ from one another in certain traits of character, formed in the course of their history. Lenin wrote of this too. We speak, for instance of the revolutionary spirit of the Russians, of the business acumen of the Americans, of the Englishmen's reserve, of the methodical and punctilious Germans, the clear-headed Frenchmen, the industrious Chinese, and so on. But these qualities do not come from biological differences between races.

---

[1] H. Kohn, *The Mind of Modern Russia* (*Historical and Political Thought of Russia's Great Age*), New Brunswick, 1955. *Basic History of Modern Russia. Political, Cultural and Social Trends.* Princeton (N.Y.), 1957. *World Order in Historical Perspective*, Cambridge, Mass., 1942. *Revolutions and Dictatorships. Essays on Contemporary History*, Princeton, 1955, etc.

They are historically formed traits and are subject to evolution. The character of a nation must be examined only in development. It is not a static or immutable thing. Especially in the case of the Russian nation, which has undergone such great revolutionary changes in the last fifty years.

Literature reflects the life and character of a people; it does not simply reflect the writer's individual psychology but actually interprets history and shows the peculiarities of a people's development.

The greatness of Russian literature must be attributed not only to the fact that it happened to be a sphere in which the Russian genius manifested itself so splendidly. Russian literature does indeed illustrate the giftedness of the Russian people: but it also owes its greatness to the eventful life and history it reflects.

Tolstoi is a great writer not only because he is Tolstoi, but also because his genius sprang from and was nourished by a great people. When Lenin called him the "mirror of the Russian revolution", he had in mind Tolstoi's ability to absorb and truthfully reflect the peasant life in its entirety, with all its contradictions and its protest against oppression and injustice, and to impart to it a universal meaning and significance.

Russia's history happened to run such an unusual course that it was always providing an object lesson for the rest of the world. The struggle of the Russian people against serfdom and tsarism, against exploitation by those who owned the land and the factories, their struggle to defend their country against Tatars, Mongols, Germans and other invaders—all this fed literature with lofty ideas and epic images, and accounted for its dream of freedom and determination to stand up in defence of human rights.

Russian literature derives its main qualities from the deep involvement of the 19th-century classics in the life and interests of the different strata of the country's population. These qualities are: first, its closeness to the people (as regards both form and content); next, its earnest yet romantic patriotism; and, last but not least, its constant defence of human rights, its profound humanism. It is this last and most pronounced quality of Russian literature which is responsible for its social and ethical spirit, its tendency to preach, and its invariably critical attitude to life in old Russia. Such are the traditions of the Russian literary heritage.

Chapter 3

Russian Literature After
the October Revolution

Conditions for a socialist revolution ripened earlier in Russia than in other countries. A progressive revolutionary class—the Russian proletariat—grew up at the factories and plants built at the end of the last and the beginning of this century. It was headed by Lenin's monolithic party armed with a revolutionary theory. The positions of the bourgeoisie were shaky. The mounting crisis, the imminent revolutionary explosion, the tense ideological and emotional atmosphere that prevailed at this point in Russian history, were reflected widely and from different angles in the literature of those years, producing new images and views in the writings of people who belonged to such apparently opposed aesthetic movements as realism, symbolism and futurism.

Alexei Tolstoi, describing the situation in his novel *The Ordeal* wrote: "In the last ten years, huge enterprises were built up with extraordinary speed. Millions were made as if by magic. Banks were erected from glass and concrete, and so were new music halls, skating rinks and gorgeous night-clubs where people were deafened by the music, and dazzled by the reflections in the mirrors, the half-nude women, the brilliant lights and the champagne. Gambling houses, brothels, theatres, cinemas and amusement parks were hastily opened." But at the same time "the spirit of destruction was felt everywhere; it seeped like a deadly poison into the fabulous stock-exchange deals of the notorious Sashka Sakelman, into the sullen resentment of the steel workers, and the twisted dreams of the fashionable poetess brooding till five in the morning in a bohemian basement cafe. . . . Destruction was considered good taste, and neurasthenia a sign of refinement. This was preached by the fashionable writers who sprang from nowhere and became celebrities overnight. To breathe the smell of the grave and feel beside you the trembling of a woman's hot body, excited by morbid curiosity—such was the mood of poetry written in those last years: death and lechery".

The First World War greatly enhanced the feeling of approaching crisis in literature. Illustrated literary magazines like *Niva* (The Field), *Solntse Rossii* (The Sun of Russia) and *Stolitsa and Usadba*

(The Capital and the Country Estate) were full of sentimental war stories, and there was a flood of songs on the "all-is-over" and "everything-is-going-to-the-dogs" theme, urging people to "take it now while you can" as recommended by Artsybashev, Verbitskaya and company. The stream of pseudo-patriotic eulogies to the tsar (which carried away even writers of such stature as Leonid Andreyev and Sergei Gorodetsky), chauvinistic verses, boastful war reports, articles, plays, declarative announcements and invectives formed, for a time, something like a united front in literature (with the exception of Maxim Gorky, Mayakovsky, Serafimovich, Yesenin, Veresayev and a few others). On the eve of the Revolution the country's literary life, concentrated in the editorial offices of the literary journals and in St. Petersburg salons and circles, the whole intellectual atmosphere in the literary world throbbed with the excitement of capitalist enterprise and a desire to either gloss over the contradictions or flee from them. But it was a "feast on a smoking volcano". This is what Alexander Blok wrote in 1919, recalling Russian literary life just before the Revolution: ". . .I am becoming more and more convinced that such wonderful Russian magazines as, say, *Stariye Gody* (Times of Old) and *Apollon* (Apollo) were perfectly crazy undertakings; leafing through those gems of typographic art today, I quite seriously almost go mad trying to puzzle out how their editors could possibly have failed to feel what we would turn into, what we'd become in three or four years' time."

From this one should not draw the conclusion that the whole of Russian literature had turned decadent and despondent on the eve of the Revolution. In fact, it was as rich in talents as before, as in the 19th century. Many outstanding writers who adhered to realism, the leading trend in literature which was headed by Gorky (with his *Znaniye* collections), produced works which are still the pride of our literature today.

Gorky's generation of writers included Korolenko, Leonid Andreyev, Sergeyev-Tsensky, Bunin, Veresayev, Kuprin and Serafimovich. All that was sound and healthy in literature, all that held promise of developing further, was at first connected in one way or another with the *Znaniye* group, and particularly with Gorky himself. Later, of course, the *Znaniye* group fell apart and these writers joined different camps. The ideological struggle waged by Gorky in his articles had a resonant public quality and was of extreme importance for the development of literature. The pessimism and morbidness which prevailed in the poetry of the time was countered by Mayakovsky's bold revolutionary spirit. Serafimovich and Valery Bryusov pursued a consistently democratic course.

Yet Gorky, who closely followed the literary life of those years and analysed various works and their main characters, especially revolutionaries in a number of articles ("The Destruction of Personality", 1909; "On Modern Times", 1912, and others), invariably drew the conclusion that "the old literature freely reflected the moods, feelings and thoughts of all Russian democrats, while modern literature meekly submits to the persuasions of the small petty-bourgeois groupings. . .inwardly demoralised and hastily clutching at whatever comes to hand. . . .".

Further on, Gorky continues: "A modern writer can hardly be suspected of worrying about the fate of his country. Even the 'elder greats', if asked about this, will probably not deny that their motherland is of secondary importance to them at best, that social problems cannot inspire their art as strongly as does the riddle of individual existence, and that the main thing for them is free art, objective art, which is superior to their country's destinies, politics and parties, and which lies beyond the interests of the day, the year, and the age."

Such, in brief, was the ideological and political baggage with which the majority of the writers met the October Revolution.

The Revolution burst into this atmosphere like a great, cleansing storm. We know how difficult it was for many to grasp what was happening at first. Even Gorky did not correctly understand the events of the proletarian revolution immediately (see his "Untimely Thoughts"). The bloodshed frightened Korolenko, a remarkably gentle, compassionate man, and confused Veresayev. Gorky's friend Stepan Skitalets left the country (to return in 1934). Ilya Ehrenburg wrote in one of his poems (included in the volume *Fire*):

> Rain falls on earth, a scorching rain.
> My lonely heart is trembling.

And in another:

> I do not know who's right, who's wrong.
> They're flying different colours.

Indeed, many were stunned by the revolutionary storm, and some, voicing the despair of the defeated class, harped variously on the theme of universal doom. Alexander Blok poked sarcastic fun at them in his poem *The Twelve*. A long-haired character says in an undertone: "Russia's finished", and the author remarks: "He must be a glib-tongued writer". . . . B. Sadovsky, whose name once adorned the pages of *Apollon, Vesy* and *Stolitsa and Usadba,* called his first book of verse published after the Revolution *The Abode of Death.* While Anna Akhmatova wrote:

> All has been looted,
> Sold,
> Betrayed.

Literary life was undergoing the same radical changes as everything else in the country. Everything was changing—people, magazines, ideas, life itself.

Nor could it have been otherwise: to begin with, for political reasons. The Revolution divided the writers into those who voted *for* Soviet power and those who were *against* it. It swept aside the reptilian servants of capitalism and opened the way to new writers from the midst of the victorious people.

In the first years of Soviet power this revolutionary process was extremely intense. Yet many failed to grasp it at the time since the issue was confused by the complexity of the general situation in the country. The situation mixed all the cards in literature, and the crushing blows it suffered from famine, economic dislocation and war were seized upon by the enemies of the Revolution in their attempts to blame everything on Soviet power, making it out to be the original cause of literature's decline.

The first change to take place concerned the collapse of the prerevolutionary pattern of literary life. The people who came and went in the editorial offices of the magazines, attended the Wednesdays and Saturdays of Countess Kleinmichel in her St. Petersburg drawing rooms (where Yesenin and Klyuev sang their ditties), frequented the salon of Zinaida Gippius and her husband Dmitry Merezhkovsky, Vyacheslav Ivanov's "tower", or the Moscow house of Margarita Morozova, the Russian Madame Récamier, and those who belonged to the Society of Free Aesthetics in Dmitrovka Street or the Literary Circle—in short, that whole world where names were made, literary fashions set and sensations born, that world of small, cheap bourgeois newspapers and respectable publishing houses, of worthy and worthless writers who moved noisily through the labyrinths of the editorial offices from morn till night, filled the drawing rooms, the exhibition halls, and dined in private rooms at the restaurants, this world which was maintained by patrons of the arts and dealers in art, and which was essentially bound up with the old landlordist Russia began to disappear in the very first months following the Revolution and especially after the closing down of the bourgeois newspapers in the summer of 1918, gradually folding up and assuming unrecognisable forms.

The threadbare fabric of the life of the bourgeois intelligentsia soon wore through and fell apart. Their streets, mansions and de luxe apartments were taken over by the working people who made up the "great-coat" audience of Demyan Bedny, and whom Mayakovsky saluted and asked rhetorically in the *Futurists' Gazette* published in 1918: "With what fantastic buildings will you cover the site of yesterday's fires? What songs and music will pour from your windows? To what Bibles will you open your souls?"

They were the people who appeared to Valery Bryusov as the implacable judges of the old world, whom Alexander Blok portrayed as the symbol of retribution in his poem *The Twelve*, and whose victory the proletarian poet Nikolai Poletayev (1889-1935) welcomed as happily as if it were a joyous family gathering.

The very elements that had fed the old literature disappeared. The Olympians and those who worshipped the Muses on Parnasus, famous lawyers and wealthy society ladies, hurried to the south of Russia, driven by animosity and fear, and from there made their way abroad. Bunin, Kuprin, Balmont, Zinaida Gippius, Merezhkovsky, Zaitsev and Shmelyov left the country. Alexei Tolstoi, swept up by the retreating wave, followed the fleeing White Army out of Russia at the end of 1918 though he was to return a few years later.

All these people were well known to the Russian reading public, and I remember how anxiously we asked each other when we met in Petrograd or Moscow immediately after the Revolution or later, during the Civil War, when we returned for a few days' leave from the front: "What side is Bunin on? Where is Leonid Andreyev?" We wanted to know where they were and whose side they were on—Blok, Balmont, Shmelyov, Zaitsev and all the other writers whose names we were so used to seeing in the literary magazines, newspapers and playbills. And I remember how happy we were to learn that Blok was with the Revolution, and how painful it was to hear that Kuprin had left with Kerensky's cadets.

Soviet literature was born as the old world came crashing down and the class struggle reached an unparalleled intensity. The drama of the situation is well rendered in both Mayakovsky's and Blok's poetry written at the time.

The class split, the Civil War and the armed intervention of fourteen foreign powers headed by England and France, at first created a chaotic situation in Russia, causing people to flee the country *en masse*, and not just the aristocracy, the nobility, the big landowners and the court, but a large part of the intelligentsia too.

Altogether, about a million people emigrated, the majority belonging to the top strata of old Russian society. This was an unprecedented case in the history of the Russian state. Later, in other countries where socialist revolution triumphed we were to witness a similar emigration of a part of the population (in the Baltic states, Czechoslovakia, Bulgaria, Rumania, Hungary, and China), but never on such a scale as after the Russian revolution.

New literary associations were formed abroad and magazines in Russian began to come out in Paris, Berlin, in Yugoslavia, Bulgaria and, finally, in the United States. Although the scale on which the Russian émigré writers launched their literary activities was pretty ambitious (they set up their own publishing houses and founded many magazines and newspapers), none–with the exception of Bunin and Kuprin–produced anything serious that could claim a place in the history of Russian literature.

Ivan Bunin is a wonderful stylist and a subtle artist. His stories *The Gentleman from San Francisco, Chang's Dreams, The Cup of Life* and others, published in 1912-1916, have been translated into many languages and brought him world renown. He was elected to the Russian Academy of Sciences for his translation into Russian of Longfellow's *Song of Hiawatha*. Bunin left Russia in 1920 and settled in Paris. In his publicistic articles he often spoke out against communism. But they are not to be taken too seriously, any more than the majority of his recollections about his contemporary Russian writers–Chekhov, Mayakovsky, Yesenin and others. In his memoirs published in Paris in 1950, the subtlety of his observations and the beauty of his style are as remarkable as his spitefulness which is like the annoying and malicious grumbling of a doting old man. Bunin does not speak well of anyone, thus depriving his work of the poetry for which his prose is distinguished.

While abroad Bunin wrote three of his major works: *The Life of Arsenyev, Mitya's Love* and *Leka*, and also some of his best short stories including *Light Breathing, Sunstroke, Shadowed Paths*.

In 1933 Bunin was awarded the Nobel Prize–the first Russian writer to receive the honour.

Bunin's prose conjures up for us a picture of the old Russian countryside with its sprawling estates, its smell of wild flowers, in which the sweetness of gillyflowers mingles with the bitterness of wormwood. His own feelings are as conflicting, and with him sorrow and joy are always intertwined. His heart is as full of sadness as it is of admiration for all that is beautiful in the world. Bunin frankly extols the charm of the landed gentry's life, but at the same time he paints the grimness and crudeness of the peasants' existence with the merciless realism of Emile Zola.

Maxim Gorky thought very highly of Bunin, calling him a superb stylist who could make an image tangible, visible and evocative, whether he was describing the desperate longing of someone in love or the boredom of provincial life. In his letters to Teleshev, written just before he died in Paris in 1953, Bunin said that he wished to return home, but this never came about because he was too old and ill and there were some financial reasons, besides. After his death, his collected works were published in the Soviet Union twice, both times in large impressions. The second, 9-volume edition includes stories written by him as an émigré.

Another émigré writer who cannot be ignored is Alexander Kuprin, who was born in 1870, the same year as Bunin. Kuprin had a vivid, ebullient life-loving talent, but he was less profound than

27

Bunin. He returned home in 1937 (and died the following year). I met him at the Metropol Hotel immediately upon his arrival, and he struck me even then as a man who had spent all his life strength and had come home to die.

Kuprin lived an eventful life, moving from his early youth in Bohemian and fast-living officers' circles. But being a democrat, he liked the company of sailors, musicians and wrestlers just as well. He described all of them in his stories. When one reads his *Emerald* (the name of a race horse the story is about) one is reminded of Tolstoi's *Kholstomer*. Kuprin's *Duel*, which has been filmed in the Soviet Union, shows how empty and hopelessly dull life was for the officers of a garrison stationed in a small provincial town in tsarist Russia. It is a dramatic story which ends in tragedy. I also remember the popularity enjoyed by Kuprin's *Captain Rybnikov* about a Japanese spy who posed as a Russian officer.

Kuprin paints his canvases in bold strokes and vivid colours—his sunlight is brilliant, his shadows deep. One is constantly aware of his passionate nature. His books make interesting reading, and they are reprinted again and again in the U.S.S.R.

Bunin and Kuprin, both realist writers of the old school, were inheritors and continuators of the traditions of Russian classical literature.

But the best writers of the older pre-revolutionary generation either stayed in the U.S.S.R. or soon returned home. One such was Alexei Tolstoi. Another was the poet Valery Bryusov. Strange as it may seem, this pillar of pre-revolutionary decadence, this exponent of symbolism and friend of Verhaeren, who was bound by a thousand ties to West-European literature, showed no intention of quitting Moscow and, what is more, was very active in promoting the cultural undertakings launched by the Soviet government and immediately after the Revolution joined the Communist Party.

Another writer who stayed behind and accepted the Revolution was Alexander Blok (1880-1921), one of the most important early 20th-century Russian poets, who can be ranked with Pushkin, Lermontov, Nekrasov and Tyutchev. No other Russian poet ever succeeded in expressing with such sincerity, subtlety and depth the torments of a man's soul which, straining towards everything radiant and splendid in life, stumbles into the filth and sordidness of the surrounding world. Blok's lyricism has a spell-binding power. His love poems, which throb with an anguished dissatisfaction with life, have an irresistible appeal.

Blok's poetry, as distinct from Pasternak's idyllic lyricism, is profoundly historical. It is filled with sensations arising from the poet's responsiveness to social reality. Block despised the Russian bourgeoisie. A dreamer and a romantic, he longed for great upheavals and great changes in this sinful life. He called old Russia a "frightful world". This is why he welcomed the October Revolution with gladness and hope. His famous poem *The Twelve* written in January 1918 can be justly called the first major literary

Alexander Blok. 1907.

work about this great turning-point in the history of Russia. The whole poem is permeated with a deep-felt acceptance of the Revolution and sympathy with it. It is significant that at the time certain lines from it were used as slogans.

Andrei Bely (the pen-name of Boris Bugayev, 1880-1934), was another pre-revolutionary pillar of symbolism who took up the cause of the new, revolutionary Russia. I saw a lot of Bely. Baldheaded, his movements somehow elusive, he was really impressive.

Some people considered Andrei Bely to be a writer with flashes of genius. I don't know about that. But I do know that there was no other poet in the world who could have expressed the premonition of an imminent revolutionary cataclysm as powerfully and originally as Andrei Bely. His style is unconventional, somewhat jerky, and based on phonetic associations, yet it conveys remarkably well the psychology of a man who is awaiting a world-wide explosion. In one of his verses he actually predicts the invention of the atomic bomb. He referred to himself as a man "with a forever staggered mind". His most important work is the novel *Petersburg* written in 1913-1914 and revised somewhat in 1922. This is indeed a poem of fear. The characters of the novel, bomb-throwing terrorists, a senator and his son playing at revolution, are more like phantoms than real people, and there is something about them that reminds one of Maeterlinck. Senator Ableukhov (the name is a distortion of slap-in-the-face) paints a magnificent mental picture of the indestructible tsarist Empire where everything is divided into cubes and squares, while his son, who puts on a red domino to go to a masked ball, has already become involved with terrorist-revolutionaries, and has actually planted a bomb in an empty sardine tin on his father's table.

To be sure Andrei Bely was a poet of crises, a medium of horrors, and yet he accepted the socialist revolution and stayed on to work in the Soviet Union.

What is the explanation for all this? How can we explain the fact that Bryusov, Blok, Bely and others (to name but a few)—people who stood so far removed from the Revolution—welcomed it as a deliverance? The explanation must be sought in Russia's unique historical conditions.

No thinking person could help feeling the stirrings of a guilty conscience as he pondered on the contrasts then existing in Russia where the aristocracy and the bourgeoisie lived in gorgeous mansions and splendid country estates while the peasants suffocated in wretched log huts and the workers froze in clapboard barracks, and where people, children too, slaved at the factories from ten to twelve hours a day. Writers were also influenced in this by the traditions of Russian literature. After all, Russian literature has always been a "literature of great compassion" as Rosa Luxemburg once so aptly described it. Another circumstance of no little importance was that Russian capitalism began to rot, unable to compete with its West-European rivals, before it had developed sufficiently to give factory and office workers such relative benefits as they were already receiving in England and the United States.

This is why even those who were entirely dependent on the patrons of the arts and the prosperous publishers, and whose livelihood actually came from the capitalists' profits (Andrei Bely put this very well in his memoirs *At the Turn of the Century*, 1930)– even these people, or at any rate many of them, renounced the bourgeoisie when the Revolution came.

But in order to picture what happened to Russian literature immediately after the Socialist Revolution of October 1917, one must bear other and probably more important things in mind. One is the fact that such well-known writers as Mayakovsky, Yesenin, Veresayev, Alexei Tolstoi, Fedin and most of the young authors whose works had begun to be published before the Revolution sided with Soviet power. Another and perhaps even more important fact is that those revolutionary years witnessed an extraordinary upsurge in artistic creativity among the literate workers and peasants. Dozens of new magazines and newspapers were started. They printed poems and stories by Gladkov, Bakhmetyev, Lyashko, Bezymensky, Gastev, Gerasimov, Kirillov, and many other beginners.

At first, much of what the working and peasant youth produced had slight intrinsic literary value. But from the point of view of its social and cultural worth, this upsurge in the artistic creativity of the masses was an extremely important phenomenon which cannot be ignored if we want to understand just what was happening to Russian literature in those years. By focusing all our attention on the outstanding writers of the time, such as Anna Akhmatova and Boris Pasternak, of whom I have more to say later on, we are liable to let these names block our view of the floodtide of popular artistic endeavour and fail to appreciate the historical process itself. Naturally, what Pasternak wrote in those years is far greater in terms of artistic merit than the poetry written, say, by Nikolai Poletayev, one of the first working-class poets. Although Pasternak did not remain aloof from the historic events of his time, in those first years his poetry was mainly concerned with the past.

The poems of Alexei Gastev and Nikolai Poletayev, on the other hand, expressed entirely new and unusual emotions, then being experienced by millions of people. Poletayev described the feelings of the basement dwellers who, after the Revolution, moved into the apartments vacated by the fleeing aristocrats and capitalists.

Alexei Gastev was a veteran industrial worker, a Communist who had been sentenced to hard labour by the tsarist government. He wrote an amazingly original book of verse entitled *The Poetry of a Worker's Blow* (1918), which in rhythm is vaguely reminiscent of Walt Whitman. By means of form and intonation Gastev sought to render the rhythms of the Revolution itself: the rhythms of movement, explosions and blows. He renounced rhyme. In his blank

31

verse he tried to create original, eloquently expressive portraits and sketches that would convey through their romantically enlarged and generalised features the thoughts and sentiments of the proletarian operating a machine. His poetry is slightly abstract, tending to draw symbolic images portraying the life of a work team, the working class as a whole, or even whole historical epochs. Man with his warmth, his soul and his anger, does not figure as a person in Gastev's poetry. His epic studies: *We Have Dared, My Life, We Are Coming, Come Out* and others are extremely original works. Later, Gastev became the director of the Institute of Labour, gave up poetry writing, and devoted himself to the task of raising Russia's technical efficiency. I should very much like to quote a passage from one of Gastev's articles inspired by Lenin's plan for the electrification of Russia. In 1920, when Gastev wrote this article, he was merely putting down on paper the dreams of a poet, and now more than fifty years later we find that most of these dreams have come true.

"Although the West European and American countries surpass us in technical accomplishments and economic scale, Russia has one fortunate peculiarity which may in a relatively short space of time turn the dream of electrification into a very tangible reality. We are a semi-nomadic, semi-civilised country. We have peoples who believe in witch doctors, and intellectuals whose theories create sensations in Europe; we have vast stretches of virgin tundra, but we also have whole areas virtually encased in steel which can rival even the United States in machinery. We are a country that has not gone rusty under the pressure of traditions, while the vastness of our land and the constant movement of the population from one region to another lend us a peculiar freshness of outlook, unknown in the West. Much of what we do is started from scratch. Ten years ago the residents of Petrograd travelled in a rattling horse tram, and then suddenly a fast, new tram came speeding down Sadovaya Street, Nevsky and Kamenno-Ostrovsky prospekts, which made the trams in Paris look ridiculous and ugly in comparison. Swamps and woods surrounded Petrograd and Moscow, the Urals and Siberia on all sides, and suddenly, one fine day, factory chimneys shot up everywhere, like bolts from the blue, and machine-tools which were considered rarities in the United States and Germany were installed where once the quag sucked people under. Does anyone need reminding that during the war Russia managed to raise such factory buildings in the wildest of wildernesses and set up such machine-tools which now stagger foreigners, fed on tales of Russian bears, into open-mouthed stupefaction. We are glad that we have not yet entrenched ourselves so deeply in stone and iron as Europe, we are glad that we have not entangled our land in railways and are free to draw straight, long roads across Russia, covering it with a new pattern of meridians and parallels."

Much of this may sound naive and rhetorical, but all of it was projected into the future like an arrow on a taut bow-string.

The colourful figure of Demyan Bedny loomed large during the turbulent period of the Civil War and the first years of socialist construction. Demyan Bedny (the pen-name of Yefim Alexeyevich Pridvorov, 1883-1945) came from a poor peasant family, but was educated at the university of St. Petersburg. He wrote political poetry imbued with civic ardour, much of which appeared in *Pravda*, a Bolshevik newspaper founded by Lenin in 1912. Demyan Bedny's association with *Pravda*, which lasted all his life, had a decisive influence on the shaping of his talent. His work was addressed to the popular masses, and his poetry came across even to the completely illiterate listeners. This explains why his writings acquired such importance in the first post-revolutionary years. That was the time when the peasants and workers, aroused by the Revolution, badly needed the vital questions of political struggle to be answered for them in clear, easily understandable terms. And in Demyan Bedny's poetry, the mass reader and listener found an explanation to the political situation of the moment, offered in an easily assimilable form and in a language that appealed to them with its plebeian coarseness, wit, idiomatic turns of speech and popular slang.

However, Demyan Bedny's poetry had its weaknesses too. He did educate his mass audience politically, but at the same time he played up, to a certain extent, to their backwardness. In his reminiscences Gorky wrote: "Lenin repeatedly and insistently emphasised the importance of Demyan Bedny as an agitator, but said that he was rather course. 'He follows the reader when he should be a little ahead of him.' "

But in the first years after the Revolution the weak points of Demyan Bedny's aesthetics went unnoticed, because what mattered more was his excellent knowledge of the people, their life, their vocabulary, their tastes and their sayings. He certainly made remarkably good use of all this knowledge for rousing people to struggle. The song *How My Mother Saw Me Off to War*, written in 1918, won Bedny truly nation-wide popularity.

In his poetry he combines narrative with a popular exposition of the Party's appeals, citations from newspapers with lyrical digressions, and ardent publicism with virulent satire. Mayakovsky in his article "How to Make Poetry" (1926), remarked on the power of Bedny's "fable-like style" and the "precision of his aim".

During the Civil War Bedny lived among the soldiers, sharing their front-line hardships, travelling with them in troop trains, bivouacking with them and sleeping in their barracks. I remember the first time I saw him. In the summer of 1919 I was escorting a freight car carrying literature from Moscow to the southern front. At one of the stations I pushed back the door a little to let in the early morning air, and a hubbub of excited voices tore in. A troop train was standing alongside ours, and I saw a crowd of soldiers making their way towards the Revolutionary Military Council train some distance away. On enquiring the cause of the excitement, I discovered that Demyan Bedny was in that train. He came down the steps of the carriage to meet the crowd of soldiers—a stoutish, portly man wearing the famous Budyonny pointed cap, a tunic with wide red collar insignia, and baggy trousers tucked into knee-high boots. He looked like a Russian *bogatyr* from Vasnetsov's painting.

After Bedny's "man-to-man" chat with the soldiers, the brochures with his verses were literally snatched out of my hands, I remember.

His poetry took the mass reader into a familiar world of customary names and notions: Grandad Sofron, Brass-Buckle Yashka the Soldier, the Mother-in-Law who has more Spite than Right, the Ivans, Kuzmas, Provs, Klims and scores of others straight out of their own lives. Each poem described some topical theme or exciting event in real life: a peasant going off to war, a deserter seeking asylum in his home village and dying at the hand of his own father, a Menshevik revealing his traitorous soul, a White general using flattery to make the peasants more tractable, and the Red Army routing the Polish interventionists. All the vital themes of the day, political, historical and moral, found some sort of reflection in Demyan Bedny's works. Taken together they form a poetic chronicle of the period.

Although the work of Demyan Bedny and Mayakovsky followed the same general trend, and had a somewhat similar content, these two poets had an entirely different style and approach. It is not simply that Mayakovsky was exclusively a town poet, while Demyan Bedny's poetry drew its nourishment from rural sources. The differences were fundamental. Mayakovsky's work presents a poetic image of the epoch. Demyan Bedny's verses (taken in their chronological order) are more like a record of events. With Mayakovsky man is inseparable from history, he is bound up with it entirely—from his most intimate emotions to his ideas on the communist transformation of the world. The poet achieves this by blending personal and social themes into one, by combining the lyrical element with the epic, and by rendering his poetry in an extremely novel manner. With Demyan Bedny, on the other hand, the purely didactic principle prevails over all else. He captivates the reader with his original manner in order to teach him. Mayakovsky awakens lofty emotions in his reader; he also teaches, but he does it in such a way as to inspire the reader with the universal aims of communism. ("Realists we are, but not grazing the grass at our feet, not bending our snouts to the ground.") His poetry is romantic. Demyan Bedny's is down to earth, and not infrequently this tendency leads to an unnecessarily utilitarian attitude to reality. Hence that preponderance of naturalism in his poetry. It is not surprising, therefore, that Lenin (according to his wife Nadezhda Krupskaya) liked his lofty dramatic poetry more than his satirical verses.

In his best poems, Bedny showed himself to be an heir to the finest revolutionary traditions of Russian literature. Bedny understood the soul of the Russian people well and, moreover, he had an excellent knowledge of Russian history, literature, and popular speech. He was probably the keenest bibliophile in Soviet Russia, owning a personal library of over a hundred thousand books.

As one of the representatives of militant revolutionary art, Demyan Bedny holds a prominent place in the history of Soviet literature. His popularity waned within a few years, and not only for political reasons (Stalin's dislike of him). This was mainly due to the aesthetic rift between the intellectual level and tastes of the new generations of readers and those feuilleton and pamphlet genres which Bedny cultivated and which were wholly geared to the current, day-to-day politics. Besides, a poet is bound to produce verbal dross eventually if he goes on writing didactic tales or feuilletons for the daily newspapers as a matter of routine, year in year out.

I once had a conversation with Bedny about this. It was some time in 1939. I ran into him in the street outside his house, and so we had a chat, remembering the old days.

"Oh well," he said, "I, too, can scrape together enough poetry to fill a volume that will be as good as anyone else's and will be here to stay. Now, you're supposed to be an aesthete. Go ahead and select what you think should stay. Let it be a volume to suit your taste."

"Very well," I replied, in the same bantering tone. "But you won't let me do the choosing in peace anyway. You'll never trust me entirely. You're sure to leave something in."

"I suppose so," he agreed. "I'll meddle in something. It's too late for me to change now. But still my star will continue to shine in your sky too."

He was right. His star shone brightly in the years of the Civil War, and it still shines for us today across the years.

Radical changes took place in Russia's literary life after the socialist revolution. Petrograd and Moscow stopped publication of such old Russian literary magazines as *Vestnik Yevropy, Russkaya*

Mysl, Mir Bozhy and others which had been coming out for decades. Some of these magazines were true masterpieces of printing, for instance *Apollon* maintained by the millionaire Ryabushinsky. The large publishing houses also closed down and the old literary life was paralysed partly due to the shortage of food, fuel and transport, but mainly because the owners of the publishing houses, print shops and magazines refused to accept Soviet power, its policy and its ideology and were leaving the country.

Dozens of dwarfish private publishers sprouted on the ruins of the past, and as early as 1919 the world's first publishing house owned by workers and peasants was opened in Petrograd. This was the State Publishing House of the Russian Federation. New Soviet magazines also began to appear in 1919-1920, among them *Kniga i Revolyutsia* (Book and Revolution) to which Konstantin Fedin contributed, and *Khudozhestvennoye Slovo* (Literary Word) published by the Commissariat for Education, with Valery Bryusov playing the leading role.

Among the magazines which acquired the greatest importance were those published by Proletarian Culture, the new mass organisation generally known as Proletkult. Printed in many cities they were more than just a haven for budding poets and writers from the masses. The leaders of Proletkult, Bogdanov and Pletnyov, expounded on the pages of *Proletarskaya Kultura* (Proletarian Culture), *Gorn* (Bugle) and other magazines their theories on the creation of a new proletarian culture. These theories ran counter to Lenin's idea that the new culture of a socialist society should be a nation-wide and not a narrow class culture.

The leftist theories of the Proletkult leaders have long been forgotten. But then they never influenced the development of Soviet literature enough to matter. Still, we might remember them if only because the Proletkult leaders attracted the notice of Lenin who found the time to criticise their "guild" attitude. In December 1920, on Lenin's initiative, the Party adopted the letter of its Central Committee on the subject of the Proletkult. This letter is interesting in that it gives an example of the way the Party strove to influence the artistic intelligentsia by persuasion. Pointing out the fallacy of the leftist approach to problems of art, the Central Committee addressed the writers as follows: "Far from wishing to fetter the initiative of the working intelligentsia in the sphere of artistic endeavour, the Central Committee, on the contrary, wants to create a healthier and more normal atmosphere that will be beneficent for artistic endeavour as such. The Central Committee fully realises that with the war coming to an end workers will be taking a greater interest in problems of art and proletarian culture. The Central Committee appreciates and respects the desire of the front-rank workers to place on the agenda the question of the individual's greater spiritual development."

Looking back over the past now, we see that both the Letter on the Proletkults and Lenin's public speeches about the creation of a communist culture, made in the first years after the Revolution, already contained those principles on which the Party has since based its policy as regards literature. After the October Revolution, Soviet literature developed under the influence of this new and fruitful factor, guided by the Communist Party's ideas, organised and aided by it in every respect. By rendering this aid, the Soviet state was performing its new educative function. Reviewing the course followed by Soviet literature we see how our art absorbed the historical experience of the working class in its struggle for socialism, how little by little it began to express this experience, thereby becoming an active participant in the struggle. It was precisely along this road that Lenin tried to direct the development of Soviet literature from the first.

Before going any further, we would do well to examine what Lenin had in mind when he spoke of "the road of development" of the new literature, and first and foremost, we should consider the principle of partisanship in socialist realism in the light of Lenin's teaching.

·

Chapter 4

Lenin on the Principle
of Partisanship in Literature.
Traditions of the Russian
Classics

The Socialist Revolution of 1917 caused a deep political rift in the writers' midst. The political "division" into those for and against the Revolution was only the beginning of a deeper ideological rift. The whole course of development of Soviet literature can only be understood if viewed as a struggle for the creation of a literature that would be "part of the common cause of the proletariat" to use the words of Lenin. In every successive decade the problem of bringing literature into closer contact with life and making it play a more active role in the communist education of the people was posed and solved in a different manner as dictated by historical conditions.

At every stage of the development of Soviet literature the Communist Party acted as an important factor influencing the whole literary process. In this respect, it represents an entirely new phenomenon in the history of world literature. As I go on, I shall acquaint readers with decisions adopted by the Central Committee, the statements made by Party leaders and the various documents which had a specially strong influence on the ideological development of our writers. But before we go any further, we must examine the philosophical and theoretical principles on which the Party bases its policy in respect to literature. We must dwell on the main concept, that of partisanship, which makes the cornerstone in the edifice of the new art being created in the land of socialism.

What is *partisanship* in art? Is it not directly opposed to the idea of artistic freedom? Does it not imply an order to engage in tendentious propaganda which may find itself at variance with the truth of life? This is precisely how bourgeois ideologists represent partisanship in our literature, and this is precisely what they aim their criticism and ridicule at, posing as defenders of individual freedom.

A correct understanding of this problem will provide us with a key to the understanding of much that is peculiar to the literary life of the Soviet Union. It will also help us to understand why the

Central Committee of the Communist Party takes all deviations from the ideological principles of Marxism-Leninism in literature so close to heart.

Lenin gave a comprehensive philosophical substantiation to the principle of partisanship in many of his works. His philosophical work *Materialism and Empirio-criticism* (1909) is permeated with the spirit of partisanship, as is also his article about Lev Tolstoi. In this connection, I can hardly do better than quote Lenin's important statement on literature and the arts recorded by Clara Zetkin in her memoirs.

"... The important thing is not our opinion of art. Nor is it important what art gives to a few hundreds or even a few thousands of a population of millions. Art belongs to the people. It must be deeply rooted in the very thick of the working masses.... *It must unite the feelings, the thoughts and the will of these masses.*"[1] (Author's italics.)

That is why Lenin also said that: "... We (i.e., Communists–K.Z.) must not stand idle and allow the chaos to develop in whatever direction it pleases. We must systematically guide this process and shape its results."[2]

Thus, for Lenin the task of intervening in the literary process, that is giving the writers ideological assistance, stemmed directly from his understanding of partisanship in art. Marx's words that formerly the philosophers only explained the world while now they had to change it are fully applicable to Lenin. Lenin was indeed a philosopher who changed the world. For him, the most abstract speculative philosophical constructions had a direct connection with reality, and above all with social struggle. This also applies to aesthetic categories, including the concept of partisanship in literature and the arts.

For Lenin this concept was imbued with profound philosophical meaning. He tied up the idea with the nature of human thinking and with his teaching on the principal link. Our thinking combines the sensations which give us our first signals of the outside world, the development of concepts and abstract ideas about this outside world and, finally, our practical knowledge of it. At all these stages an essential role is played by a person's ideological attitude, which organises his relations with the outside world and his social invironment, and is the guiding principle that shapes people's behaviour, being connected with their social relationships and their life's aims.

From the flood of life's impressions the artist selects that which he wishes to portray. In the broad philosophical sense this can be

---

[1] *Lenin on Literature and Art*, Russ. ed., Moscow, 1957, p. 583.
[2] Ibid., p. 582.

called a committed selection. Partisanship in this case may be interpreted not only in its social sense (as devotion to a party), but also as an aesthetic category.

Beauty is bound up in one way or another with the concept of those elements of which it is compounded. The partisanship of socialist realism will be revealed to us in its aesthetic aspect through the portrayal of the beauty of the socialist forms of life, through the portrayal of the spiritual beauty of people struggling for communism.

Some people writing about the partisanship of socialist realism (both in this country and abroad) wrongly equate it with tendentiousness in art. Tendentiousness means championing through definite social and political ideals, and is to be found as far back as Aeschylus and Aristophanes, Dante and Cervantes. Schiller's drama *Kabale und Liebe* is charged with a definite political bias. Engels, who also wrote about tendentiousness in the art of the past, linked the integrity and strength of the characters portrayed by the Renaissance artists with the fact that these artists wholly shared the interests of their age and took part in the political and social struggle of the time.

Partisanship in art can be considered as a further development of tendentiousness. It implies the artist's deeper understanding of the philosophical meaning of his art, of its social purpose and his own role in the social struggle.

Lenin's theory of partisanship in literature is an offshoot of Marx's and Engels's views on the subject, and represents an elaboration and development of these ideas. His article "Party Organisation and Party Literature", published in 1905, expounds the basic principles of this theory. Although written more than sixty years ago, the article is still frequently referred to in discussions on the nature of art, artistic freedom, and so on. This alone goes to show how vital the problems raised by Lenin were and the importance of the conclusions drawn by him for the development of world literature. In any case, none of the books published abroad on the subject of Soviet literature fail to bring this article up.

Attempts have been made by critics and writers both at home and abroad to interpret Lenin's article "Party Organisation and Party Literature" as simply referring to those practical aims which Lenin pursued in his desire to bring order into the Party press. This view is definitely erroneous. Lenin's aim was not merely to settle the contradictions and the difference of opinion among the Party workers and help them to organise their activities more efficiently in the interests of the Party. In this article Lenin examined such problems of fundamental importance as: can an artist or a writer be entirely free and independent of society? If he cannot, then what is he dependent upon in capitalist society? What will literature be like in socialist society?

The best way to answer these questions is to quote Lenin himself: "One cannot live in society and be free from society. The freedom of the bourgeois writer, artist or actress is simply masked (or hypocritically masked) dependence on the money-bag, on corruption, on prostitution.

"And we Socialists expose this hypocrisy and rip off the false labels, not in order to arrive at a non-class literature and art (that will be possible only in a socialist extra-class society), but to contrast this hypocritically free literature, which is in reality linked to the bourgeoisie, with a really free one that will be *openly* linked to the proletariat.

"It will be a free literature, because the idea of socialism and sympathy with the working people, and not greed or careerism, will bring ever new forces to its ranks. It will be a free literature, because it will serve, not some satiated heroine, not the bored 'upper ten thousand' suffering from fatly degeneration, but the millions and tens of millions of working people—the flower of the country, its strength and its future. It will be a free literature, enriching the last word in the revolutionary thought of mankind with the experience and living work of the socialist proletariat, bringing about permanent interaction between the experience of the past (scientific socialism, the completion of the development of socialism from its primitive, utopian forms) and the experience of the present (the present struggle of the worker comrades)."[1]

This statement is perfectly applicable to modern Russian literature as well. One might say that it is an embodiment of Lenin's idea of what the literature of the future should be. Soviet literature reflects the interests not of the "top ten thousand" but of millions and millions of working people who represent the country's élite. It draws its sustenance from the activity of the people building communism, describing that activity and expressing the ideals of the progressive sections of society which lead the country along the road to communism.

When planning a new book, the Soviet writer—just like any other—is faced with a number of problems involving the selection and the aesthetic arrangement of his material (plot, imagery, style, etc.). In solving these problems the Soviet writer feels and regards himself as a participant in the people's struggle for communism. He finds that his aesthetic problems are intrinsically bound up with his ideas and his world outlook. As Sholokhov put it, a Soviet author writes at the bidding of his heart and his conscience. And his heart

---

[1] V. I. Lenin, *Collected Works*, Vol. 10, pp. 48-49.

beats in unison with all that he serves, with that for which the Communist Party is struggling.

The stream of images and life's impressions crowding the mind of the artist is always organised into a pattern by a definite idea. The attempts of some writers to give a sort of tape-recording or a shorthand report of the fleeting thoughts and impressions streaming through their mind (for instance, James Joyce or Dos Passos), or in other words, attempts to demonstrate raw, unorganised material, can make no claim to any great aesthetic significance. This way could well lead to the tape-recording of delirious ravings (of someone sleeping, drugged or demented) being passed off for an artistic achievement. But this means a withdrawal from Man. It means dehumanising art. However, abandoning all ideological positions in art is in itself a sort of ideological position, negative though it is. Asserting chaos as an alternative to organisation is also a world outlook of sorts. But this is a stand worthy of an ostrich, the position of a creature which hides its head in the sand when it senses trouble, instead of squarely facing the truth. Agnosticism is neither an evasion nor a renunciation of philosophy. It is another philosophy, a defeatist one.

Modernistic literature, literature "without ideas", without plot, theme or even sense (like abstract paintings) may still be of some interest to a comparatively small circle of bourgeois readers, those "top ten thousand" mentioned by Lenin. It may give them a thrill and even amuse them with its absurdity. But the reading public at large, the majority who seek aesthetic pleasure and enlightenment in books, are left completely unimpressed by the sort of literature which is manufactured for the "top ten thousand". It is socially alien to them.

Contrarily, books which by their aesthetic pattern and the ideals they champion show their affinity with the interests of the masses acquire nation-wide significance. They are not "just something to read", to kill time. They become part of the people's spiritual life. They inspire people, give them solace, advice, and aesthetic delight.

Because of its partisanship, ours is a literature of the people and for the people. Partisanship and affinity with the people are interrelated features of the new world's free literature. This is how Lenin understood it; and such is Soviet literature.

The desire to address the widest circle of readers and to embody the vital interests of the people in their books was common to all the greatest writers of pre-revolutionary Russia as well.

But affinity with the people meant one thing to the Russian classics and something quite different to modern Soviet writers. In his article about Lev Tolstoi, Lenin wrote that it took a revolution to make his works known to the entire nation. The same can be said about Pushkin, Lermontov, Turgenev, Nekrasov, Herzen,

Dostoyevsky, Chekhov and other Russian authors, who did not actually become known throughout the country until after the Revolution of 1917. This was due partly to the fact that two-thirds of the population were illiterate, partly to the fact that the classics were brought out in insufficiently large editions.

The very notion of affinity with the people was different in the 19th century because the people's life was different. Lenin divided the revolutionary movement in Russia into three stages, and the concept of affinity with the people underwent a change with every stage. At the first stage, its spokesmen were revolutionary noblemen like Pushkin and Lermontov. In the second stage, revolutionary democrats came to the fore. Their works were already closer in spirit to the people, whose life they reflected more fully. This new stage is best expressed in the works of Nekrasov, Chernyshevsky, Dobrolyubov and Saltykov-Shchedrin. The third and last stage is distinguished by the historical rise of the working class which, in alliance with the peasantry, won political power in 1917. The proletarian revolution brought radical changes into Russian life, and under Soviet power the people themselves rose to a new level of social consciousness and culture, which even affected the Russian character, as we have already seen. In the works of Soviet writers from Gorky and Mayakovsky to Sholokhov, affinity with the people is displayed in a new aspect, illumined by party spirit in the struggle for communism.

In Soviet literature we find an alliance of life's truth with the social ideals of the writer. In the old society, a realist writer who wanted to be faithful to the truth of life, often found himself contradicting his own political sympathies. Thus, although Balzac and Gogol were monarchists they actually served the cause of revolution with their writings.

The ideals of kinship with the people upheld by the Russian writers of the past were varied in their historical meaning, and Soviet literature rests upon the more progressive and democratic traditions of our classics.

A word about these traditions. The Russian classics had a keen sense of responsibility to the people. All the great Russian writers—Pushkin, Lermontov, Belinsky, Chernyshevsky, Nekrasov, Turgenev, Herzen, Lev Tolstoi, Dostoyevsky, Chekhov and Gorky—believed that the purpose of their work was to reflect the pain and anger, the joy and hopes and the sense of beauty which they drew from the life of their people. Suffice it to recall Lev Tolstoi's famous treatise *What is Art?* (1898). For all the ideological contradictions contained in this work, when it came to the most important thing—that is, stating his own social standpoint and his views on the relation of art to life and the role of the individual—the first principle Tolstoi invariably stressed was that a writer must not forget his responsibility to the people.

In this treatise Tolstoi writes that the art of the future will not simply continue today's art, but will emerge on the basis of new and entirely different principles that will have nothing in common with the ones by which the art of the upper classes is guided today. The judges of this art will be the entire people and not just the wealthy class alone, the way it is now. For a work of art to be considered good, to be approved and popularised, it will have to satisfy the requirements not of the few who live in identical and often unnatural conditions, but of the whole people, of the large mass of people living a natural life of toil. Nor will the works of art be produced merely by those few men from the élite minority who either belong to the propertied classes or are closely connected with them, but by gifted men from the entire population, who ever will show an ability and aptitude for artistic activity.

The time of which Tolstoi was writing has now come. No one can fail to see how close the traditions of the Russian classics are to us today. And they are further developed by our Soviet literature. I could cite hundreds of statements made by other Russian authors, besides Lev Tolstoi, on the importance of books being written by, of and for the people, but I shall limit myself to quoting a passage from Saltykov-Shchedrin, a great Russian satirist of the 19th century. His statement, besides proclaiming the popular principle in literature, also speaks of the educational role of literature, and in this sense he is not shy of using the word "propaganda". Such concepts as "literature" and "the people" are used with a very precise meaning.

This is how this revolutionary-democratic writer reasoned in 1869, a century ago: "Literature and propaganda are one and the same thing. This may be an old truth, but literature itself is still so little aware of it that there is good reason for repeating it. Every great, bright thought that literature voices and every new truth it discovers wins it so many converts that we must not fail to treasure this precious quality it has to conquer darkness and win over the most stubbornly prejudiced people. Roughly, the same can be said about delusions as well. Literature which propagandises a carefree, happy-go-lucky existence has no chance, of course, of imposing its everlasting influence on the world, but it may retard progress considerably and from time to time deal it such blows as will be all the more painful because the agents of progress are mere men, after all, and as such are not always indifferent to blows received."

Five years earlier Saltykov-Shchedrin had written that "...Literature undertakes to call forth these new forces from the darkness, point them out to society and convince it that thereafter its existence will be fatalistically bound up with them. Literature can have no other duties and no right to give society anything other than that which lies latent within itself."

I trust my readers will excuse me for this slight digression in order to present the views of a Russian writer who was not as well known, perhaps, to the general reading public abroad as Lev Tolstoi and Dostoyevsky and who, moreover, lived a hundred years ago. But Saltykov-Shchedrin did more than play an important role in cultivating a revolutionary self-awareness among the Russian intelligentsia. His views, like the views of the revolutionary democrats Belinsky, Chernyshevsky, Dobrolyubov and Herzen who lived earlier, show how deeply rooted were those traditions in Russian literature according to which a writer could not be regarded as a person wholly preoccupied with himself alone. The Russian classics were always aware of their responsibility to the people, and this is why the thesis "art for art's sake" always went against their grain.

The thesis of partisanship as one of the basic elements of socialist realism means a continuation and development of these traditions in the new historical conditions. The task which Soviet literature has set itself is to point out the new forces to society and convince it that its very existence is inevitably bound up with them.

In his essay *Lev Tolstoi* Maxim Gorky records what Tolstoi once said against anarchism and the so-called "absolute freedom of the individual". Here is an excerpt from Gorky's account:

"I remember how Sulerzhitsky got hold of Prince Kropotkin's puny little brochure, got inflamed by it and for the rest of the day told everyone about the wisdom of anarchism, philosophising ruefully on the subject.

"Tolstoi said to him with some annoyance: 'Oh, stop it, Lyovushka, you make me tired. You're like a parrot, harping on this word freedom, freedom. But what does it mean? For if you were to attain freedom in your sense of the word what, do you imagine, would happen? In the philosophical sense, there'd be a bottomless void, and in life, in actual life you'd become a sluggard, a beggar. What ties will you, a free man in your sense of the word, have with life, with people? Look at the birds, they're free but still they build nests. You won't even bother to build a nest, you'll satisfy your sexual urges just anywhere, like a dog. Think about this seriously and you'll see, you'll feel that freedom in the final sense is emptiness, an infinite void.' He frowned angrily, and after a minute added a little more calmly: 'Christ was free, Buddha was too, yet both took upon themselves the sins of the world and of their own free will surrendered to the bondage of earthly life. No one went further than that, no one. And you, and we—oh, what's the use of talking! We, all of us, seek freedom from our duties to our neighbour, whereas it was precisely our awareness of these duties that made us human in the first place, and if it had not been for this awareness we'd be living like animals. . . .' "

This was Tolstoi. But even Dostoyevsky, who saw no creative force in revolution and wrote his anti-revolutionary novel *The Possessed*, even Dostoyevsky, a religious man who was against social transformations, hated the system of bourgeois exploitation. Even Dostoyevsky realised the falseness of the slogan of freedom in capitalist conditions. In the chapter entitled "About the Bourgeois" in his book *Winter Notes on Summer Impressions* he wrote: "What is *liberté*? Freedom. What freedom? Equal freedom for all to do what they please within the limits of the law. When can you do anything you please? When you have a million. Does freedom give everyone a million? No. What is a man without a million? The man without a million is not a man who does whatever he pleases but the one to whom anything anyone pleases is done."

Actually, Dostoyevsky's writings, motivated by his love for the "insulted and the humiliated", was a protest against this situation where anything at all could be done to a man.

Such were the views even of Tolstoi and Dostoyevsky, the authors whom Gorky rebuked for poeticising the "Asiatic" anarchic traits in the Russian character.

Before and after Tolstoi similar thoughts against the so-called "absolute freedom of the individual" were voiced by many writers: Gogol, Herzen, Saltykov-Shchedrin, the revolutionary-democrat critics Belinsky and Chernyshevsky, the poet Nekrasov and others. And, of course, Gorky, who wrote more than anyone else on the subject, and who sarcastically called the claims to this so-called absolute freedom "a tape-worm of individualism".

From the philosophical and theoretical point of view absolute freedom is unattainable because man, whatever his level of cultural development, has always been and still is a creature of historical determinism compelled to reckon with the objective conditions of life.

This explains why the Soviet press spoke out so sharply against abstract paintings and sculpture, and also against certain films and books which give a distorted picture of real life.

Would you call this meddling in the artist's work? Yes and no. Yes, in the sense that artists are set certain limits for the manifestation of their anarchistic self-will which might otherwise threaten to violate the natural norms of the community. Such limitations also exist under bourgeois democracy, for instance with respect to pornographic films and literature (unfortunately, this is not practised everywhere and not always consistently even where it is). There are also other restrictions in capitalist society, restrictions of a political nature, for instance.

In Soviet society where the policy in respect to literature as "a part of the general proletarian cause" (to use Lenin's expression) is more frank and more consistently implemented, the criticism of anything that goes against the interests of the people is also more frank than in the West.

The ideologists of bourgeois democracy in the West are trying to present the Communist Party's policy in respect to literature as a violation of the very principles of democracy. This surely invites the question: what sort of democracy? The people who are straining all their efforts to build up a new economy and a new culture in the Soviet Union, determined to eliminate centuries of backwardness, these people can hardly be expected to settle for the kind of "freedom" which serves as a breeding ground for semi-pornographic films, strip-tease, trashy comics and literature devoid of all ideas.

Art that is wholly preoccupied with entertainment and sex is obviously unsuitable for Soviet conditions where the struggle for communism is being waged on a nation-wide scale. Naturally, each society creates and cultivates the sort of literature and art which best answers its spiritual requirements and fits into the pattern of its life. The question of the Party interfering in their work never occurred to either Mayakovsky, Sholokhov, Fadeyev or Alexei Tolstoi. They felt no discrepancy between their creative plans and the Party's interests. Mayakovsky, for instance, wanted "the pen to be given the status of a bayonet" and poetry to be discussed as seriously at Party congresses as the output of iron and steel. Alexander Fadeyev, speaking at the Writers' Union in 1951 on the occasion of his fiftieth birthday said that he still dreamed of writing his major work, that he still had to sing the main song of his life: a song about the Communist Party.

All this goes to show that there have always been and always will be different types of writers, taking their dependence on outside circumstances, their determinism, in various ways. Pushkin wrote:

> I need another, better freedom.
> Dependent on the tsar, dependent on the people,
> What difference? It's all the same.
> I want to be subservient to none,
> I want to serve and please myself alone,
> And not prevaricate or cower
> To gain a higher rank or power....
> (From "Pindemonti".)

Of Mayakovsky it can also be said that it was himself he served and pleased when he extolled Lenin and the Party. Pushkin, too, was a people's poet. Yet his sense of involvement in the people's struggle was different. He extolled freedom and between the lines revolted against Nicholas I. Mayakovsky, by extolling Lenin, extolled freedom. Herein lies the historical distinction and the historical connection between these two Russian poets.

The principle of partisanship advanced by Lenin in the literature of the new society answers the new historical conditions. In order to make the leap from the "kingdom of necessity" to the "kingdom of freedom" (to use Engels's expression) it is imperative for the new society to mobilise all its forces, tense itself for the effort and exercise the strictest self-discipline. It is to this sharpest of sharp turning-points in history, this tensest of periods that Lenin's principle of partisanship in literature corresponds. The old bourgeois world may not like this principle, but then that is only natural. After all, it was born of the renunciation of the old world, and it is one of the weapons used in the battle with the old world.

Chapter 5

Maxim Gorky

Maxim Gorky. 1928.

In 1928, soon after his return to the Soviet Union from Sorrento after his long stay abroad, Gorky invited the poet Selvinsky and myself to come and see him at his place. The house in Malaya Nikitskaya Street which the Soviet Government gave Gorky for his private residence, had once belonged to Ryabushinsky, a millionaire who had fled abroad after the Revolution.

I felt a touch of panic as I crossed the gravelled fore-court adorned with flower beds and entered the house. The world fame of our host made me apprehensively tongue-tied during the first few moments of our meeting. When speaking with celebrities–and I have met many famous people in my life: actors, writers and political leaders both at home and abroad–you often find your illustrious interlocutor trying to impress you with his superiority. And this always has the effect of inhibiting both the conversation and your memory of it. But I have had the great fortune in my time of meeting two men who had the gift of instantly lifting this embarrassment–the gift of natural democracy. These two men were Lenin and Gorky.

Lenin was amazingly democratic by nature and there was not the slightest hint of affectation in his manner. There was more of the actor in Gorky and he could turn on his charm at will. One felt irresistibly drawn to him, fascinated by his wisdom and experience.

Gorky, a tall man wearing a blue shirt, with the typical face of a Russian craftsman and a smile which lifted up his moustache–welcomed us at the dining-room door. We fell into conversation there and then, standing as we were. Gorky began by asking Selvinsky and me to explain constructivism to him (we both belonged to this literary group at the time) and to tell him our literary news. Perhaps no other Russian writer had ever had such a strong sense of proprietorship over the Russian Muses or of responsibility for them. Gorky felt he had to know all that was happening in Russian literature, and world literature too, for that matter. His sense of responsibility for literature was really quite astonishing.

Gorky was a truly remarkable figure. The enormous range of his interests and the insatiable curiosity with which he studied life in order to re-organise it had no parallel among his contemporaries and bring to mind the legendary giants of the Renaissance, men like Leonardo da Vinci. Gorky took an interest in all the spheres of Russia's art, science, technology and economy. As a novelist, publicist, critic and organiser of a literary movement, he established contact with thousands of his contemporaries, writers, scientists and workers (he penned no less than 8,000 letters in his time), and with millions of readers for whom he embodied their dream of a better future and whom he gave confidence in their own strength. One may say that the Russian people made of Gorky a symbol, a means of self-cognisance, an expression of their latent powers and talent.

Maxim Gorky (the pen-name of Alexei Maximovich Peshkov, 1868-1936) rose to the pinnacle of fame from the lowliest beginnings. His father, a cabinet-maker, died when Alexei was still very young, and he was brought up by his grandfather, an upholsterer, who was a morose and cruel man. Gorky began to earn his living very early in life, working as a dishwasher, then a scribe and then a baker, and knew well what manual labour meant. As a young man he went wandering about the country, from the middle reaches of the Volga right down to the Caucasus. He stored up a wealth of impressions from his travels and came to know the life of the people intimately.

His rich personality and penchant for fantastic and romantic imagery were not the main source feeding his art. He first gathered impressions and experience on his travels, and only then took up the pen to tell the world about Russia and her people, their life and their hopes, and the meaning of happiness. That is why philosophical reflections and description occupy so much space in his works.

It so happened that Gorky embarked on his literary career at the same time as the Leninist party emerged on the historical scene in Russia. It was a period marked by a sharp upswing in the workers' movement and a rapidly mounting revolutionary situation. Gorky's stories reflected the psychology of a people roused to energetic action. In his early works he portrayed the lowest strata of society—artisans, tramps, dreamers and rebels—presenting them in vividly romantic images. His characters tend to argue about the purpose of life, to pose questions to the reader and answer them themselves.

In a letter to Chekhov, Gorky wrote that a writer's excessive fidelity to facts "kills realism". The old method of realism no longer satisfied him. He was even less inclined to render the drab colours of life by naturalistic means. What he needed was to find a new method that would render life more romantic, that would raise the readers above drabness, awaken in them an interest in the beauty and goodness of life and spur them on to action. He began to introduce this romantic element in his works, especially in his revolutionary parables, poems and legends (*The Song of the Falcon, The Stormy Petrel* and others). It is always present when he is depicting characters from the "lower depths" of society, which as a rule have a fantastic appeal to the imagination.

Gorky's famous play *The Lower Depths* (1902) is alive with this spirit of revolutionary romance. It has been staged by theatres in all the world's largest cities. In Russia, the tsarist censors put up a stubborn opposition to the staging of the play although none of the characters in it actually call for the overthrow of the established order. But in his portrayal of the "lower depths", Gorky showed such a thirst for beauty along with crushing poverty that his play became an indictment of a society where such conditions were possible. The main characters—thieves, prostitutes, a déclassé Baron, a former actor—these dregs of society living in the stench of a basement doss-house, all seemed to cry out to the audience: "This mustn't go on!" Small wonder that Luka, the old man preaching meakness and acceptance is disliked by most of the inmates and especially by Satin, the rebellious drunkard who refuses to take his fate lying down.

Gorky's equally famous novel *Mother* is permeated with the same romantic spirit. The novel is about working-class life and the class struggle waged by the Russian workers at the beginning of this century. Gorky's purpose was to show how people developed spiritually in the course of revolutionary struggle. In this respect, the book is of basic importance, for it enables us to see how the method of socialist realism drawing its material from life itself was originally conceived. Prior to Gorky, beginning with Schiller's *Die Räuber*, revolutionaries had usually been portrayed in literature as destroyers of society. Gorky presented an entirely new view that: initiation into revolutionary struggle enriches and straightens out a man spiritually. It is on this principle that he moulded the characters of Pavel Vlassov and his mother Nilovna. It is interesting to note that the main characters had real, living prototypes. Pavel Vlassov, for instance, was based on Pyotr Zalomov, a Sormovo worker, who died only recently.

Gorky's role as a sort of live bridge between Russia's two literary epochs is perhaps most evident in *Mother*. The basic idea of the novel is that the aim of historical progress should be the good of man. In this sense Gorky was following the emancipatory traditions of 19th-century Russian literature. But there is a new angle in his treatment of the theme: he does not only show suffering men (as Dostoyevsky did) but also men who work changes in the world and become all the more human for it.

Gorky's *Mother* has proved to be one of his most popular works with workers both in Russia and abroad. It has been reprinted time and again in millions of copies. Gorky wrote it during his American trip in the summer of 1906, and it was first published in English in the *Appleton Magazine* in 1906-07. In May, when Lenin met Gorky at the Fifth Congress of the Russian Social-Democratic Labour Party in London, he congratulated him on the novel which he had read in manuscript. Gorky records this conversation in his reminiscences of Lenin. "I told him that I had been in a hurry to write the book, but before I could explain why, Lenin nodded and himself explained the reason: it was very good, he said, that I had hastened to write it. It was a much needed book. Many workers had joined the revolutionary movement spontaneously, instinctively, and would find reading *Mother* very useful. 'It's a very timely book,' he said. That was all the praise he gave me, but it was extremely valuable to me."

Gorky devoted a large place in his works to the portrayal of the former masters of Russia—factory owners, merchants, and intel-

52

lectuals linked economically and spiritually with the wealthy classes. During his wanderings Gorky came close to understanding those "men of iron" or "masters of life", as he called them. Very often they were interesting, gifted people, self-made men in many cases. Gorky was by no means prejudiced against them simply because they were capitalists. If anything, he actually showed something like admiration for those heroes of his, whose seething vitality found an outlet in drinking orgies, eccentricity and frenzied money-making. But he showed the harmful effects of this life on the "private owner" himself: how it cripples his soul, cultivates greed and cruelty, teaches him to lie and fills him with dissatisfaction and boredom. This subject reoccurs in a number of Gorky's plays (*Vassa Zheleznova, Yegor Bulychev and Others*) and in several of his novels and stories *The Three, Foma Gordeyev, The Life of Matvei Kozhemyakin*, and *The Artamonovs* (1925). The latter novel covers the life of three generations in a Russian merchant-class family. The head of the family is Ilya Artamonov–a man as mighty as an oak reared in its native soil. There is something fine about this man of boundless energy, ever launching new plans. He wants to use his money to transform the sleepy provincial town where fate has brought him. But his activities are based on exploitation, and his sons and grandsons degenerate and become smaller men, wallowing in the ugly slough of accumulation, indolence and aimlessness.

While romantically extolling Man (Gorky wrote the word with a capital M) he was emphatically opposed to individualism. Gorky's well-known article "The Destruction of Personality" (1909) is a passionate philosophical treatise against the "tape-worm of individualism".

Gorky's last and biggest work, *The Life of Klim Samgin* (a book in four volumes, on which Gorky worked the last ten years of his life) is also devoted to the theme which had always engaged his attention: how a person gets poisoned by Philistinism and individualism and what happens to him as a result. The main character of this story, which gives a panoramic view of Russia from the 1880s to 1917, is Klim Samgin, a lawyer, a typical Philistine individualist. Since childhood Samgin had learnt never to commit himself, and never give a straight "yes" or "no" for an answer. He claims to be a defender of the poor, a champion of the people, but in actual fact he depends on the rich for his livelihood. He is a born chameleon and traitor. He takes good care of himself in everything: in joy, in sorrow, in his relations with the state and with the different political parties. He sides with everyone but belongs to no one. He poses as a good friend of the revolutionaries and of the capitalists, of the police and of the street walkers, of the students and the merchants. He is the larva of a man, a genius of adaptability.

Fortune is kind to him and he plays a certain role in society. But he is a dehumanised person, a typical child of that age when masquerade and manoeuvre became the guiding principle of behaviour. For its psychological depth, *Klim Samgin*, in which Gorky is polemicising with Dostoyevsky, is indisputably one of the masterpieces of world literature. In Gorky we find none of the sentimentalising over the "little men", which we often do in Dostoyevsky.

When Gorky began work on *Klim Samgin*, there were some who felt the subject and the period it covered were too remote from the times, and somehow incompatible with his brilliant publicistic writings. But this could only have seemed so to the superficial observer. In fact, Gorky the artist was not at odds with Gorky the publicist. Indeed, it is precisely this last work of his which, for the generations to come, may be of supreme importance in the struggle he waged against reactionary views and trends.

Artists have a tendency to present the rout of fascism by the forces of progressive mankind as the killing of the dragon. But defeating the dragon is only half the battle. It still remains to examine thoroughly the field where the dragon had planted its teeth. Fascism must be defeated morally and politically. It is imperative that the majority of mankind should see the historical and psychological roots of fascism laid completely bare, exposing its nature from the larval stage.

Gorky's *Klim Samgin* does just this. Probably nothing as profound as this book has ever been written about the degeneration of man.

In the years during which he was engaged in writing this four-volume philosophical epic (which Gorky himself for some reason chose to call a short novel), he also wrote many brilliant articles on current political themes which were simultaneously printed in *Pravda* and *Izvestia*. Those that had the greatest impact were: "If the Enemy Will not Capitulate, He Must Be Destroyed" (1930), "Whose Side Are You On, Masters of Culture?", and "The Answer to American Correspondents" (first published on March 22, 1932). The first was levelled at foreign aggressors who were preparing a war against the U.S.S.R. In it Gorky wrote: "This obliges the working class to actively prepare for self-defence, for the defence of their historic role, for the defence of all that it has already created for itself, and also for the instruction of the proletariat in all lands, in the course of its thirteen years' heroic and dedicated endeavour in building up a new world."

Generally speaking, Gorky's articles reflected his change of mood more strongly than did his words of fiction. In 1930, making the final changes in his essay on Lenin, he accurately defined the difference between Lenin's and his own approach to life's phenomena. He wrote: "He (Lenin—K.Z.) was a politician. He had that perfectly trained, straight-forward vision essential for the helmsman of a huge, heavy ship, as unwieldy as peasant Russia.

"I have a physical aversion to politics, and have little faith in the wisdom of the masses in general, and the wisdom of the peasant masses in particular. Wisdom does not make a creative force until it has been organised by an idea. In the wisdom of the masses there is no idea so long as they are not aware of the community of interests of every one of them."

Gorky's words about having "a physical aversion to politics" sound rather surprising, of course, especially in an article on Lenin. For Gorky did take an interest in politics—and a very keen one, too, sometimes. There were his articles "Untimely Thoughts", for instance, which appeared in the newspaper *Novaya Zhizn* (New Life) in 1918 and later came out in brochure form. Years later, Gorky himself condemned these articles as a mistake. Articles of this sort, often written under the impression of odd isolated incidents (like his article "Russian Cruelty", 1922) are not infrequently used by anti-communist propagandists in the West as proof of their allegation that even Gorky agreed with some of the charges made by the bourgeois press against the Communists and the Russian people as a whole.

However, it is ridiculous to try and find in Gorky's writings a barb aimed at his own people or the Communist Party. In his articles he really sings the praises of the Russian people and their great achievements after the Great October Socialist Revolution. This was the essential thing in Gorky. He was above all a *people's* writer of the proletarian epoch in the true meaning of the word.

Gorky can in full justice be called not just a social writer but a socialist writer. His aim was not simply to portray the society of his day in all its class aspects (like Balzac), but also to portray those processes in the life of society which determined its future.

Gorky was a highly intellectual writer. In his writings, the intellectualism and the urge to fathom the world and world history, typical of world literature in the 20th century—take Anatole France, Bernard Shaw, H. G. Wells and many others—found its traditionally Russian and yet entirely new expression. The newness stems from the inquisitiveness of the people who, feeling they are the masters of life now, are anxious to understand it, reorganise and beautify it in their own fashion. That is why Gorky always wrote about work with such genuine inspiration.

"...I believe that never in the world, never in all history, has work revealed its fantastic power to transform people and life as vividly and convincingly as it is doing today, with us, in our state of workers and peasants," wrote Gorky in his *Correspondence with Readers* in 1930.

With Gorky, descriptions of everyday life and historical episodes, made in his usual bold manner and with enthusiasm for his material, alternate with dialogues and long discourses by the characters themselves. In view of this, his big novels have less compositional unity, to my mind, than his stories. His artistry is most apparent in his psychological studies. His Lev Tolstoi (in the article of the same name) has been painted by an artist as great as his model, while his portrait of Lenin is probably unequalled by anything else written or said about him by his contemporaries and friends.

Gorky emerged on the literary scene at a time when it was customary for writers to present the people through a veil of compassion for their sufferings, almost as something holy which was being desecrated. Gorky rejected this tone of pity. He spoke in the voice of the people telling their own story. He criticised, describing Russia's frightening philistine world, the poverty and the self-banishment of men from civilised society. His harsh criticism was as uncompromising as that of the critical realists of the past, yet through it broke a glowing faith in life, in himself, in Russia and the Russian people.

Gorky raised his voice against the most highly esteemed names in world literature, Lev Tolstoi and Dostoyevsky, where their preaching of humility and non-resistance to evil acted as an obstacle in the struggle for the liberation of mankind from the world's dark forces. "Submit, proud man," said Dostoyevsky. But Gorky said: "Man! How fine! What a proud sound it has!" Father Zosima, Dostoyevsky's beloved character in his *Brothers Karamazov*, used to say: "Indulge not and multiply not your needs and desires." But Gorky taught: "Be greedy for life. Nature is yours to take and make into a beautiful thing!"

In Russian literature Gorky with his hymn to Man, to culture, to peace and sunlight, was like a young *bogatyr* emerging from the ocean depths of the people and confidently stepping ashore. Of himself he used to say that he had come into the world to challenge the leaden sordidness of life, to challenge and defeat it. For a pen-name he chose the word Gorky, which means bitter, thus symbolising his bitter pain for the people and his desire to speak the bitter truth about it. This he did, but he also told people that Man is a splendid creature and that if all men joined together and built their own kingdom of reason and labour they would be able to do wonderful, extraordinary things in this world.

Gorky did not believe in leaving things unsaid, in resorting to vague allusions or allegorical figures of speech. His emotions were strong and pure. He thought in terms of history, present and future, and his mind was occupied with the issues and ideas of the epoch.

His hatred for fascism came as natural to him as breathing. He once wrote to some school children in Irkutsk: "A fascist who knocks a worker's head off his spinal column by kicking him in the chin, is not even a beast, but something incomparably worse than a beast, a mad animal that must be destroyed."

Gorky was the first author of his kind. And readers the world over felt it at once. In his writings he embodied all those progressive ideas and thoughts which had long been ripening in Russian literature, and led it forward. No Russian writer since Pushkin had been so brimming with optimism and love of life. No literary critic since Belinsky and Chernyshevsky had been so profound and versatile and as capable of organising the minds of men. Since Saltykov-Shchedrin Russian literature had not known a more merciless critic of old Russia's evils. But apart from all this, Gorky had also enriched literature with new ideas drawn from the people, the workers' movement and Lenin, and had developed them in his articles, novels, and plays—ideas engendered and fostered by the people's revolution. He showed, more convincingly than did any of his predecessors, the inevitability of the socialist renovation of Russia.

Thus Gorky, the founder of the method of socialist realism, is rightly esteemed as the father of new Russian literature.

Chapter 6

Mayakovsky

Vladimir Mayakovsky. 1924.

When the cruiser *Aurora* fired its historic salvo on October 25th (November 7th), 1917, announcing the start of the socialist revolution, many writers of the older generation felt too confused to face up to the changing world. A few days later, Anatoly Lunacharsky, the People's Commissar for Education, decided to assemble the writers in order to find a common language with the Russian intelligentsia. Only a few people turned up. Among them were Alexander Blok and Vladimir Mayakovsky.

Blok was a subtle lyricist, a man of tremendous sensibility who keenly felt the crises and contradictions of the age. His poem *The Twelve* is the music of the times, a dream of beauty which is the soul of a popular revolution.

Blok was only 41 when he died in 1921. What he had not had time to say about the Revolution was expressed by Mayakovsky.

When anyone mentions the name Mayakovsky, I automatically think of the word "revolution", by association. The reader of his unconventional poetry, packed with politics and topical events, will surely say: "Yes, a poet like that could only live in a period of radical change in social relations."

I saw Mayakovsky for the first time at a sailors' gathering in Petrograd in the winter of 1918. He was reading his *Left March*. With his deep, thundering voice he managed to outshout the noisy audience who were in no mood to listen to poetry. Most of the sailors had come there to have a dance with their girls. But gradually they began to listen, captivated by the power of Mayakovsky's faith in his convictions, his drive and his revolutionary verve. I made his personal acquaintance later, in 1920, and often met him between then and his tragic death. The literary group he headed, known as "LEF", was probably closer to the Party line than the group of constructivists in which I played the role of theoretician and ideologist. In the second half of the 1920s we had many disputes with the former group. However, this did not prevent us becoming friends, especially as I started on my literary career under Mayakovsky's wing, so to speak, writing for his magazine. He had a peculiar attraction that none could resist. His personal charm was compounded of a variety of qualities: he was full of youthful daring, a gentleman, and a man of revolutionary honour.

Mayakovsky was born in 1893 in Bagdadi, a small village in the valley of the Rion River in the Caucasus. His father was a forester and died young. Soon after his death the family moved to Moscow. As a boy of fifteen Mayakovsky joined an underground social-democratic circle. He was arrested for distributing proclamations and kept in prison for eleven months, and this experience left a deep impression in his mind.

Mayakovsky studied painting, but became a poet. He began writing in 1912 during a new upswing in the social movement. He appeared on the literary scene as a futurist breaking with the aesthetic canons of conventional art. But his example shows that Russian reality gave a different content to literary movements which sprang up simultaneously throughout Europe. Mayakovsky's futurism had no relation to the futurism of the Italian poet Marinetti. The Russian futurists did not make a cult of machines, speed, or military power. In short, they did not cultivate the aesthetics of aggression.

Mayakovsky's poetry was centred on Man. He was full of compassion for Man. "I'm there where it hurts, everywhere," he said in his early poetry. "I'm all injury and pain", "nothing but heart wounds everywhere". He was not a direct successor to nor a follower of Gorky, and it would be stretching a point to call them the representatives of the same school, for they had nothing in common as far as style was concerned. Yet they were close in spirit. What they did have in common was their militant revolutionary humanism. They joined hands on the flagpole of the banner carried aloft by Russian literature and inscribed with the words: "Fight for Man Who's Worthy of the Name!"

A book of Mayakovsky's verse with the intrigueing title *As Plain As a Moo* came out during World War I. The poetry included in this volume expressed a wide range of emotions: from anguish to protest, oratorial fervour and anger. It denounced "bedroom" lyricism and decadence. Mayakovsky began his famous poem *Cloud in Trousers* with the lines:

> *I'll tease your thought,*
> > *daydreaming on a softened brain,*
> *Just like a bloated lackey,*
> > *lolling on a greasy couch,*
> *I'll tease it with a rag torn from my bleeding heart,*
> *With insolence and spite,*
> > *until I've had my grouch. . . .*

He was indeed a poet with a "bleeding heart", an apostle of the new religion which preached complete renewal.

Still, his entire pre-revolutionary output makes up just one of the thirteen volumes comprising his collected works. Mayakovsky is very much our contemporary, a poet of the popular struggle for socialism. Just as the wind helps the eagle to straighten out its wings, so did the Russian Revolution of October 1917 help to shape Mayakovsky's talent and make him into a fully-fledged poet. The masses were his family. Promoting inspired inventiveness was his passion. Starting people off on a new way of life, purged of all past filth, was his purpose. "Comrades! To the barricades! To fight for hearts and souls!" he called. He put people's dream of the ideal man into words. The way to the achievement of this ideal, he realised, lay through popular struggle. Although it meant bloodshed and great sacrifices, the struggle was unavoidable. Thus he understood his mission as a poet of the Revolution, and awareness of his responsibility determined the character of his work.

There have, of course, been other great poets in world literature who glorified liberty and man freed from his chains. Rousseau,

Byron, Lermontov, Heine, Walt Whitman, Petöfi, Hugo and many others expressed in their poetry mankind's age-old dream of a free and noble man, at the same time reflecting the historical essence of their period and a definite stage in the development of society. We speak of them as the poets of freedom.

However, no words are more over-used than freedom, humanism, and affinity with the people. What made Mayakovsky a great poet of the proletarian revolution was that the object of his poetry was not man in general (as with Walt Whitman), nor even the man who protests (as with Byron), but the man who fights for the liberation of mankind. With Mayakovsky, all these words—freedom, humanism, affinity with the people—acquire a new historical meaning, expressing the interests of the progressive circles of society. This is what enabled Mayakovsky to create a new kind of poetry. This is why he sings a hymn not to some abstract, free man, but to the man in socialist society. Whereas before Mayakovsky the tendency in Russian poetry had been to set the individual apart from the state, with Mayakovsky we find precisely the opposite desire to merge the state and the individual into one.

He said:

> *Let Gosplan,*[1]
> > *debating from dusk till dawn,*
> *My yearly assignment set.*
> *And let the people's commissar*
> *The thought of the times direct.*

He visualised poetry not as a "sweet-smelling bunch of pinks", nor as Baudelaire's "black flowers of evil", nor even as Prometheus's proud challenge to the world. For him a poet was a soldier, a worker at his lathe.

A Russian national poet, Mayakovsky championed a new type of patriotism which was inalienable from the cause of building socialism in Russia. Each of his verses gives you a charge of energy directing your actions and thoughts, and in each of his words— condensed and positioned with a powerful hand—you seem to feel the presence of this big, broad-shouldered man, striding into the future.

Mayakovsky's poetry represents a unique chronicle of revolutionary events from 1917 to 1930 (the year he died). It made no difference to him whether the theme happened to be "lofty" or "lowly". He wrote about everything under the sun that was topical in those

---

[1] *Gosplan*: State Planning Committee of the USSR Council of Ministers, a Soviet government body whose function is to draw up the plans of economic development and verify their fulfillment.—*Ed.*

days: the state loan, a factory worker moving into a new flat, the conference in Genoa (at which he imagined himself representing the people's interests), rubber dummies for village babies, love and friendship, the death of Yesenin, and literary debates. He ripped every theme apart in order to show the seed of poetry inside it, a glimpse of the road leading into a radiant future, and its appeal to the revolutionary conscience of men, mobilising their strength.

In his moving poem *Vladimir Ilyich Lenin* Mayakovsky succeeded in creating a monumental image of Lenin moulded by history itself, and also in conveying the people's boundless love for their leader. The poem *Fine!* expresses the jubilant feeling of people who have won freedom with their own hands and have built up their own state.

Mayakovsky's poetic images are like Cyclopean structures. Hyperbole and extravagant metaphors are piled on top of one another. Every word and rhyme is packed with meaning and feeling. His comparisons, his neologisms and his metre are strikingly bold. Gogol used to say that Derzhavin (a prominent poet in the reign of Catherine the Great) used hyperbole and allegory as a "supernatural force" which rendered a figure "so very much alive that it seemed to stare at you with a thousand eyes". Mayakovsky's images also look at you with a thousand eyes. Some appalled by the tragedy of life, others glowing with affection for people, and still others shining excitedly from the sheer joy of being alive. Like Gogol's prose, Mayakovsky's poetry is alternately ironical and lyrical. Irony and satire, which Mayakovsky called his pet weapons, give his poetry its special colouring and its ode-like, emotional tone.

For all its formal innovation, Mayakovsky's poetry echoes many of the themes and sentiments of the 19th-century Russian classics. I think I can say with all justice that no poet has ever expressed the revolutionary sweep, the generosity, daring and courage of the Russian nature as powerfully as Mayakovsky. He was a Russian through and through.

After everything that has been said here, Mayakovsky's suicide may seem to defy explanation. It happened on April 14, 1930. People often ask why he did it. Why did Mayakovsky, whose whole poetic output was directed towards the goal of communism and served the one aim of building a new society, why did this poet who called himself an agitator, a brawler, a ringleader, and who really did invent new poetic forms that brimmed with revolutionary boldness, why did this man suddenly kill himself?

In a letter written just before his suicide he wrote that he was doing it for personal reasons: "My love boat has been smashed against the commonplaces of life," "I wouldn't advise others to do it."

For his last poem *In Full Voice* addressed to his "comrade descendants" he found some powerfully penetrating words which reveal to some extent what he was feeling then:

> Scribbling love songs for you
>   would suit me as well,
> Even better—
>   for pleasure and purse.
> But I,
>   I'd trample,
>   My voice to quell
> On the throat of my own verse.

Further on he says:

> A poet licked away
>   consumptives' clots,
> With the rough tongue
>   of posters that he made.

I think that Mayakovsky was being unfair to himself when he said this. He was a tribune of the socialist revolution in the full meaning of the word, so what other "song" can we associate with him? Various remarks of his and lines of his poetry have become proverbs and slogans. His statue in the square named after him in Moscow is the meeting place of young poets who consider themselves his successors and heirs to his revolutionary boldness and energy.

Mayakovsky said about himself:

> I love the hugeness of our plans,
> The boldness of our mile-long strides.

We shall probably be nearest the truth if we put Mayakovsky's suicide down to extreme nervous stress.

He was a true townsman, he was well-travelled in Europe, and had also taken a trip to Mexico and the United States. He was a living embodiment of the revolution itself with its lust for life and world-sweeping energy. Mayakovsky was immensely proud of being a citizen of the Soviet Union (remember his *Poem About the Soviet Passport*). He never worshipped bourgeois culture even in those years of near chaos, when little had yet been built and poverty and destitution peeked out of every unmended hole. It was Mayakovsky who wrote: "We Soviet people have our own special pride: we look down our noses at the moneybags." His satirical plays *The Bedbug* and *The Bath-house*, in which he takes a vicious stab at bureaucracy, are playing to full houses to this day.

In his lifetime his physical hugeness formed a sort of barrier to my understanding him, and I suspect I was not the only one affected like that. Russians have a preconceived notion that all big men have big hearts. These *bogatyrs* can cross themselves with a 50 lb. weight in their hand, yet they wouldn't hurt a fly, let alone harm a single hair on a child's head. We were like children, making a nuisance of ourselves and wanting him to bounce us on his knee. We tugged and pulled at him, and never let him alone. Everything about him was huge: his height, his hands, his feet, his close-cropped head, and his eyes which were so bulging and attentive that they seemed to absorb whatever they were peering at. Alexander Fadeyev in his novel *The Rout* wrote that Levinson's eyes made Morozko think of strange lakes. Why strange? Because you can go on and on gazing into them without ever being able to fathom them. Fadeyev puts it very neatly. Mayakovsky's eyes were also like strange lakes. It was the strong undertow or the magnet in them that drew you on, sucking you in with all you contained. All his features were prominent: forehead, nose and chin.

I repeat, in his lifetime I did not understand Mayakovsky, and I am sure I was not the only one.

His powerful physique concealed a tenderness and an extraordinary sensitiveness. He was a very intelligent man. His intellect had such a vast range that it seemed to embrace the life of millions of people. It was an intelligence that stretched beyond the horizon, as it were.

The next most amazing thing about Mayakovsky was his nobility and delicacy of soul. He was noble in the fullest sense of the word. In this respect he was indeed a *bogatyr*, and we were mere children playing with him. I never saw him go to pieces or even show that he was badly upset. But I did hear from two women who knew him well that they had seen him sobbing. In his recollections Gorky also says that after reading his *Cloud in Trousers* Mayakovsky burst into tears. This is something one has to know in order to really understand Mayakovsky, to appreciate his self-control and his respect for other people which made him try so hard not to break down in public. Mayakovsky could deafen an audience with his thundering voice and for all his self-control suddenly burst into tears.

We once sat together on the executive bureau of the first federation of Soviet writers in which the different movements and groupings were represented. There were the RAPP[1] members (Russian Association of Proletarian Writers) and the "village-oriented" writers and poets. Leonid Leonov, whose face had a sculptural expressiveness, and Abram Efros, wearing gold-rimmed spectacles

---

[1] *RAPP*–Russian Association of Proletarian Writers, existed from 1923–1932 (abolished by decision of the C.C. C.P.S.U.)–*Ed.*

and a well-groomed beard, represented the Writers' Union. There too, Mayakovsky could be a different person. Perhaps what impressed me most strongly was that this loud-voiced heavyweight, who could magnetise an audience weighing a thousand tons, could become transformed into the most vulnerable and delicate of men. When speaking with someone, he would finger the chords of the other's soul with the gentle touch of a doctor, for fear that he might cause them harm. There was the Mayakovsky famous for his thundering voice, and another Mayakovsky, shy and thoughtful, and yet another Mayakovsky—meek and apologetic. I knew him like that too.

There is a shorthand record (unedited) of one of Mayakovsky's last public appearances in which he recalled his reading of *In Full Voice* at a conference of the Moscow Association of Proletarian Writers, and asked me afterwards what I thought of it, to which I had replied that it had sent shivers down my spine.

At this conference (which, if my memory doesn't fail me, was held on February 6, 1930) Mayakovsky read his poem with a note of challenge, and also with great anguish. He had the look of a man taking aim at a distant target, firing over the nearer ones.

The constructivists held a meeting of their own the night before at the Business Club in Myasnitskaya Street (now Kirov Street). There we decided that Bagritsky and Lugovskoi would join the Russian Association of Proletarian Writers. Lugovskoi prepared for the occasion with solemn eloquence, while Bagritsky took it as a matter of course and even as a nuisance, judging by his snappish tone.

Thus the three of them—Mayakovsky, Lugovskoi and Bagritsky—were admitted to the Association that same evening, having written more or less uniform applications. Leopold Averbach who presided did not conceal his satisfaction and positively glowed with delight as he glanced about him through the thick, gleaming lenses of his pince-nez. Mayakovsky read his poem, drumming with his fingers on the green baize table and glancing now and again at a piece of paper in his hand (obviously he had not yet memorised the poem). He read with inspiration and bitterness in a resonant voice that drowned out all the other sounds:

> *I do not care a damn*
> *for bronze piled up in tons. . . .*
> *Let socialism built in battle*
> *Stand as a common monument*
> *to all of us!*

He was wholly obsessed with one subject all his life. He never stopped thinking about it. It was always there at the back of his mind when he sat silently at a meeting, thundered at an audience, joked or brooded. This subject can hardly be called simply politics. It spread out like circles on a pond. Thinking of politics he began to think of people, then of mankind, and then of the beauty and goodness of life. He gave a political interpretation to everything, to people, events, and his own poetry.

He never accepted compromise. Never a concession! And he rendered the atomic fire of the epoch of transition from one social system to the other more compellingly than any other poet.

Mayakovsky has won world-wide recognition, and his popularity will grow with the ages. He is, to quote Gogol, "visible from far away, from all the corners of the earth".

Mayakovsky once said to Aseyev, and later repeated it to me almost word for word, that if the Party needed him to he would be willing to start writing in iambs. Another time he said that he had placed his pen in service... "mind you," he added, "in the service of the moment". This, coming from a poet who attached the greatest importance to the form of expression! He treated words like a lion tamer, making them turn somersaults and chasing them about. He also invented new words. Was it not Mayakovsky who said he was afraid that poetry might be reduced to "cracks from the gallery and the nonsense of a ditty".

But when politics called him, he threw all other considerations overboard. I think he was prompted by a magnificent anger at anything that might hamper the achievement of communism. Like Cyclops he could hurl rocks. And when he felt some personal weakness getting in his way, he was even capable of turning this anger against himself.

> *I'd trample,*
> > *my voice to quell,*
> > > *on the throat of my own verse.*

He was something of a fanatic in this, like Father Avvakum, one of the founders of the Old Believers' sect in Russia in the 17th century, who was as frenziedly irreconcilable and chose to be burnt alive rather than renounce his beliefs. The main thing for him was "the red of his republic's flag", and it was constantly on his mind. Probably the only other writer who could have put it like that and who had felt like that was Nikolai Ostrovsky.

The Revolution shaped some amazing characters. They were not fanatics: their spirit was fantastically fired with enthusiasm. And Mayakovsky was one of those at whom people will never cease to marvel.

Chapter 7

Yesenin

Sergei Yesenin. 1922.

The very name Sergei Yesenin evokes an image of sheer beauty and humaneness. True, a feeling of anxiety is also associated with it, for his poetry expresses pain and confusion caused by the spectacle of the great revolutionary upheaval. At times his emotions were at odds with his reason which clearly saw the road stretching away into the future. But the main impression his poetry leaves you with is a feeling of lightness in your heart, the joy of contact with something beautiful. And this is why Yesenin's lyric poetry, like all real art, like music, has that peculiar healing power. Contact with the beautiful ennobles us, gives us new faith in life and fresh strength.

Lyric poetry, we know, has its own means whereby a poet can tell a story of life or lay bare the secrets of his soul with a revealing power that could not be achieved by any other expressive media. I think that the greatness of Yesenin as a lyric poet lies in the amazing frankness with which he expresses emotions and reveals the wealth of the human soul in images and in the very music of his words. No wonder Gorky had said that "Yesenin was more of an organ of feeling created by Nature exclusively for poetry, than a man of flesh and blood".

Sergei Yesenin was born on October 3, 1895, into a peasant family in the village of Konstantinovo on the Oka. In those days, Ryazan region was one of the poorest and most backward in Russia. People were compelled to leave their home villages and seek seasonal work elsewhere or jobs in the towns. Yesenin's father, Alexander Nikitich, worked as a shop assistant at a butcher's in Moscow. As a child Sergei lived with his grandfather and went to the parish school. The poet awakened in him at an early age and for all the wretchedness of village life he saw the beauty of it and lost his heart to it forever. He developed his feeling for poetry by reading Pushkin, Lermontov, Nekrasov, Koltsov, and *The Lay of Igor's Host* whose poetic images he adored. It is no exaggeration to say that his native country was to him a spring of magic water which gave him a vision of all that is beautiful in the world.

Yesenin's poetry conjures up for us a picture of rural Russia with her roads bathed in moonlight in winter and brooding thirstily in summer. This Russia with her colours and smells is a big, inhabited world, the home of man, the poet's Motherland, and he loved everything in it. All his comparisons, images, metaphors and expressive verbal means he drew from the peasant life that was his and which he understood.

Yesenin likens the sun to the plough and the new moon to a lamb or a shepherd's horn. Such metaphors and comparisons fill almost every poem.

The Russian landscape and life in the countryside are the subject matter of Yesenin's early poetry in which his enchantment with this natural world blends with his passionate feeling for Russia. The landscape, his home village and Russia are combined in his poetry in a single profound feeling of beauty. His patriotism was one of the mightiest sources feeding his poetry.

Yesenin has described the charmingly modest landscape of Central Russia with a love so tender and profound as if it were a living creature. And because he felt it thus, he showed it in movement and not contemplatively. The night "leans over the stream, and in the white water bathes its blue feet"; the grass "collects the copper pieces from the wind-blown willows"; the twilight "dances"; the pine "has put on a white head scarf" or again it has "bent in two like an old woman"; the warm evening "thievishly nibbles the tree stumps in the meadow"; the crescent moon "polishes its horns"; the marsh "blows clouds of smoke"; the willows "click their rosaries", and so on. The sky, rivers, sunsets, dawns, shrubs, marshes, the new moon, fields and grasses—everything in Yesenin's poetry is in motion and thereby comes into poetic relation with man, with life itself. His very soul has no existence apart from his native land, and he says:

> *Land beloved! In my heart-dreams*
> *I see suns in meadow streams.*
> *Oh, to lose myself forever*
> *In your glory-ringing greens!*

Yesenin brought into literature images of his native countryside, its speech and songs. His close, direct contact with folk songs and, consequently, the tradition of Koltsov whom Yesenin recognised as one of his teachers is everywhere in evidence.

As a whole, Yesenin's poetry is wistful in mood, but there is in it an infinite healing power, an inexpressible kindness that puts your soul at peace. This is one of the secrets of Yesenin's appeal.

Sometimes his imagery is so unexpected and his feelings so inexplicable that his poetry becomes rather involved. But in essence it is very simple. He brings his readers, whose mind has grown sophisticated with the abstractions of modern mathematical logic, cybernetics and all the intricacies of modern culture, back to those primordial affections and sufferings with which man emerges from his cradle and whose origins are lost to sight in the dim remoteness of history. Loving your mother, and loving your homeland. Sleeping out in the open and hearing a song through the mist. Simple joys and simple pain.

> *The sadness of my bestial verse*
> *I fed on mint and mignonette....*

But Yesenin does not come to us in sadness, bringing solace in moments of grief. Yesenin also sang his hosannahs to life.

Fine is the title Mayakovsky gave to his poem dedicated to the tenth anniversary of the Russian Socialist Revolution. His "fine!" is an exclamation of joy, a glad affirmation of all that the Revolution has given the working people. It expresses the jubilance of emancipated labour.

Yesenin puts a different meaning into the word. How fine it is to be alive! How fine life is!

His amazingly fresh and keen perception of life as a thing of beauty finds expression in his frequent use of such exclamatory openings as:

> *T'would be wonderful smilingly munching hay*
> *with the snout of a crescent moon!*
> *It's good in the autumn freshness*
> *Your apple-tree soul to shake down. . .*
> *It's fine getting out of your system*
> *The nail of your blood-heating verse. . .*
> *It's fine through the grass to go wading*
> *Alone, on a moonlit night. . . .*

Yesenin had the gift of sincerity, the gift of laying bare his soul. He was a poet of the heart, and that is why his voice, over-coming all language barriers, the voice of humanity itself, a voice tense with the drama of our epoch's revolutionary battles and cataclysms, reaches people everywhere. Poetry, he believed, should "caress the souls of strangers with the warmth of blood". With all the passion of his tender nature he responded instantly and whole-heartedly to pain in men, animals and even plants. Mayakovsky used to say that he was everywhere where there was pain. But I think Yesenin might have said that about himself with more emotional right and a greater force of conviction. He shared the pain of the bitch whose pups had been taken away from her. He suffered for the cow led to slaughter. It hurt him when flowers were crushed underfoot, when fruit and grain were gathered for food.

There are different kinds of humanity and love. Love can be a creative power. Love can mean pride in what one holds dear. Love can be compassion. And although Yesenin wrote that he envied those who "spent their life in battle, defending a great idea", his was not a fighting nature. Even though he said, rejoicing, that:

> *The whirlwind has dressed up my life*
> *In a flowering cloak of spun gold. . . .*

he was always thinking of other people, of people who were "even unhappier, even more downtrodden". He had seen their eyes which were "sadder than a cow's", and he cried:

> *Who'll cast a stone into this pool?*
> *Don't touch it. Let it be.*

70

In one and the same year (1924) Yesenin extolled the heroism of revolutionaries ("Ballad of the Twenty-Six", and his wonderful "Song of the Great March") and worried about people whose "blood had turned rancid and mouldy, like water in a stagnant pool". What could be done for these people? Surely man cannot be treated as refuse? Yesenin's heart could not reconcile itself to this. To be sure, there is a great weakness in this love-compassion which has its roots in the "sentimentality of the patriarchal village world". It is not the same kind of humanism as that praised by Gorky and Mayakovsky. For instance, Mayakovsky said of Lenin:

> *With friends*
> *he'd be the very soul of kindness.*
> *With enemies,*
> *as hard as hardest steel.*

Here you have humanism not born but "hammered into shape" in the course of proletarian struggle. Yesenin's humanism was inborn, he loved his neighbour as a Christian should, and was "the very soul of kindness" with friend and enemy alike. And this was the weak spot in his world outlook, reared on patriarchal soil. In his poetry even Lenin was transformed from a leader of the proletariat's steel armies into just a "good old soul" who went sleigh-riding with the "snotty kids" in winter.

Yesenin's ideological position and his concepts of humanism are indefensible against historical criticism. But what can you do if Yesenin, like old Brotteaux in Anatole France's *Les dieux ont soif*, had a "perverted instinct", as Anatole France ironically calls it: he could not stand the sight of blood and no philosophical theories, however correct, could defeat this "unnatural trait" in his character. But then, such is the power of art that even the profession of erroneous ideas cannot prevent us from succumbing to the charm of defencelessness if it is embodied in the image of a big, suffering heart. And we have to admit that we do succumb to this feeling of love-charity which Sergei Yesenin, like Romain Rolland and our kind-hearted Korolenko, communicates to us so compellingly.

Yesenin began to write poetry at the age of sixteen or seventeen and died when he was only thirty years old. He gained artistic maturity and ideological stability during the revolutionary years, and it was then, in the latter period of his creative life, that he produced his most important works.

His commitment to the people was manifest in the political stand he took, siding with the revolution from the start. He has written some beautiful poetry about Lenin, the "Ballad of the Twenty

Six" in which he sang a hymn to the heroism of the Baku commissars, the wonderful "Song About the Great March", and *Anna Snegina*—a poem which can be ranked with the best in Soviet poetry. Gorky was very fond of his dramatic poem *Pugachev* about the peasant revolt against the autocracy in 18th-century Russia.

But alongside these epic poems, alongside his lyric poems about nature and love, Yesenin's lyric poetry speaks of something else, stemming from the old to which he was bound. He meant every word of it when he said:

> *I'm not a new man. Can I hide it?*
> *I'm stuck with one foot firmly in the past,*
> *While with the other I keep falling, sliding,*
> *To catch up with the steel-clad force that moves too fast.*

What was the "old" the traces of which we find in Yesenin's poetry? In the first place, an abundance of religious images and themes, especially in his early poetry. Yesenin himself wrote: "The most controversial stage was my religiousness which left a very distinct imprint on my early poems. I do not regard this period as creatively mine. It was conditioned by my upbringing and my environment when I first embarked on my literary career. . . . I would ask my readers to treat all my Christs, Virgin Marys and St. Nicholases as the fairy-tale element in poetry. All these proper names must be taken in the same way as we take such names, which now belong to mythology, as Osiris, Oannes, Zeus, Aphrodite, Athene, and so on. In my poems the reader should turn his attention mainly to the lyrical feeling and the imagery which has shown the way to many, many young poets and prose writers."

All these themes and the verbal pattern of many poems with their predilection for archaisms reflected Yesenin's idealisation of the patriarchal village. And as a result, naturally enough, his protest against capitalism did not have a consistently revolutionary character. He glorified democratic freedom as in "Marfa-Posadnitsa" or gave vent to his feeling of protest in devil-may-care rowdiness.

There is one other weak spot in Yesenin's literary heritage. I mean his verses, few as they are, of the "Moscow Tavern Life" kind. In this and other such cycles Yesenin glamourises free-living and casual love-making ("Your blue eyes, soaked in drink", or "Sing then, sing, play your cursed guitar" and so on) which are alien in spirit to a Soviet person. These morbidly Bohemian themes are the direct result of the pernicious influence which life in a bourgeois city and in a set of decadent poets had on Yesenin.

I can well understand the desire to idealise one's favourite poet. But, frankly, I would not care for Yesenin more if he were a marble Adonis with not a thought wrinkling his brow and not a line of suffering on his face. I hold more precious the poet who fearlessly laid bare his restless soul, who had known both the glory of success and the tragedy of failure, who had known the dazzling happiness of communion with beauty, and also the bitterness of denied understanding, the pain of suffering. The Yesenin who was prepared to "caress the souls of strangers" with the warmth of his blood is dearer to me. Maybe he was not as handsome as Adonis, but he was more human.

When we meet one of Yesenin's heroes out in the open, in the countryside, more often than not we find him to be a good Russian lad with a touch of bold recklessness and also much tenderness in his soul. But when Yesenin paints the same character against the background of a big city, we see this same lad trudging along the moonlit street to some dive, and whining to some hoodlums or tarts about his finished life. In the Soviet reader, a character such as this can evoke nothing but condescending pity.

Yesenin committed suicide in the Hotel Angleterre in Leningrad on December 28, 1925. In the last two years of his life his wonderful poetic talent blossomed in all its splendour. He had freed his poetry of the affectation and intricacy that was alien to it, and it now clearly revealed its kinship with the Pushkin tradition. Yesenin himself used to say at that time that Pushkin's poetry had the strongest appeal for him.

Carlo Levi, the well-known Italian author, wrote in one of his articles that, in his opinion, the works of Russian literature which had the greatest influence on Italian writers, especially young writers, came from the pen of Lev Tolstoi, Dostoyevsky, Chekhov and Yesenin, "affecting to a large extent the whole of later Italian literature".

When I was in Rome in 1958, I asked Carlo Levi if Yesenin's influence could not perhaps be explained by the fact that in Italy the importance of the peasantry is as great as it had once been in Russia.

"Does it surprise you that Yesenin is so popular with us?" he asked.

"Of course. After all, there's only Russia in his heart."

"Yes, but your Russia is the human heart. Tolstoi and Dostoyevsky too, they belong to those whose hearts shine for all mankind. And there can be no poetry if there is no heart."

It was well put. Humanity is a part of the Russian tradition, of the tradition of Russian literature. And we remember with tremendous affection the good name of Sergei Yesenin because humanity is our motto, because in a country which is building communism the most honorary title is Man.

Chapter 8

The 1920s.
Emergence of the New Prose

What characterises Soviet literature of the 1920s as a whole? How did it develop in those years? In the West, this period is not infrequently described as a sort of golden age in Soviet literature. True, in those years Soviet literature was mostly judged from hearsay–I remember this well and all the better for living almost the whole of 1926 in Paris. People had a very vague knowledge of it. Those newspapers which were hostile to us spoke of Soviet literature with biting irony. Translations into foreign languages were made of books in which the West-European readers could find some criticism of Soviet society and the new way of life. To be sure, Russia in those days did present a picture of backwardness and poverty. One had to have a progressive, revolutionary world outlook to be able to penetrate the outward shell into the essence of the historical processes and see the forces which had undertaken to completely transform the old, backward Russia. The majority of the literary intelligentsia of the time and the writers of the older generation had not prepared themselves for writing from this stand-point which would have enabled them to show the phenomena of the new life in the process of development and to give readers a glimpse into the future. This is why the West clutched at such works of literature as Mikhail Bulgakov's plays and his story *Fateful Eggs* (1925), Pilnyak's novels and Panteleimon Romanov's *Comrade Kislyakov* which was published in France under the title *Three Pairs of Silk Stockings*. Does anyone still remember that dime novel? What the story boiled down to was that the intelligentsia had been reduced to such straights that a foreigner could buy any Russian woman for just three pairs of silk stockings. Plays like Valentin Katayev's *Squaring the Circle* were translated. It is a witty play, but is faithfully modelled on the old French vaudeville comedy where everything hinges on misunderstandings, confusion and muddle between lovers, misaddressed remarks, and so on.

The 1920s were the years when the foundations of Soviet literature were laid in conditions of sharp, ideological class struggle, when the new type of writer was shaped, and the first important works of socialist realist literature were produced. Readers began to lose interest in many of those writers who (like Pilnyak) chiefly played up the seamy side of Soviet life. The novels of Serafimovich, Furmanov and Fadeyev, who had grasped the essence of the historical process, grew in popularity and importance.

Last but not least, the 1920s saw the great poet of the revolutionary epoch, Vladimir Mayakovsky, in his prime. In the eyes of the whole world he came to symbolise those great and splendid changes which the socialist revolution had made in Russia.

But let us return to the story of our literary life in those years. The problem of creating a new socialist culture and literature was not really tackled until after the end of the Civil War, when the armies of the tsarist generals Kornilov, Denikin, Kolchak and the various White atamans in the South of Russia, Siberia and the Far East, had been defeated, the intervention forces of the fourteen powers headed by Britain and France had been routed, and the new Soviet regime had been finally established. The entire life of the country was entering an important new phase. The immediate task was to prove the viability of the new principles of labour organisation and production relations.

Methods of compulsion had prevailed in the preceding period, known as war communism, when war was on and the entire country resounded with the roar of guns. The new period was marked by the adoption, at the instance of Lenin, of a New Economic Policy, known as the NEP. Small private enterprises, shops, commercial agencies and publishing houses, were opened in the towns. Although all the key positions, such as large factories, banks and land, remained in the hands of the victorious proletariat, the New Economic Policy changed even the ordinary street scene. This apparent revival of the recently defeated enemy perplexed the romantically inclined poets from the Proletkult (Proletarian Culture) workshops.[1] It also perplexed that part of the old literary intelligentsia who, like Blok, had allied themselves with the proletarian revolution for reasons of the highest moral order. Thus, for instance, Marietta Shaginyan said (in her article "How I Taught Weaving", 1920) that the writers welcomed the Revolution in the first place because of the moral demands which it advanced. The maximalism of these moral demands appealed to the writers most strongly and evoked a response in their hearts. The New Economic Policy, on the other

---

[1] Proletkult was founded in 1917 and functioned for a few years. Its theorists, A. A. Bogdanov and V. F. Pletnev, developed views alien to Marxism and contradictory to the Party policy. They held that the working class had to reject the achievements of world culture and artificially build up its own "proletarian" culture. These harmful theories were sharply criticised by the C.P.S.U. and in the first place by Lenin.

hand, with its seeming renunciation of that heroic radicalism which marked the period of the Civil War was not understood by everyone.

Lev Nikulin, a well-known author, later described this period picturesquely in his memoirs entitled *Time, Space and Movement*. He recalled how the signs of revived capitalism had shocked him after his front-line impressions.

"We came back to Moscow at the end of August, 1922. Myasnitskaya Street was gaudy with shop signs. 'Haberdashery. N. Zakharov and Isidor Krants' ran across the whole frontage of the building which we had left bearing the laconic inscription 'Glavbum'; the place where I had been issued with coupons for men's hats (for the members of our mission) had the lettering on the sign, 'M. Mezheritsky. In Business since 1889', freshly covered with gold paint. 'The Mutual Credit Society' announced that it was in existence, and 'I. Majoffis, Jeweller' was displaying an assortment of wedding rings and silver dippers painted with Vasnetsov's *bogatyrs* and *bogatyr* steeds, on trays lined with cherry coloured velvet. To tell the truth, we were perplexed by this splendour, and it planted the seed of alarm in our souls."

Alas, all this splendour, or what the young writer fancied it was after life in the trenches, was rather shoddy. Those long years of war–World War I and the Civil War–left Russia looking pretty drab, or in other words the way it actually was. The Revolution had removed the thin veneer of wealth and well-being belonging to the aristocracy and the capitalists, and now that they had fled abroad the country was left with its miserable hovels, poverty-stricken towns, cobblestones, wretched, peeling houses badly in need of repair, and poor lighting.

Wherever you turned you saw a picture of poverty and backwardness. It took a genius like Lenin to see through the years and visualise Russia ablaze with electric light, built up with splendid new houses lining broad, asphalt streets, and to trust in the people like he did, confident that they would be able to achieve all this with their heroic creative labour.

H. G. Wells, who visited Russia at the time, wrote a book of impressions about the new revolutionary country and called it *Russia in the Shadows.*

But life has an amazing ability to heal its wounds and sprout new corn and flowers where ruins still smoulder. This applies especially to life in socialist society with its system of planning and organisation of labour. With tremendous enthusiasm the working people set about restoring the old factories and plants. Fyodor Gladkov described the beginning of peacetime construction in his novel *Cement* (1925) which scored a great success with readers in the Soviet Union and abroad. This success, however, was due not so much to the writer's skill or the book's artistic merits, as to its informative character.

The period of rehabilitation was completed by the middle of the 1920s, and the Fourteenth Congress of the Communist Party adopted a programme for Russia's industrialisation which provided for the construction of new factories and plants, with priority given to heavy industry and the machine-tool building industry. This total re-equipment and reconstruction of Russia continues to this day. But it was then, back in the mid-twenties, that the slogan to overtake and surpass the developed capitalist countries was proclaimed, and it was then that the groundwork was laid for that rapid pace of development which made this a realisable ambition for the first time in Russia's history.

Looking back through the mist of time at the period I am describing, it appears as exciting and as full of contradictions as youth generally is. And indeed it was the youth of Soviet literature, the season of search, experiment, and budding talent. Early in the 1920s publication began of the first new literary magazines: *Pechat i Revolutsia, Krasnaya Nov, Novy Mir, Oktyabr, Molodaya Gvardia* and others.

From the outset these magazines published articles and stories contributed by both the established authors of the pre-revolutionary generation and by gifted beginners. These young writers who had just finished fighting in the Civil War came to the editorial offices of our first magazines still wearing their army coats.

The first question which confronted Russian literature immediately after the October Revolution was: to accept or not to accept Soviet power? After the end of the Civil War the question resolved itself. Those who did not accept Soviet power gradually drifted abroad. And the ones who did were faced with new ideological problems: how should they interpret the new hero, the historical tasks of the Revolution and its aims? What had actually happened in Russia and where was she heading?

The prevailing genre during the years of the Civil War was poetry—rousing and satirical verses, or introspective poems that begged the reader to turn away from what was happening about him, withdraw into his inner world and find oblivion in poetic visions.

The 1920s mark the birth of Soviet fiction. If we were to classify the writers according to trends, very roughly of course, we would find that actually they fall into just two major trends, despite the fact that the 1920s were notable precisely for their abundance of literary groupings and associations. There was the Russian Association of Proletarian Writers (RAPP), the "Kuznitsa" (Smithy) society, the Peasant Writers' Society, Mayakovsky's literary group

77

"Left Front" (LEF), and the constructivists whose programme was based on principles of organisation, of kulturträger-ship, which in conditions of our economic dislocation and poverty had an especially strong appeal.

Nevertheless, I repeat, we shall not go far wrong if we divide the writers into two main trends. What distinguished the first group was that in their depiction of reality they never lost sight of the beckoning light ahead–the aim set before the new society by the Party and Lenin. The second group were more impressed by the many contradictions inherent in the life about them which, as I have said, was full of sharp contrasts in those years and not very attractive outwardly. The first saw Russia as "Washed with Blood"– the title of Artem Vesely's romantic novel–but still advancing towards its historic goal. The second saw Russia devastated and in the shadows, and in their books the horizon was obscured by the dark clouds of ignorance, narrow-mindedness and corruption–all of which was really there but only as the negative, dark side of reality and not its decisive aspect.

Naturally enough, the theme of the Civil War had the strongest appeal for both the authors of the pre-revolutionary generation and, especially, for the young writers just back from the fighting fronts. It was the first great experience of the new society which had just established its right to existence, and it was natural that it should be the theme of the first novels. How was this experience to be interpreted? The writers belonging to the first group accentuated the heroism of the struggle. The others were affected most strongly by the spectacle of the "muzhiks' war" with its brutality and filth: indeed, most of the Red soldiers had been "muzhiks", peasants who had changed their antediluvian bast sandals and homespuns for the greatcoats and tall leather boots which the state had issued them with (and of which, incidentally, there were not enough to go around).

One of the first novels about the Civil War which won immediate popularity was Dmitry Furmanov's *Chapayev* (1923). It is a semi-documentary and semi-autobiographical book. The author had served with Chapayev, the legendary hero of the Civil War, as his division commissar. Although Furmanov was a young writer (and he died as a young man in 1926) he succeeded in moulding a very impressive image of a truly popular hero, an embodiment of inexhaustible energy and purposefulness in establishing the new state system. When you read his novel (which became widely known from the film of the same title made by the Vasilyev brothers) you see whom Lenin had in mind when he assured H. G. Wells, who was polite but doubting, that the Russian people would be able to rebuild their country.

The early short stories and novels of Sholokhov, Vsevolod Ivanov, Malyshkin, Vishnevsky, Leonov (*Badgers*), and Fedin (*Towns and Years*) were all inspired by the events of the Civil War. This same theme, however, is rendered in an entirely different manner by Boris Pilnyak. He was unquestionably an original, talented writer, and in his collection of stories which came out in 1919 under the general title *Past and Gone* he presented the confusion of life in those years in the style of topical satire. He was indeed the first to write about the revolutionary events in Russia.

Boris Pilnyak (1891-1938), whose real name was Vogau, was born into the family of a veterinary surgeon in a village near Saratov. His romantic infatuation with the Revolution was blended with his exaltation of dark, elemental "muzhik" forces which the Revolution is supposed to have released. He takes up this theme from various angles in many of his works, among them: *The Deadly Fascinates, Machines and Wolves, The Barren Year*, and *The Third Capital*.

In *Machine and Wolves* he writes: "In 1917, Stepan Razin was at large in Russia again—hostile to towns, to statehood, to trains. He ravished Russia.... A jolly and frightening snowstorm swept across Russia, howling, roaring with laughter, and wanting to ravish everything in its path."

Pilnyak gives this liberation of the muzhik elemental forces a peculiar admixture of sexual freedom and carnal anarchy. The people in his stories are always making love, greedily and hurriedly, falling into each other's arms with casual abandon. The country is at war, there is hunger and devastation everywhere, but their sensual delight in life is only sharpened by the possible nearness of death. This blend of sensuality, death and revolutionary ardour attains its zenith in the story *Ivan and Maria*. The main character is a titled woman, a Princess, who becomes head of the CHEKA. She is an erotomaniac and executions give her a perverted thrill. She even says that the whole Revolution "smells of sex organs".

The chaos of the Civil War epoch, the striking contrasts, the mass migration from one part of the country to the other in quest of food, and the desolate waiting rooms at the ruined railway stations where men, women and children, crawling with lice slept on their bundles, made the main theme of Pilnyak's romantic canvases. All of this was presented in the manner of a romantic Grand Guignol. Pilnyak's prose style is especially suited to his purpose of rendering the music of chaos. The plots of most of his stories are meant to stagger the reader with the paradoxes of revolutionary Russia. Pilnyak describes princesses and priests who turn Bolshevik; muzhiks who become governors and governors who become night watchmen; he describes Communists from among the anarchists; bears at large in the streets; the torments of "Slav souls"; drunkards who dream of communism and Communists who become drunkards.

It is not surprising that until the first industrial achievements under the five-year plan programmes made people abroad ponder on the reasons for these socialist accomplishments of backward Russia, Pilnyak's books enjoyed considerable popularity with foreign readers, especially in the United States.

Serafimovich (*The Iron Flood*) and Malyshkin (*The Fall of Dahir*) are writers of a different trend. In contrast to Pilnyak's characters, the commander in *The Iron Flood* is an embodiment of self-discipline and purposefulness. Serafimovich describes the march of an insurgent army, surrounded on all sides by General Pokrovsky's Cossacks. This army was not a regular military unit, but a disorganised, semi-anarchic mob, capable of killing even the commander they had themselves elected. The story is constructed as an epic narrative, the mood changing now to romantic lyricism now to tragic rhetoric. The human avalanche presents a picture of spontaneous heroism, suffering, terror and strength: exhausted, barefooted men and women, children dying in their mothers' arms, scenes of madness, despair, love and cruelty. . . . On the other hand there is Commander Kozhukh–proletarian staunchness, composure and purposefulness personified. Kozhukh is a gifted organiser, and does not have to use coercion all the time because he knows how to appeal to the best in men. So, at the end of the march, when this insurgent army breaks through the enemy encirclement, the men carry their commander on their shoulders and the women cry out in admiration, enthusing over Kozhukh's blue eyes as though they had never noticed them before.

The Iron Stream is rather naturalistic in its idiom, and yet I would call it a romantic novel.

Another prominent prose writer of that period was Isaac Babel. His style was a blend of extraordinary emotionality and vividness of expression with the terseness and lightness of French prose.

Isaak Babel was born in Odessa in 1894 into the family of a tradesman. He was brought up on the Talmud in a Jewish school, and at the same time studied the French language and literature. (His first stories were written in French.)

Babel's literary legacy is not very large: two collections of stories *Odessa Stories* and *Konarmia* and two plays: *Sundown* and *Maria.*

In his earlier stories he gives free rein to his apparently inexhaustible imagination. The following sentence from his *Italian Sun* should show what I mean: "Sidorov, the bored murderer, tore the pink wool of my imagination into shreds and dragged me into the corridors of his rational madness."

His word-painting evokes tangible images which you can smell, see and feel. There is a concentration, a dreamy earnestness in his manner. "The blue roads flowed past me like sprays of milk squirting from many breasts," he writes in *Italian Sun*.

In most of his stories we find such "physical" comparisons as: "the wine smelt of sunlight and bedbugs", or "the girl's feet had the sweetish stench of slaughter-house beef."

The chief characters of his *Odessa Stories* are the local apaches and picturesque gangsters speaking a peculiar solemnly-ironical jargon.

Babel's *Konarmia* (Cavalry) is composed of scenes and episodes from the march of Budyonny's Red Cavalry in the war with Poland in 1920. Babel served in the Cavalry and describes the campaign from personal experience. The fabric of these stories is woven of an original mixture of pride in and admiration for the Soviet soldiers, with superimposed pictures of violence, hand-to-hand fighting, and the execution of spies. The peasant masses are portrayed thus: "Monstrous, unbelievable Russia shuffled in her bast shoes on either side of the train, stamping like a herd of lice." And again: "The typhus-ridden rustics pushed before them the hearse bearing the customary soldiers' death." (*The Son of the Rabbi*).

However, it should not be imagined that such morbid notes prevail in *Konarmia*. The battle scenes are rendered emotionally: "Their gorgeous flags mounted on guilt poles, adorned with heavy velvet tassels, swayed in the clouds of orange dust. The riders had an air of regal and arrogant coolness." (From *Afonka Bida*).

His art had strong inner links with the Russian revolution, with its great aims, its dream of mankind's revival, and its thirst for beauty. But his manner of presenting life, his style packed with romantic hyperbole, his very artistic method testified to his ideological weakness. After all, only a writer whose imagination had run away with him could have compared a crowd of Russian peasants to a herd of lice, and because he was so carried away by his flights of fancy the historical meaning of this crowd eluded him entirely.

Many of the young and gifted writers appearing on the literary scene in the 1920s were unduly fascinated by the country's backwardness, poverty and the negative aspects of life generally. And life, alas, did abound in negative aspects then. When a new house is being built, and even more so when an old one is being reconstructed, the first thing that strikes the eye is the rubble heaped round the building site. But if you know what the architect has set out to construct you will be able to envisage the future palace from the bare framework alone. At least you will be able to appreciate the architect's idea, and want to know more about the project. A writer who cannot see beyond the rubble will, in spite of himself, adopt a contradictory attitude to the actual process of realising the project.

This is what happened to the gifted writer Mikhail Zoshchenko. There is no gainsaying that his satirical stories—and Zoshchenko was above all a satirist—have their great merits. He has a fine contempt for Philistinism. But there are two planes to all his stories—one shows his "little man's" absorption in petty cares and trivial interests, and the other—the way his human dignity is hurt by this philistine form of existence. Zoshchenko displays the same warm affection for his characters as Chekhov. But his humanism has a dual nature: he ridicules sentimentality, yet he waxes sentimental on the subject of ridicule. He satirises the "little man" and yet he also wants to console him.

Zoshchenko's funny little man of the nineteen-twenties is usually a junior clerk. There is nothing dramatic about his plight, nothing claiming the attention of society (unlike the tragic poverty described by Yuri Olesha). He is quite willing to laugh at the ridiculous situation he has landed in, and will dismiss his troubles by making a joke of them. Zoshchenko's racy style suits these stories perfectly. But his attempt in *The Blue Book* to render some scenes from world history in the same "glib patter" (to quote Gorky) was a complete fiasco. The form clashed with the content, and the result was an anecdote.

Passive lyricism is the underlying mood in Zoshchenko's writings; both his satire and his mocking language are no more than a screen for his vulnerable heart.

This was also the period of Yuri Olesha's rise to fame with his novel *Envy* (1927). Olesha makes a philosophical study of the clash between two truths, two worlds—the old and the new. The new world is personified by Babichev, director of a food industry trust, a "great sausage-maker, confectioner and cook". Babichev is full of animal spirits, he is an optimist, he loves a good business deal, and believes in calling a spade a spade. Ranged beside him are Volodya and Valya, a young student and his girl, healthy young people who happily bask in thoughtlessness.

The old world wears a shabby look—it is personified by Andrei Babichev's dissipated brother Ivan, an ace among the rakes, a crank bordering on idiocy who walks about the streets hugging a pillow, and another young man of no fixed occupation, Cavalierov by name. But then the whole rainbow of human emotions and feelings, all the subtleties of perception which Olesha describes with such brilliance, belong to them, to the people of the old world. According to the plot of the story they meet their end, and the people of the new world triumph. But only according to the plot. The entire "music" is so constructed that the new world plays tunes on a sausage, and a whole symphony departs with the Cavalierovs. Olesha's underlying theme is a sort of Chaplin series about a little, defenceless man, with an individualistically blossoming soul and dreams of happiness, who is denied understanding by the soulless, machine world of big business, by a state in love with pork.

Envy is an ethical novel, probing and laying bare the deepest conflict of our epoch, the conflict between a man's right to personal happiness and the general weal. But here the plea for the individual, for the small man, is voiced more loudly and more convincingly. At that time Pasternak wrote in his poetry *To a Friend* dedicated to Pilnyak:

> *Do I not use the five-year plan for measure?*
> *Do I not fall with it and rise?*
> *But what about the thing that in my chest I treasure,*
> *That die-hardness, the hardest one to die?*

As if in answer to the poet's question, Olesha replied that emotionally, as an artist, he could not really feel yet the heroic poetry of socialist construction. The romance of the personal was stronger in him than the romance of the state's cause. Gorky said in one of his articles that in his opinion many of the writers suffered from a sort of "emotional illiteracy": in their minds they understood and fully sympathised with socialist revolution and approved of the revolutionary changes in general, but their emotions lagged behind their reason.

Last but far from least among the writers of the 1920s we should mention Mikhail Prishvin, a superb artist who chose for himself the neutral theme of nature and life in nature. It cannot be said of him that he withdrew from politics altogether, but nonetheless when the entire country was subordinated to the main task of asserting the new ideas and consolidating the new statehood Prishvin always kept away from the topical questions and major issues. Still, Prishvin's books are genuine works of art, inspired by his love of man and all that is beautiful in nature, and imbued with a faith in life. In the same way as the classics influence the shaping of our minds and emotions, so will Prishvin, with his exquisitely subtle appreciation of nature—its springs, dawns, sunsets, rivers, lakes, fields and skies, help our young people to start out in life the richer in spirit for this feeling for beauty.

Mikhail Prishvin (1873-1954) was a trained agronomist, and having stored up some interesting observations on the habits of birds in the Karelian lake district, he put them down in a book *The Land of Undisturbed Birds* which came out in 1906. He made no claim to any artistic merits, but the book was immediately recognised as the work of a first-class writer and it served to launch him on his literary career. He took shape as a writer in the period of the first Russian revolution of 1905, and the years following its defeat.

At this time many intellectuals and writers who like Prishvin had taken part in the revolutionary movement renounced it and turned to mysticism, decadence, intellectual emotionalism (like Leonid Andreyev) and so forth. Whatever Prishvin had of the petty-bourgeois intellectual in him would not let him become a proletarian writer, but then his wholesomeness as a realist artist, which was strongest in him, kept him safe from the putrid forms of bourgeois art. Later, Prishvin wrote in *The Home of Cranes*: "I solved my own problem by admitting that it was not the revolution but myself who was 'redundant', and by withdrawing not into the world of petty, everyday cares with Chekhov's heroes, but into that life where poetry is born, where there is no essential difference between man and beast. What guided me there was my long dormant instinct of a pathfinder and hunter."

Prishvin describes his escape into this depersonalised world and his gradual return to the life of men in his autobiographical novel *The Ogre's Chain* (1923-1930). The main character is Alpatov, an engineer. He matures "between the cross-currents of decadent aestheticism and revolutionary asceticism" to gradually arrive at the "open sea of natural creativity" where all living things obey the supreme law: "if you think the time has come for you to die, plant rye for those who will come after you". The whole novel is written in the tone of a confession and has two distinct converging lines: the author's growing acceptance of the new reality, and the legend about Alpatov. But once again this reality is not a historical, social reality, but an awareness of the new creativity going on all about him, with the proletarian revolution as its highest expression.

The temporal and the eternal, the historical and the natural are combined in Prishvin's work. His main theme is nature, the scene of infinite creativity, to which he devoted his best works: *Berendey's Springs, The Home of Cranes, Gin-seng* and *Spring Is Coming*. No other writer in Russian literature has ever spoken of nature with such poetic power and understanding. He wants to discover the human in nature, in its creative genius. He wrote that he was obeying an inner urge to discover "the myth of things created in the innermost depths of nature".

In his stories and charming thumbnail sketches he writes about the early morning frost, the migration of birds, the taming of a hedgehog and the habits of a field mouse as if they were the most exciting myths of nature. All that is human dissolves in this "sea of natural creativity". Occasionally the author himself says: "I carried all that inside me, I wondered about it, and saw myself in my origin."

With Prishvin these myths of nature merge into a sort of social myth about the happiness of man dissolving in nature and wisely acting in unity with its creative processes. There is no denial of civilisation à la Jean-Jacques Rousseau in Prishvin's myth. A person's understanding of the world is enhanced by the experience of all human culture, he says. For him this meant mainly technical experience. Social experience and social creativity were still foreign to his art–a consequence of his withdrawal from the revolution. But for all that, it was after the socialist revolution, in the years of socialist construction that Prishvin's talent blossomed to the full. This happened because the poetry of Prishvin's writing and his researcher's attitude to nature fell in with the socialist idea of emancipating endeavour in all spheres and treating nature as a field of the entire people's creative drive. Unlike certain American writers (Henry Thoreau, for instance), Prishvin does not rise in protest against the town and the established pattern of life. He extols creation and Man–the creator.

Prishvin evolved his own peculiar narrative style. It has the lyrical quality of a diary (the story is often told in the first person singular) with little stories apropos intricately woven into it; there is always a central theme–a myth or an image, told in parts. Frequently Prishvin turns to folk mythology as well. His idiom is wonderfully limpid, evocative and precise. Maxim Gorky used to call Prishvin his teacher.

Prishvin turned to nature as an escape from bourgeois society and its false intellectual values. But socialism restored nature to people, so to speak, and with it Prishvin returned to society. There is no doubt that Soviet writers will yet develop Prishvin's theme on the sources of creativity in nature, re-interpreted as a theme of socialist creativity.

* * *

Thus the 1920s were the years when the foundations of Soviet literature were laid, and when the first young Soviet writers entered the literary scene. Those were also the years when the basic problems of Soviet literature, later to be developed or amended, were first outlined.

I shall speak of four more writers whose work reflected most vividly the different and conflicting trends of our age: they are Fadeyev, Alexei Tolstoi, Pasternak and Fedin. These writers truly belong to the 1920s, despite the fact that they continued to attract as much of the readers' and critics' attention in the 1930s, and indeed in subsequent years as well.

Chapter 9

Fadeyev

Alexander Fadeyev. 1936.

I can still see him today as if he were standing there before me,
alive. A tall man with his silver-grey head thrown slightly back,
slender and erect, with cold grey eyes. His erect bearing was not
that of an officer. It was the attitude of a proud man with a keen
feeling for beauty, a man who felt elevated by the ideas he served.
I first met him in 1927 when he came to Moscow from Rostov
(where he worked on the newspaper *Sovietsky Yug*) with the

manuscript of his novel *The Rout*. This novel holds a place apart in the history of Soviet literature. It marked the ascent of Soviet literature to a new level. The fact that *The Rout* was acclaimed so unanimously is not surprising: it was the first real success on the road to achieving what we now call the art of socialist realism.

What was so basically new in this novel of modest length? First of all, Fadeyev's approach to the portrayal of the real makers of Russia's new history. He made a profound psychological study of their characters and, what is more, showed them "from below", from the point of view of the popular masses who accomplished the Revolution.

Before Fadeyev, portraits of Bolsheviks were made more in the nature of tentative pencil drawings or rough sketches. They were men modelled on a single pattern, all dressed in leather jackets (as with Pilnyak). Ilya Ehrenburg in his story *Impcomman* (abbreviation of Improved Communist Man) drew a cartoon of such a schematic Bolshevik. In his novel *The Grab-All*, where he described how people's private-ownership instincts ran riot in the early 1920s, he portrays a communist whose characteristic feature is an absence of any private life. "At the very mention of Artem (the positive hero— K.Z) we involuntarily begin to speak in journalese, simply because the wealth of this man's inner world (like that of many others of his age) was derived from the frankly appalling paucity of his so-called private life." What was to be done? "For Artem to become a story hero, he had to stop being just a hero and, following the example of his younger brother, liven up his days by going in for rape, robbery, maudlin tears and savage debauchery. Modifying the well-known saying, we make bold to assert that good Communists have no biographies." And so Ehrenburg paints his "heroes"—Nikolai Kurbov, Mikhail Lykov and other Communists— in the "good, old style", with sentimental words, spiritual debauches and psychological self-rape. In an effort to dilute the new hero's dry rationalism he poured all sorts of emotional and psychological elements into him (in doses large enough to kill a horse), but even this method failed to give the reader a real image of the new man. But at least a bridge was thrown across to the old hero. This familiar hero, for whom literary tradition had already evolved its definite forms and methods of portrayal, became so widespread in the NEP period mainly because of the writers' inability to probe deep into reality and bring out its essence. All these linear sketches of the new man symbolise, above all else, his historical function: organisation, planning, and a strong-minded, sensible intrusion into the order of things. In one of Leonid Leonov's earliest stories (*The Petushikhino Breakthrough*, 1920) we also read an episode written along these lines: "... A leather man with a gramophone arrived at Petushikhino. He showed the chairman his mandate and his revolver, called all the available men and women together, wound up the gramophone, and it began to speak." The gramophone instead of human speech, the revolver, the leather coats—all these were external signs of the obdurate and the mechanically coercive. Readers today will find it difficult to sort out all these symbols, so numerous in early Soviet literature, and see where the author, subjectively sympathising with the revolution, got over his misapprehension and began to voice his protest or to caricature its motive forces in the manner of a bourgeois lampoonist. Seven years later Leonov, in his novel *The River Sott*, already painted the solid figure of a builder of Soviet industry, the Bolshevik Uvadyev, with bold brush strokes and vivid colours, describing the man's energy, broad-mindedness and the American scale of his ambitions. But, alas, even here: "he saw everything except the coming construction in its extremely simplified form, and love itself was just fuel that would double his strength for tomorrow's effort." As a human being Uvadyev is a narrow-minded utilitarian like Babichev in Olesha's *Envy*. Uvadyev himself says that he is simply a "machine, adapted for independent existence". Emotion or tenderness—whatever is kept under the hard shell of his common sense—is all supposed to be foreign to the rationalistic hero of the new world.

In complete contrast to these one-dimensional images of the new hero, there came a long file of devil-may-care atamans (in Vyacheslav Shishkov's story *The Band*, in Artem Vesyoly's novel *Blood-Washed Russia*, and many, many other books). Such an ultra-romantic interpretation of the new hero showed that deep down the author saw the proletarian revolution as the elemental "muzhik" forces running riot. In books of this type the picturesque portrayal of the leaders always went together with naturalism in language and a play on dialect.

Furmanov's *Chapayev*, Seifulina's *Virinea* and Serafimovich's *The Iron Stream* were the first novels to portray the new hero realistically. Fadeyev's *The Rout* went a step further. As a boy Alexander Fadeyev lived in the Far East where he later joined a partisan unit to fight against the White Cossacks and the Japanese interventionists. It was on this personal experience that he based his first novel which answered all the vital questions posed to our young Soviet literature by life itself. These questions concerned the new hero and his human qualities, the part played by the peasantry in the proletarian revolution, and the organisation and guidance of the masses.

From the very first pages of the novel the reader finds himself in a strangely ordinary, everyday world which clashes with the romantic notion of the revolution, then popular in literature, as a sort of splendid procession of the masses, striding forward with shining eyes, amid a glorious orgy of the elements, and so on. *The Rout* is written as a simple, truthful narrative, the straightforward tone of which holds a challenge to the sham picturesqueness and the sham romancing common to a whole number of books about the Civil War.

Fadeyev planned to show the role of the people at the bottom of the social ladder in the proletarian revolution without embellishing anything. The young writer, a mere beginner, went bravely towards his goal, unafraid of showing the sharpest contradictions and the most difficult impasses. The title itself speaks of the author's approach. The partisan unit is routed. Almost all the men are killed. And yet, on closing the book, the reader does not have a feeling of hopelessness, but, on the contrary, is filled with profound faith in the invincibility of the revolutionary movement. The fairness of the people's life and struggle stands out in all its splendour in spite of the fact that the men who personify it are in their majority still ignorant, illiterate, and not yet free from many prejudices and vices.

The everyday prose of revolutionary struggle makes the fabric of the novel: the partisan hospital in the taiga, the village, encounters between the partisans and the peasants, partisans on the march, scouting, men dying, internal affairs of the unit—quarrels, fights, everyday conversation, and the hardships of forest life during the partisans' retreat.

The heroes of the novel are the peasants from the Suchan villages. The author intentionally makes no saints of his heroes—those former miners and farmers. For instance, one of them—Morozko—steals melons from the kitchen gardens. But at the same time Fadeyev stresses the historic importance of what these people are accomplishing. The main conflict is rendered in the psychological clash between two characters—Levinson, the commander of the partisan unit, and Mechik, an intellectual who belongs to the Socialist-Revolutionaries.

Levinson loves people. His humanism is exacting, it compels people to take up arms, an axe or a shovel, and become fighters for the most just social relations worthy of man, for communism. After his conversation with Mechik one night, Levinson decides that such worthless characters, as poor in spirit and will power as Mechik, can only sprout where men are exploited, where there is poverty, laziness, ruin and spiritual emptiness. The purpose of Levinson's existence on earth is to overcome all this wretchedness and the "leaden ugliness" of life (as Gorky put it). "But what talk can there be of a new, splendid man," he says to himself, "as long as millions of people are forced to lead such a primitive, sorry, and incredibly frugal existence?"

This explains Levinson's hatred for falsity of any kind. It also explains the strict demands he makes upon himself and others, the way he will stop at nothing if the people's goal is at stake.

Mechik, the intellectual, is quite different. He is a romantic, poetic nature, with inbred courtesy and gentleness. In different circumstances, not requiring a person display courage, will power, perseverance, and other such qualities every day, he might have become known for a good fellow, as "not a bad sort at all". He joined the revolutionary movement and the partisans not because he was called up, but from an inner craving for romantic adventure. His habit of posing even when alone developed into a vital need to live in a world of romantic conventionalities, and people the life about him with them.

In Lenin's works we can find not just a political but also a psychological analysis of different human types who, in Lenin's opinion, are suitable or not suitable for the proletarian revolutionary movement. This is what he wrote as far back as 1908 about the vacillations of the Socialist-Revolutionary maximalists (and Mechik, it must be remembered, belonged to this party too): "It is the logic of the keyed-up intellectual, of hysteria, of incapacity for steady, stubborn work, of inability to apply the basic principles of theory and tactics to altered circumstances, of inability to carry on the work of propaganda, agitation and organisation in conditions sharply differing from those which we recently experienced."

Mechik is not suited for the role of a proletarian revolutionary, as Fadeyev proves in a number of episodes. Needless to say, it was entirely his own idea. He may well not have read that particular work of Lenin's from which the above paragraph comes. Fadeyev took his examples from life. As a participant in the revolutionary movement in Primorye and as a partisan he met a great number of people with vastly dissimilar spiritual qualities, abilities and opportunities. Now, as an artist, he drew generalisations from this material in the light of the ideas which had made him join the ranks of the proletarian revolutionary fighters. Levinson, being one of the leaders in the revolutionary struggle, is portrayed as a very complex personality. He has his moments of doubt, and by and large no human emotions are foreign to him (unlike the portrayal of the Bolsheviks in Pilnyak, the early Ehrenburg, and other writers); but Fadeyev stresses the main, essential features which must be in character with a man who has undertaken the revolutionary reconstruction of the world.

In his *The Life of Klim Samgin* Gorky says: "We have to say goodbye to those heroes for an hour, because what we want now is heroism for life, the heroism of a labourer, toiling for the revolution. If you are not capable of such heroism, step aside."

Through Mechik's spiritual conflict with the partisan unit Fadeyev reveals the weakness, the bankruptcy of the old moral principles. In this sense Mechik holds a place of supreme importance in the plot. The author does not present him as an outright enemy of the socialist revolution. Mechik's sympathies do lie with the people, and he believes that he is prepared to die for them. But Fadeyev shows by accurate artistic characterisation that Mechik has not got what it takes to become a fighter for the people's just cause. His entire background has prepared him for something quite different. He has absorbed the philosophy and psychology of the exploiter classes. He is an individualist, an egotist. For him the revolution is just a beautiful, romantic opportunity to manifest his "inimitable personality". He approaches everything from the point of view of his own personal interests.

A believer in realism, Fadeyev copies much of Lev Tolstoi's manner although he does not, of course, attain Tolstoi's plastic force and depth in his portrayal of people. In Tolstoi's novels and stories the people seem to live their lives independently of the author's will. Even though, quite naturally, his interpretation of some characters was somewhat biassed (for instance, Napoleon in *War and Peace*) he nevertheless always looked at a person out of a hundred eyes, as it were, catching the very flux of existence and thus attaining an extraordinary plasticity of moulding.

By using Tolstoi's techniques of realistic portraiture, Fadeyev created psychologically convincing and significant characters. But at the same time, he belongs to Gorky's school, for his writing is more tendentious, and the ideological bias is more overt. Thus, his books have a more obvious and direct educational influence—like Gorky's *Mother*, which has exerted a political and moral influence on workers in Russia and throughout the world.

I may have devoted a disproportionately large number of pages to this not very large book, but I had my reasons. *The Rout* has been translated into twenty foreign languages and fifty-eight languages spoken in the Soviet Union, and since it is so popular all over the world, it can serve as a fine example of the method of socialist realism. Readers will gain from it a tangible idea of what this method means, and they will be able to see how their own impressions of one of these earliest works of Soviet socio-psychological prose compare with my analysis and conclusions.

Anti-communist propaganda loves to misrepresent the method of socialist realism as a sort of Party directive which our writers must blindly follow. *The Rout* serves to show how the ideas and images which make the basis of Fadeyev's writings as a whole were conceived.

In his speech, addressed to a large gathering of intellectuals in Paris, in 1949, Fadeyev said, recalling the time when his world outlook was taking shape and the first poetic images were born in his heart and mind:

"People will always remember it as the time of the Civil War. It is also called the time 'when fourteen foreign powers marched on Soviet Russia'. We had to choose whose side to take. . . . It was not difficult for us to choose. The life of the workers and the peasants was closer to us.

". . .We joined the Revolution, full of youthful hopes, and carrying a small volume of Gorky and another of Nekrasov in our school bags.

"We were full of a liberating fervour because by that time Admiral Kolchak's power had become established in Siberia and the Russian Far East, and it was more cruel than the old regime. We were full of a patriotic fervour because our native soil was being trampled upon by the hob-nailed boots of the interventionists.

"I owe my birth as a writer to that time. I came to know the finest qualities of the people to whom I belonged. I was with the partisans for three years, we shared an army coat at night and the gruel in our mess tins, and together we covered thousands of kilometres of road."

So much for "directives" and "instructions" in those days when socialist realism as a term had never yet been mentioned in Soviet critical reviews, or in the press generally.

In the 1930s (and then after the war, too) Fadeyev worked on his novel *The Last of the Udeghes.* The novel remained unfinished (five out of the six parts intended were written). The author himself was not satisfied with his book and he meant to revise it completely and, among other things, write in the figure of Sergei Lazo, one of the great heroes in the struggle for Soviet power in the Far East. Lazo was captured by the Japanese interventionists and, together with Fadeyev's cousin Vsevolod Sibirtsev, burnt alive in the furnace of a locomotive.

There is much that appeals to me personally, as a reader, in this novel. There are many pages which, in my opinion, surpass *The Rout* and *The Young Guard* in artistic merits. Thus, the Bolsheviks Pyotr Surkov and Alyosha Malenky are deeper and more convincing than even Levinson in *The Rout*, let alone Protsenko, Lyutikov or Barakov in *The Young Guard*. The aim of the novel was to show the development of modern society from capitalism to Soviet power via the proletarian revolution. Not back to nature (in the spirit of Rousseau, which misdirected Knut Hamsun to the adoration of the "strong man" and eventually, towards the end of his life, brought him to the dead-end of Hitlerism), but forward, to industrial communism. The Udeghes, a small hunting people in the Sikhote-Alin Mountains, who had preserved the features of primitive communism in their way of life, were meant to play a prominent part in the story. But very soon they were overshadowed by scenes from the class civil war in the Far East. Yet it is a unique sort of "book of life". The main hero in the first part is Seryozha, a young man endowed by Fadeyev with certain autobiographical features. Then the circle of characters widens. The reader is led into the drawing rooms of the Vladivostok rich society (the story begins in pre-revolutionary days), into the birch-bark wigwams of the hunting tribes, workers' hovels, factory shops, and the town's dives; to meetings, the partisans' campfires in the taiga, the military port of Vladivostok, the meeting of the Revolutionary Committee, the Korean congress, the headquarters of the hun-hudses, and the military units of the Japanese and American interventionists. Fadeyev paints a whole gallery of portraits: Vladivostok businessmen, Udeghe hunters, White scouts, officers and civilians, political figures, and Communists. *The Last of the Udeghes* is a wide epic canvas which makes the background for the artist's ethical and psychological investigation of those social forces which came to the forefront of history in the twentieth century and also those which remained bound up with the past both spiritually and economically. Although on the way out, the latter forces were still capable of poisoning everything round them and striking out at the new world emerging from the great revolutionary cauldron.

In *The Rout* neither the partisans nor even their commanders discuss politics, the word Party is never mentioned, and the author's whole attention is focused on problems of ethics, the purpose of life and human psychology. In *The Last of the Udeghes*, on the contrary, it is the Party interests of the Communists which are given prominence. It is precisely in this light that the two main heroes—the Communists Pyotr Surkov and Alyosha Malenky—are portrayed. The former is a leader of the Party movement behind the Japanese interventionist and White army lines. The latter is a representative of the regional Party Committee who has made his way to the fighting front from Vladivostok. One of them has a working-class background, and the other comes from the democratic intelligentsia. The idea is that communism does not reduce people to schemes, does not encase their spirit in a uniform. Fadeyev presents in detail how differently Party directives are assimilated by different individuals, in this case Pyotr and Alyosha. He shows how people argue and what they disagree about; how they make friends, and what they quarrel about; how they love and what they dream of. One particular dialogue between Alyosha Malenky and a peasant who has a strong private-property instinct and is nobody's fool, is worth describing. What Fadeyev himself once dreamed about was to come true some thirty years later. Alyosha says (the year is 1919) that after victory the workers will make good use of the iron ore, copper and zinc lying uselessly in the bowels of the surrounding mountains. They might even look farther ahead and picture the day when the Communists will harness atomic energy.

"The peasant gave Alyosha a surprised, sidelong glance, wondering if he was making fun of him, but Alyosha's face was perfectly straight. It wasn't fancy talk either—he spoke of travelling to other planets as calmly and casually as though the matter had long been decided, and so the peasant began to listen to him attentively again, his expression turning glummer and glummer. 'Now if we could utilise atomic energy, for instance,' Alyosha continued. 'Think of the power! It gives you the creeps just to think of it, and yet some day it will be utilised. Atomic energy, eh?' he shouted, looking merrily at the peasant."

This was written at the beginning of the thirties. Today, when we have atomic reactors, the *Lenin* icebreaker, atomic submarines and atomic power stations, these words acquire a prophetic meaning, linking the dreams of the people who fought for Soviet power with the achievements of their grandchildren who are already building up the material base of communism.

At the end of the Second World War Fadeyev wrote his novel *The Young Guard*, telling the true story of the underground struggle waged by a group of young patriots against the German occupation forces in the town of Krasnodon in the Ukraine. The novel is based on factual material, and not even the names are fictitious. The five leaders of this group—Oleg Koshevoi, Ivan Zemnukhov, Ulyana Gromova, Lubov Shevtsova and Sergei Tyulenin—had the title of Hero of the Soviet Union conferred on them posthumously.

Fadeyev's characterisations are as powerful as they are convincing. The idea of the novel was to reveal the romantic faith in the triumph of justice, natural to very young people, and cultivated by the Soviet school and the Komsomol, as it was manifested by the Young Guard in the struggle against the nazis who had seized their home town. Here Fadeyev gives the ghastly picture of the atrocities committed against the Soviet people by the nazis. In the original version of the book Fadeyev, romanticising the patriotic fervour of Krasnodon's youth, left the older generation altogether in the shade although in actual fact the Young Guard's underground activities were directed by older, experienced men. The novel was criticised for this and rightly so because an historical novel on a modern theme cannot ignore historical facts.

After Stalin's death (and especially after the death of Fadeyev himself who had defended the second version of his book) a heated polemic began about this in the press. Some critics and writers—Konstantin Simonov, for one—supported the first version where the poetic accent was on the young patriots. It does not seem right to me at this late date to re-examine the amendments made by the author and to blame everything exclusively on the cult of Stalin's personality. Objectively it must be agreed that there was more to it than Stalin bringing pressure to bear on Fadeyev. I am inclined to think that Fadeyev was persuaded to change his mind by the new facts that came to light, and that his amendments, which lent the novel greater breadth and depth, were made in precisely the same spirit as he wrote of Communists in his earlier books.

The Young Guard is a beautiful poem in prose, a dramatic affirmation of all that is young and fine. Like *The Rout*, it emanates confidence and hope in spite of the fact that it describes such tragic events. A tendency to poetise life, which became especially pronounced in the late forties, was already evident in *The Young Guard*.

Fadeyev's artistic method, practised by all Soviet writers, tended, on the one hand, to intensify the romantically affirmative means of expression when describing good characters and, on the other, to make wider use of scathing satire and grotesquerie when portraying bad characters. This general tendency was most apparent in *The Young Guard*. But the results can be unfortunate if this tendency is followed dogmatically: one has only to recall some of those novels about kolkhoz life written in the early fifties.

The very nature of Fadeyev's talent urged him to write for young readers. And youth has always been in need of poetry and romance. His most essential quality was the way he glorified with such generous warmth not just the exceptional heroes whom history, or even more so they themselves by their deeds, had placed upon a pedestal, nor even Soviet society as such, but the ordinary working people.

His commitment to the people and the Party was an organic part of his creative personality, and in this sense Alexander Fadeyev is a typical figure in Soviet literature—a writer reared by the Communist Party and the Soviet reality.

In his article "On Lu Hsin" printed in Peking and Shanghai newspapers on October 19, 1949, Fadeyev wrote: "In Western Europe and the United States there still exist writers who are extreme individualists, dwelling in ivory towers and championing art for art's sake.

"They are liar-writers. They know perfectly well whom they are serving.

"Art which does not influence men's souls, art 'without man' is a degenerate art; indeed it is no longer art. The personality of a real writer is shaped by the people that gave him birth ... and the better he serves his people, the nobler and the richer his personality will be and the greater writer he will become."

These last words can be regarded as Fadeyev's own ideological action programme. As a writer he consciously served the people and the Communist Party, the people's advance guard and leader. As a citizen he engaged in useful, many-sided public activity. In this respect Fadeyev represents the new type of writer bred in the Soviet Union.

Fadeyev was a prominent figure in the country's public life: he was a member of the Central Committee of the Communist Party, a deputy to the Supreme Soviet, and head of the Writers' Union. He represented Soviet public opinion at peace congresses, beginning from the congress in Wroclaw, and was elected vice-president of the World Peace Council. He was a critic of merit and a competent theorist of socialist realism. A sizeable volume of his critical and theoretical articles was brought out after his death. Fadeyev introduced a number of original ideas into the theory of socialist literature and art. One of his pet ideas was blending realistic and romantic colours in portraying the revolutionary struggle for communism.

Fadeyev's sad end (he shot himself through the heart on May 13, 1956, at his country home in Peredelkino) appears to lack a motive and clashes with the entire image of Fadeyev as writer and public figure. But it does not repudiate the truth of his writings and all his work. His novels and the characters he has created continue to stir readers with the beautiful passion of his very human heart.

Chapter 10

Alexei Tolstoi

Alexei Tolstoi. 1937.

Alexei Tolstoi is one of the most widely read Soviet authors, and maybe the best loved. A complete collection of his works was re-published twice in quick succession, and both times more than 600,000 people ordered it in advance. Whatever he writes about Alexei Tolstoi always delights the reader with his easy, flowing style and the gay sparkle of his colourful language. His books make one think over what one has read again and again because, for all the outward variety of his themes, his works present an integral picture of Russian life in the first half of this century.

Alexei Tolstoi—a writer with the temperament and range of a novelist and playwright, and a flair for journalistic writing, a deputy to the Supreme Soviet of the U.S.S.R. and a member of the Academy of Sciences—looms large as one of the striking figures of our age.

There is something puzzling about his life story, a sort of riddle to which the answer is right there in his person and his writings. This phenomenon of "Tolstoi solving the riddle of Tolstoi" makes a most absorbing study, giving one a better understanding of many aspects of Soviet life and literature, and the character of its democracy. As an impressive example of continuity in the development of Russian prose in Soviet times, Alexei Tolstoi is second only to Gorky. From Tolstoi's example it will also be seen how strongly a person's character and talent can be influenced by his sense of spiritual closeness to his people, by his sense of kinship, and an inner need to be with his country and people at all the stages of its historical course. Tolstoi's very talent—so full of health and vigour, so versatile and all-embracing—proved equal to those exacting demands which Russian life and literature made on the writers of the first half of this century, particularly after the Great October Socialist Revolution.

If one were to try and find an explanation of the tremendous vitality of Alexei Tolstoi's talent which illumines all he has written, his life and his person, one would discover that the answer lies in his organic affinity with the people.

Alexei Tolstoi (1883-1945)—a big, imposing man with good-breeding written on his face, and hair worn in a long, straight bob—was the son of a Count. His childhood, however, was spent in the company of village children on a farmstead in the Volga steppeland. This farmstead belonged to the man, a nobleman of modest means, for whom his mother left his father. Tolstoi's mother— A. L. Bostrem—was the author of two novels, *Backwoods* and *Restless Heart*, but was better known as a writer of children's books. Tolstoi's childhood impressions were embodied in one of his best and, I am tempted to say, most "fragrant" books—the autobiographical story *Nikita's Childhood* (1920, published as a separate edition in 1922).

Nikita's Childhood can be ranked with such classics of Russian literature as Aksakov's *Family Chronicle* and Lev Tolstoi's *Childhood and Adolescence*. It least of all resembles the story of a young aristocrat. It is rather a poetic picture of Russia with her alluring spaces, her fairy tales and legends, a poem of a child's affirmation of his roots, of his sense of belonging to his native land and people.

Alexei Tolstoi's first works were short stories, and then came his novels (*The Funny Old Couple, The Lame Prince, Mishka Nalimov* and others) which formed a whole cycle under the general title *In Volga Country*. These novels brought their author far-reaching fame. Their subject matter was the spiritual and material disintegration of the country-seat life under the influence of the prosaic, greedy and cynical worship of Money-Making—the new god of the twentieth century. The heroes of these novels and stories, sketched by Tolstoi with the quick strokes of a fluent pen and shown in a harsh, almost grotesque light, were the impoverished nobility, the fast living scions of once great families, gentlemen who had drifted into blind alleys, "superfluous people" like Prince Alexei Krasnopolsky, the principal character of *The Lame Prince*, gamblers, duelists, daydreaming young ladies and resentful servants—in short, that motley, spinning Russia in the epoch of crisis and the ripening of revolutionary events.

In his next stories we find rootless intellectuals, "gentlemen wearing pince-nez", people in the slough of despondency, citizens without country or family ties, men gambling away their lives, the "Black Friday" men who had tasted the wretchedness of existence in its various combinations and in all parts of the globe. All these characters belong to those years and we can meet them in the books of other European writers too. In Tolstoi's story *The Ancient Route* a mortally ill young Frenchman, Paul Torenne, is making his last voyage across the Mediterranean, and, as his ship sails on, visions of ancient civilisations pass in succession before him. He dies with a painfully nostalgic feeling of the senselessness of life. This story brings to mind *The Gentleman from San Francisco* by Bunin, the true father of the "frustrated generation".

In Alexei Tolstoi's pre-revolutionary stories we can easily trace his literary links with his contemporary writers, Russian and foreign, and particularly French writers, like Anatole France and Henri de Regnier. Tolstoi began writing in the period when symbolism held sway in both Russian and European literature, when the poison of decadence and pessimism tasted so sweet, and Baudelaire's "flowers of evil" were tenderly cultivated in all the fashionable magazines and in the hothouses of literature. Tolstoi's realistic talent had to make its way through all these tempting fads and find a foothold for itself at a time when realistic traditions appeared to have been elbowed out. Make his way he did, and without abandoning the tenets of classical realism.

However, Tolstoi's adoption of the socialist ideology was not a simple or easy conversion for him. To begin with, in 1918 he happened to be in Odessa, on a literary tour, when the town was occupied by the Whites, and when the Red Army advanced on the town. He left the country, and settled down in Paris. He lived as an émigré for four years, and his writings were printed in anti-

Soviet magazines. When he finally returned home in 1923 he was not ready ideologically to immediately set about the business of creating a new art—the art of socialist realism. It took him some time to find his bearings and discover himself anew, so to speak. It is no exaggeration to say that his talent really blossomed only in those first Soviet years, which gave him a deeper understanding of our history and revealed to him in a new way the essence of the Russian people's life. His most important books, we find, are the work of an historical writer, not so much in their subject matter as in their approach to facts. His talent shed its delicate tracery of stylisation, and the pure gold of his writing emerged in all its glory.

What do the words "discovered himself anew" really mean? What is the nature of Tolstoi's talent, and precisely what qualities did it display upon coming in touch with the revolutionary reality? These questions deserve dwelling upon in greater detail for the example of Tolstoi sheds some light on the nature of talent as such, illumining it first of all from the angle of its relation to the age in which it has its being. Today, the theory of "art for art's sake" is no longer very popular anywhere in the world. But just the same there is a widespread notion in the West that an artist's talent is a spontaneous force, and that an artist's world outlook cannot affect the quality of his work. A poet simply expresses his feelings, he moulds or creates his images from the material provided by reality, merely obeying the "divine will" of his genius. He creates his images because he is driven by an inner, aesthetic urge to mould, to imitate, to reproduce one detail or another. All this has filled whole tomes of aesthetic theories. The poet is "indifferent" to his material, and even a vice—if it is described or reproduced with talent—becomes an aesthetic virtue. The business of the artist is merely to stir the reader's senses, never mind what sort of emotions are aroused.

This attitude was not entirely renounced even during the Second World War. There were poets in England, for example, who held that poetry should stay out of the war. However, such a deliberate withdrawal from history, sanctifying the poets' release from all moral obligations at a time when everyone's moral feeling, outraged by Hitlerism, was high, evoked the protest of English critics. This indifference contained a desire to disclaim any connection with the struggle, to stand aside from it, and consequently, to all intents and purposes, to lend the enemy moral support.

A highly developed moral sense has always been a feature of Russian literature. Lev Tolstoi is probably the most convincing and compelling proof that a high moral sense can go together with strong, uninhibited writing. And, what is more, that it can be the pivot and the driving power of creativity itself. The whole of Dostoyevsky is a "poem of conscience", an example of how a writer's moral sense develops into a force that shapes the plot and the characters. It was this moral sense that prompted the Russian classics to show reality in a critical light. They chose this angle because the reality of tsarist Russia provoked their moral sense, outraged it, and invited revolutionary protest. This was what determined the main trend in the literature of the past—the trend of critical realism, as Chernyshevsky named it.

Such a critical attitude to Russian life, satirically magnified in the works of Gogol and Saltykov-Shchedrin, was misinterpreted by some readers, foreign readers mostly, who began to wonder about Russia and the character of the Russian people generally, and to doubt the writers' loyalty to their country. But this scathing ridicule and indictment of vices, this attention to what was happening in the country, was precisely how Russian literature expressed its patriotism.

It must be said, however, that even within the movement of critical realism in 19th-century Russian literature we can hear life-asserting notes, a definite affirmation of hopeful faith in life and in the people. This hosanna to life takes its beginning from Pushkin and, spreading in a thousand rivulets, makes itself heard in the books of many Russian writers of the past. Even Gogol is not all criticism. Suffice it to recall his poetic vision of Russia rushing like a troika through the vastness of history. There is affirmation of Russian life in Turgenev, Herzen, Lev Tolstoi, Chekhov and Gorky. But only in Soviet times, when the chains fettering the creative genius of the people had been smashed, did this life-asserting melody ring out with full power.

Mayakovsky entitled his famous poem *Fine!* and it sounds like a joyous sigh. He says:

> *I've been all over the world in my time.*
> *Well, life is good,*
> > *and living is fine!*

Both these currents in classical Russian realism are embodied vividly and distinctly in Alexei Tolstoi's work. He entered the literary scene as a critical realist, continuing the Gorky tradition, by-passing symbolism, decadence and futurism. But in his criticism he goes to the lengths of grotesquerie, like Gogol, in portraying the landed gentry and the intellectuals of old Russia. Some of them, like his travelling magician (*Count Cagliostro*), are almost phantasmagoric. In their drunken despair his heroes may wallow in filth and shamelessness, yet afterwards a character like Prince Krasnopolsky (*The Lame Prince*) will crawl on his knees all the way from the railway station to his country estate to implore his wife to forgive him. The critical light in which Tolstoi shows up his heroes is harsh, relentless and spiteful, and the shadows it casts are ugly.

But the most important quality of his talent has always been its life-asserting power. Gorky had good reason for calling Tolstoi's talent "jolly". Indeed, under his pen everything acquires an elusive optimistic hue, everything is given the hope of a chance. He does not lose faith even in those men who have sunk to the lowest depths of moral depravation.

This life-loving quality of Tolstoi's talent finds expression in the most various forms. For instance, he loves to write "playfully" (take his *The Golden Book of Love*, 1919, and his *Wonder of Wonders*, 1926) and enjoys a literary joke (the stories *Paramour*, 1925, *An Extraordinary Adventure on Shipboard*, 1930, and others). Or take his earlier stories (*The Jasper Book*, 1909, and others) written in a satirical vein in an elegantly stylised 18th-century manner, the language as pure and transparent as water-colour. This life-loving quality was reflected in the very style of his writing, especially in his short stories. Their plots develop quickly and lightly. There is no morbid psychologism in Tolstoi (such as is typical of Dostoyevsky, for instance), and naturally no wallowing in horrors (as with his contemporary, Leonid Andreyev).

Tolstoi's realism and artistic method are rooted in the Pushkin tradition, although in his earlier works, as we have already mentioned, there is also a certain amout of Gogolian grotesquerie. Still, the predominant mood in Tolstoi's writings has always been good-natured rather than critical.

In order to understand what we mean by saying that Tolstoi reached ideological maturity in his Soviet years, let us compare his historical stories written during his émigré days in Paris with those written after his return to Soviet Russia when he had acquired new experience.

In his story *The Day of Peter* written in 1918, the great Russian tsar is shown as a gangling young fellow, cruel and erratic, strong in will and in his passions. The "barbarity" of late 17th-century Russia is rendered most pungently, but the vividness of this description left no room for a deeper probing into the historical significance of the age or even Peter's character. It is interesting that when he returned to the same theme ten years later Tolstoi, by then the richer for new experience drawn from Soviet reality, approached the character of Peter and the problem of humanism not abstractly but historically.

In the years following the Revolution of 1917, the problem of humanism arising in connection with the relationship between the individual and the state was more or less of common concern to a great many Soviet writers. The question posed by Dostoyevsky—

may blood be shed in the name of mankind's supreme aims?—has been raised in many works of Soviet literature (for instance, Konstantin Fedin's novel *Towns and Years*, 1924, the earlier short stories of Leonid Leonov, Mayakovsky's poems, particularly his 150,000,000). Alexei Tolstoi, who was extremely sensitive to the changing spirit of the times, also introduced this theme in his writings. However, he handled it more in the tradition of Dostoyevsky, with a bias in favour of man, but man as an abstract concept, as the centre of the universe and not as a member of that living organism—a historically developing people. Tolstoi poses the problem of humanism in his historical plays of that period *The Death of Danton* and *The Golden Book of Love*, but he resolves it in an abstract manner, as a conflict between the eternal categories of good and evil. The same is the case in his story *Charity!* (1918), the exclamation mark making the title sound like an unconditional demand.

When he returns to the problem of humanism in the relationship between the individual and the state in his later works, the trilogy *The Ordeal*, the tragedy *Ivan the Terrible* and the novel *Peter the First*, he shifts his accents.

If I dwell on the novel *Peter the First* in somewhat greater detail, it is because in my opinion *Peter the First* and Sholokhov's *And Quiet Flows the Don* are the peaks of Soviet fiction, unchallenged by anything else written in all the fifty years since the 1917 Revolution. *Peter the First*, which Tolstoi himself considered his masterpiece, renders the language, the characters, the details of life, and the whole scene of late 17th-century Russia with such inspired accuracy and insight that he might well be writing about things he had seen with his own eyes.

The theme of Peter the Great intrigued many Russian writers because it embodied both the cardinal problem and the age-old drama of the Russian people. Peter, whose face was "terrible to see" as Pushkin wrote in *Poltava*, was both the "terror" that set upon Russia's backwardness, and the "hope" for the way out of this backwardness. Debates raged continually round the subject of Peter's personality, and Peter himself was time and again used as a figurehead by those sections of Russian society (such as the "Westernisers") which stood for progress and Russia's inclusion in the group of European powers. Lev Tolstoi also studied the reign of Peter the Great and wanted to write a novel about him. But he never got beyond the first few chapters. His anti-state, anarchic views prevented him from really feeling the poetry of Peter's ambitious plans for the transformation of the country.

As I see it, it was precisely Alexei Tolstoi's constant interest in state matters, which was naturally heightened by the spectacle of the Russian people building up their new Soviet statehood, that prompted him to take up the theme of Peter the Great. He later wrote: "I suppose it was more by instinct than consciously that in this theme I tried to find the key to the Russian people and Russian statehood." And again: "In order to understand the secret of the Russian people, and its greatness, one must study its past thoroughly: our history, its main turning-points, and its tragic and creative epochs in which the Russian character was shaped." (*Autobiography*).

There are, of course, no direct parallels in the epoch of Peter the Great and the Soviet epoch, and Tolstoi did right to tell his readers not to look for any sort of hints or resemblances in his novel. But there is no doubt that through Peter and his reforms Tolstoi wanted to arrive at greater understanding of the dramatic and creative epoch of Russia's transformation into a socialist state.

It is the end of the 17th century. Russia—huge, dark and barbarous. Deserted roads. Wretchedly poor villages, with smoke pouring from the doors of the squat chimneyless huts. . . .

The opening scene of the novel is set in a hut like that belonging to Ivan Brovkin, a manor serf of the nobleman Volkov. The plot develops up the social ladder, so to speak. There is Alyoshka, Brovkin's son, who finds himself first in the household of gentlefolk and then in Moscow as an army recruit. The circle widens more and more, and there before us is the palace, the Kremlin, the boyars, and then the noblest boyar of all—Princess Sofia's perfumed "gallant", Vasily Golitsin, who has been educated in Europe. Peter is only a boy. He reigns together with his brother Ivan, while his sister Sofia rules the country.

Tolstoi takes us from the chimneyless huts to the throne room where foreign ambassadors are received, and to the council hall where the boyars sweat in their heavy, fur-lined velvet coats; then into the patriarch's prayer room, from there to the royal apartments teeming with monks, wet nurses, and clowns; and thence to the German settlement in Moscow. Little by little he unfolds before us a panorama of Russia with all her startling contrasts and ruthless internal strife. There are the merchants' daughters learning "politesse" and "outlandish" European dances by order of the tsar; the friend of the young tsar General Lefort, easy-going and gay, elegantly dressed in a coat of pink velvet and a golden wig; the socials and the assemblies, the court theatre, the Dutch seamen, the builders of the future St. Petersburg, the self-taught painters, the fugitive serfs, and the convicts working in the shipyards and the cannon factories.

Gradually, the figure of young Peter emerges as the central character of the narrative. He is gathering together a group of his closest associates from among common folk and noblemen who are in sympathy with his plans. On the one hand, there is the indolent, sleepy existence of the courtiers ruled by Peter's mother Natalya Kirillovna and Patriarch Joachim, and on the other–Peter's impressions from his encounters with people from the West, merchants and seamen arriving in Russia. He hates the boyars' traditional way of life, and this hatred makes him feel painfully and acutely aware of Russia's musty, sluggish backwoods existence. "Russia lies there as sleepy, destitute and clumsy as ever," Peter exclaims. "Talk of shame, indeed! It's the rich and the strong who have shame. And here I don't know how to shake the people awake, how to make them open their eyes. . . . Are you men, or have you shed so many tears and so much blood in a thousand years, despairing of truth and happiness, that you have rotted like that tree, drooping down to the moss?. . ."

And "I felt as if claws were dug into my heart–I was so tortured by remorse, by anger at our own people, at the Russians, and by envy for the smug merchants who'd unfurl their great sails and start for home, for their wondrous lands. And you–back you go to the wretchedness of Moscow. Maybe I should issue some frightening order or something?"

But when one of the foreigners tries to adopt a superior tone in speaking of Russia, Peter feels that his national pride and his human dignity have been wounded.

The character of this "carpenter-tsar", this tireless crowned toiler, one of the most remarkable men in history, who managed to heave Russia up out of the rut and Europeanise her is revealed from every angle, psychological and historical. This is no romantic barbarian, no petty tyrant obsessed with the idea of enlightenment as he had hitherto been portrayed (by Alexei Tolstoi himself).

While sacrificing none of the historically authentic details, none of the picturesqueness of the wild and violent nature of this man from the Russian Middle Ages, Tolstoi shows the greatness of Peter's creative personality, as a statesman and patriot. All that was really progressive in Russia naturally rallied to Peter. They were people of different estates–boyars, merchants, commoners, and peasants.

One of the most successful characters is Menshikov, who began his career as Peter's batman and rose to commander of the army and the first noble of the land–a reckless, thievish, gifted and insanely brave man.

Another remarkable figure is Ivan Brovkin, a former serf who becomes the tsar's assistant in procuring provisions for the army.

In this novel Tolstoi's pen is full of colours, it sparkles with the brilliance of his characterisations and descriptions, immensely varied and always apt whether he is writing about Peter's amorous adventures in Moscow's German settlement, about his foreign travels, amusements at court, or battles. But the best thing in the novel is Russia herself, Russia building and praying, groaning and weeping, forging weapons and building ships, singing and swearing, destitute and contradictory. Russia giving birth in intense travail to a new energetic Russia, with a fantastic effort bringing it forth from the depths of her immobile Byzantine past so that she might unfurl her sails and travel over all the seas and oceans of the world along with the ships of the other leading powers.

Peter the First invites one to reflect on many things, and most of all on the nature of the Russian.

Tolstoi's other major novel was his trilogy *The Ordeal*, on which he worked for twenty years, finishing it on June 22, 1941, the day nazi Germany attacked the Soviet Union. In it Tolstoi expressed his thoughts and reflections about the Russian land and the destinies of the Russians during the first thirty years of this century. The book gives a panoramic picture of the Civil War, but it is at the same time a chronicle of events, a historical novel, and an intimate diary all rolled into one. Russia looms so big, so very big in this novel. The story moves from towns to villages; we see the seething life of the country about to flow over like a river at flood-time; we watch the battle of passions developing; we hear the roar of guns and voices raised in frenzied debate. We see people from different walks of life: aristocrats, peasants, intellectuals, lawyers, doctors, soldiers and workers. We see them in drawing rooms, in trenches and dug-outs, in military hospitals, in factory workshops, and in the field where the land must be ploughed. Everything in this book is infused with the author's anguished love for Russia, distressing in her very vastness and her contrasts, yet dauntlessly striding forward and calling men to follow her.

In *The Ordeal* the female characters are the best, especially the two sisters, Katya and Dasha. All of Tolstoi's heroines seem to be bathed in Turgenev's gentle glow and emanate grace and moral loveliness.

The idea of the novel is to trace the arduous road that had to be traversed before the new Soviet statehood was finally established. The author had good reason to devote so much space to anarchism. The conclusion he draws is that unruliness, to which human nature tends, if given free rein, will inevitably lead to fascism.

Telegin says to Katya: "Remember how much we talked, how boringly senseless we thought the rotation of history, the fall of great civilisations, ideas reduced to sorry parodies.... Under the starched shirt front there's the same hairy chest of a Pithecanthropus.... Lies! The veil has been torn from our eyes. All our past life is nothing but crime and lies! Russia gave birth to a man.... And this man demanded that people should have the right to be people. It is not a dream, it's an idea, it's borne on the ends of our bayonets, it's realisable. A blinding light has illuminated the half-ruined vaults of all the past millennia. Everything is in order. Everything is logical. The aim has been found. And it's known to every Red Army soldier."

The poetry of the great aim—to give men the right to freedom and human dignity—the poetry of humanism, permeates the whole trilogy which describes the ordeal of the Russian people in the name of this cause.

Since the purpose of my book is to give readers a general idea of Soviet literature I cannot, of course, review all of Tolstoi's work which fills ten large volumes. Still, there is something I particularly want to draw attention to.

Tolstoi's *The Viper* is one of the best Civil War stories in the Soviet literature of the nineteen-twenties. The author liked this story very much himself, and invariably included it in his collections. *The Viper* was what the tenants of a packed communal flat called Olga Zotova, an unsociable, solitary woman made up entirely of sharp angles. When she was a girl of seventeen her parents—well-to-do people of the merchant class in Kazan—were murdered by bandits who had then set the house on fire. Olga barely escaped with her life. "The film of ice on which she once dreamed of building her fortune: marriage, love, family, a solid, happy home, turned out to be so appallingly thin. This thin ice concealed an abyss. It cracked, and life, raw and passionate, swept over her with its turbid waters. . . . She accepted it as such: life was a fierce struggle (they tried to kill her twice and failed)... a crust of bread for today and the mad excitement of yet untasted love." Yemelyanov, a Red Army officer, takes her into his cavalry unit. Their love is as brief as a flash of lightning, scorching her with its pure flame. Yemelyanov is killed, and Olga begins life anew for the third time. She is expected to adapt herself to the life of an ordinary Soviet typist, ruled by office hours and crushed by routine. Seemingly trifling things pile up, compounded of pettyness, kitchen gossip, meanness, until unable to take any more Olga, "the viper" discharges her revolver into the face of the apparently harmless Lyalechka. What is that woman they call "a bitch with a cocked revolver"—a victim of the war, or a child of the Revolution?

In Tolstoi's earlier works (especially in his cycle *In Volga Country*) women play a large role. His women, like Sasha and Katya in *The Lame Prince*, personify goodness, and their hearts are big, generous and warm. In a woman like that a man finds a haven of solace. Tolstoi believed that this all-forgiving gentleness in women was one of the main features of the Russian national character. Dostoyevsky also believed that it was in his Tatyana (from *Eugene Onegin*) that Pushkin "giving the glorified ideal of the Russian woman" created the positive type of a Russian. Alexei Tolstoi's female characters can really be traced back to Pushkin's poetic prototypes. They must have the right to love, to lavish the generosity of their hearts. That is the tragedy of Olga Zotova in *The Viper*. Life dashed her to the ground when she was only a girl, broke her, and gave her no chance to express what was in her heart. But for all that she is a wonderfully strong, forthright person, a soldier of the new world who hates the shabby world of the Philistines.

Metallic notes come into Tolstoi's voice beginning with *The Viper* and he begins to poetise strong characters. There is another interesting point in Tolstoi's artistic development: whereas before, in his earliest period, he embodied goodness in his female characters, in his later work the Russian national character is personified by men who perform feats of statesmanship and themselves make history. The idea of humanism becomes more profound and acquires an historical meaning.

Alexei Tolstoi devoted the latter part of his life mainly to work on large novels and series of novels. Yet our knowledge and understanding of him will not be complete if we ignore his political articles and essays. It can be said of Tolstoi that he was perfectly at home in the Russian language, and revelled in its beauty. But he could also use it as a weapon. And that is what he did during the war with Hitler's Germany. His voice resounded "like a tocsin in an hour of calamity or popular festivity", to quote Lermontov. He expressed his fury, his pride, his sense of outraged dignity, and his boundless admiration of the people in words that flew like red-hot sparks from under his pen, scorching readers and radio listeners. In those years his passionate desire to really fathom the Russian people, its history and the sources of its strength was fanned into a burning obsession. This is how he qualified Russian patriotism in 1942:

"Only a revolutionary socialist plan could venture to raise Russia to the economic level of advanced civilisation; only science could accomplish what twenty years later was called a miracle by foreign observers. Only socialist revolution could save Soviet Russia from that wretchedness to which fascism reduced Europe. Russia was saved by the great socialist plan. It is based on the humane principle of encouraging the national development of the numerous peoples and tribes inhabiting the country and of lending this development extensive material and cultural assistance. The socialist plan envisaged our country as a single, complex organism, as a large collective Man, whose every part and member—separate individuals too—must develop freely and exist simultaneously as a part of the whole and as an integral whole." (From the article "Indestructible Fortress".)

I am by no means an apologist of everything ever written by

Alexei Tolstoi. He also has his weak points, his trivial writings, especially among his plays, such as the one about the last Russian Empress and Rasputin. All this must be put down to "literary overheads", so to speak. Every writer, even Lev Tolstoi, has his poorer works. But Alexei Tolstoi, to my mind, however strictly one judges his works, is a genuine adornment of Soviet literature in its entirety. Just as one cannot know or understand old Russia without reading Lev Tolstoi, one cannot understand the new Soviet Russia nor the course of Soviet literature's development without reading Alexei Tolstoi.

He has recorded everything—the contradictions of history, the pain, the drama, the greatness, the strength—all that fermented and seethed in the country during the decisive phase of its history.

Chapter 11

Pasternak

Boris Pasternak. 1946.

The unfortunate, and now old story about Pasternak's novel *Doctor Zhivago* made his name known throughout the world. The publication of this novel abroad, the awarding of the Nobel Prize to the author (which Pasternak had declined), and the public indignation aroused in the U.S.S.R. by these facts created an unhealthy stir round the poet's name.

The story is unfortunate because the excitement started by the bourgeois newspapers about Pasternak made his name into a trump card in the cold war, in the game of nerves. It is a pity because all this sensationalism overshadowed the main thing in Pasternak–his poetry. His name was shifted into the sphere of politics, whereas Pasternak by the very nature of his talent was farther removed from politics than anyone else. His poetry is his glory, and so let us dwell on it first of all.

Pasternak was undeniably one of the most remarkable poets of the passing age of aestheticism with its refined individualistic lyricism. However, he did not wholly belong to those poets who dwell in ivory towers. He was closer to the feelings of a modern man who cannot turn away from the events of our quickly changing age.

Boris Leonidovich Pasternak (1890-1960) was the son of a well-known artist. His native milieu was the bourgeois intelligentsia, and he began to write in the period after the defeat of the first Russian revolution of 1905 when decadent, defeatist and erotic moods were becoming widespread in Russian literature.

His first books of verse (*The Twin in the Clouds*, 1914, *Over the Barriers*, 1917, and *My Sister, Life*, 1922) were remarkable for their extremely involved system of metaphors. His syntax was like a crossword puzzle. Even then, however, Pasternak did not shun social themes entirely. But he turned them into material for his metaphoric word-game. His semantic riddles acquired an importance in themselves. As a result, the titles of his poems and their content were often at odds. There was his poem *The Tenth Anniversary of Krasnaya Presnya*, for instance, dedicated to this anniversary of the Moscow workers' revolutionary revolt. One would have thought that the author could not help but make at least some mention of the workers' bloody battle with the police. But no; this is what Pasternak wrote in 1915:

> *The frost cared nothing for the moans,*
> *And firing caressed with love the snow,*
> *The streets were innocent as always,*
> *A plea.*
> > *Unviolable,*
> > > *sacred.*

It is surely rather far-fetched that firing should want to caress the snow, and then why were the streets "innocent like a plea"? No normal logic can explain anything here. Further on Pasternak compares windows with "slits in horsecloths" for the horses' eyes.

Pasternak's subjectivity, capriciousness and paradoxicality were indeed unprecedented in poetry. Yet whatever he touched with his magic wand he turned into a glorious festival. Symptomatically he exclaimed in bemusement as a very young poet:

> *Oh, freshness! Oh, the drop of emerald*
> *Amid the grapes intoxicated with the rain!*
> *Oh, glorious, divine minutiae!*
> *Oh, sleepy fleece of disarray!*

Needless to say, the essence and importance of Pasternak is not to be sought in this monophonic word play. I have cited this example more in support of my belief that Pasternak became so completely carried away by the play of sounds or the fascination of his unorthodox comparisons that he had no thought for their meaning. It happened for the simple reason that he was obsessed with the joy of living; because he was as happy as a nightingale rejoicing in its trills, and this happiness was an infectuous thing. Everything in life, from trifles to the Universe, was included in the happiness of his poetic play, in his *joie de vivre*. But what about politics, was it included too? Politics, the focal point of the life of society? It may be the focal point for others, concentrating the interests of hundreds of thousands of people. But for Pasternak, in his uninhibited world, in his primordial chaos, it appeared no larger than a grain of sand, it was a poetic toy like the sun, the stars, the smile of his beloved, the trilling of a nightingale, a fly on the wall of a tea-room at some intermediate railway station. One of his poems is actually called: "Flies in a Muchkap Tea-Room".

Tremendous events occurred in our world: the First World War, the October Revolution, the German Revolution, millions killed, the fall of Kaiser Wilhelm's empire, crowns rolling off the monarchs' heads, the fall of the tsarist empire, famine and cold, the sufferings of hundreds of millions of people. But from Pasternak's poetry you would never guess what, if anything, was happening in the world. In his amazingly talented poetry in the book *My Sister, Life* dated summer 1917 we find these lines:

> *Well muffled, I'll pull my window slightly open*
> *And call out to the kids below:*
> *What century is it today, d'you know?*

Pasternak shocks you twice: first, with the sound and structure of his poetry, its monophonism and the startling unpredictability of the metaphors and comparisons. But all these were storms in a tea-cup and there comes the second shock: the narrowness of his social horizon. Blok was sensitive to history. Mayakovsky was a

Hercules of history, handling great rocks of it and piling them up with ease. Pasternak's field of action was the size of a jeweller's or a watchmaker's work table.

Be that as it may, I remember how in 1918-1920 we all took down Pasternak's poetry by hand (Valery Bryusov wrote about this too). I took it down in my note-book too, and then copied it into my diary as something out of this world, as extraordinary as a nightingale bursting into song in winter.

Pasternak's poetry cannot be re-told in your own words. It goes to your head like wine.

His poetry is turned to all that is peaceful, kind and beautiful. Its very essence is rejection of violence; it is tremendously human. The patriotic feeling which was manifested in Pasternak's poetry in the years of war against fascism (his book *Early Trains*, 1943) was not simply a tribute to the times. This poetry belonged to our world and none other, it was truly related to what we were accomplishing and what we were defending. The war simply awakened his patriotic feeling. To me Pasternak is not only a poet of general significance to all mankind for all time, but a talent that could only have developed in the soil of Soviet literature.

In character, Pasternak's lyrical self-expression is akin to our Soviet humanism. His poetry is much more human than that of T.S. Eliot whose world lies in ruins, or of the Italian hermetic poet Eugenio Montale who dwells in the labyrinths of his confused images.

There are two really captivating things in Pasternak's nightingale trills: unreserved courage and trust in people. Pasternak treats the universe as if it were his own private room. He tousles and runs his fingers through the images of the world as familiarly as he would play with the hair of his mistress. He takes as much delight in his phenomenal game of sounds, metaphors and rhythms, as a child splashing about in a stream. His intentions, implications and manner of speaking which poetry alone can justify must be understandable to all, he believes. Who else could have called our harsh life so trustingly "My Sister"? This in itself is poetry, it lives a life of its own, blissfully oblivious and delighting in this oblivion. But how can idyll make a place for itself in history?

Pasternak's element is not history but nature, and as a rule he reflects some phenomenon of nature rather than its essence. But this is his sphere, and in it he discerns what no one else can see. The discoveries made by him can be cited *ad infinitum*. His poetic penetration and microvision are staggering. He has seen "mountain springs hanging down in twisted threads", a rose "dishevelled after a dress fitting in the night", the dust "swallowing the raindrops", and a heliotrope transmitting its "earthy smell to the saltiness of sailors' overalls hung up to dry". He has sensed "the breath of a waterfall on freshly broiled Caucasian mutton", and he has a gift for describing the forest behind the trees. Pasternak's poetic phenomenology would be really wonderful to learn.

He never lets us forget that apart from rhymed descriptions and a rhymed statement of ideas there must also be "magic", the breath of poetry, or what Pushkin called the "magic crystal".

Pasternak's poetry is addressed to intuition. He is unequalled in his genius for creating a monophonic surge of sounds and words that carry thought, for inventing rhythmic patterns and variations, and combining all this with unexpected metaphors and comparisons.

However, there was one danger he did not escape—mainly in his first books. This was the danger of reducing his art into meaningless word-weaving. After all, the soul of poetry is the thought and feeling invested in it by the author. This being so, poetry must have the sensitive precision of realism. Its soul cannot endure phenomenological formalism, and it will elude the fingers of the empiricist.

Pasternak's evolution was a complex process. A key to the understanding of this poetic evolution will be found, I think, in one of his articles on Paul Verlaine printed in the newspaper *Literatura i Iskusstvo* on April 2, 1944.

This article may be regarded as a poetic expression of Pasternak's character and feelings. He wrote that the new urban reality which Verlaine encountered was not the same as Pushkin's, Merimée's or Stendhal's. "The 19th century with its whims, industrial arbitrariness, financial storms, and a society comprised of victims and favourites, was nearing its end when still in its heyday. The streets had just been asphalted and illumined with gaslight. Factories, which sprouted like mushrooms after the rain, closed in on them, and the daily newspapers grew as excessively. Railroads were stretched to the utmost limit, and they became part of every child's life depending on whether it was his own childhood which flew past a sleeping town in the train, or whether it was a night train flying past his poor fringeland childhood."

There are two notable things in this passage. The first is that Pasternak condemned the system which we call the capitalist system under which people are divided into favourites and victims. He also speaks of industrial arbitrariness, financial storms, and so on.

The second is that he seems to find a justification for his poetic experimenting and the confusion of his syntax in the changing world scene. Technical progress, he believes, brought confusion and impressionism into life, into the being of every child (and, consequently, every poet as well), and either his childhood flew past a sleeping

114

town in a train, or the night train (and planes, let us add) flew past his poor fringeland childhood.

I beg leave to quote Pasternak once more, for his own words express with wonderful clarity his attitude to the most important thing in our life—our Great October Revolution: "Everything became displaced and mixed up," he wrote. "Conventions were swept up in a maelstrom, and there was a distant premonition that the most important thing of the age was approaching—socialism, and its foremost event, the Russian revolution."

Some people forget that Pasternak thought socialism the most important thing of the age, and the Russian revolution its foremost event. This should be remembered by those who, for their own ends, wanted to make of Pasternak the only surviving open enemy of the Soviet system.

The third and very essential thing about Pasternak's creative evolution was his growing need to utilise the poet's material—words—not as something to play with but as a means of confessing what he has experienced. This was most evident in his poem *Waves* (1931). His tendency towards simplicity and emotional authenticity grew steadily in the years that followed, and that is why we take what he has said about Verlaine in the same 1944 article to be a confession: "Like every great artist he demanded deeds not words even from poetry; that is, he wanted poetry to contain what has really been experienced, or at least the eye-witness truth of an observer."

Why then did Pasternak, who called socialism the most important thing to happen in our age, who wrote a poem about the Russian revolution of 1905 in which he extolled Lt. Shmidt, the wonderful hero of the mutiny on the battleship *Potemkin*; who had glorified the anniversary of the October Revolution in verse and created an amazing poetic portrait of Lenin on the speakers' platform; who praised Blok for his realism and for his feeling of history, a quality inalienable from genius; why then did this singular poet, an intelligent man of profound feelings, and a truly brilliant translator (of Goethe's *Faust* and Shakespeare's *Hamlet*, *King Lear*, *Othello*, *Anthony and Cleopatra* and *Macbeth*), why did this great poet who had attained such heights suddenly go and write *Doctor Zhivago*? The more so, considering that, like Blok, he was not a very good prose writer.

In my opinion the main reason was that Pasternak came from that camp of pre-revolutionary Russian poets to whom any revolution, and more especially a socialist proletarian revolution, was an alien thing.

Possibly, his need for historical associations found an outlet in his translations of Shakespeare and Goethe. But it was an emergency exit. What he really sought was contact with Soviet reality.

> Am I a freak,
> And does the good of millions
> Mean not as much to me
> As does the empty happiness
> Of just a hundred odd?

Pasternak addressed this question to his friend Boris Pilnyak in that decisive period when the first five-year plan was being completed and the second launched. That was the time when Ehrenburg wrote his novel *On the Second Day* and Valentin Katayev his *Time, Forward!*

But, of course, Pasternak was not a freak and he understood that "stumbling blindly in the darkness, our ignorance would never see the light". He understood everything, but his heart would not be reconciled to the application of force which is inevitable in any revolution, the more so a revolution that has triumphed and taken over the reins of state power. The state, as everyone knows, is an instrument of coercion which has been brilliantly shown by Lenin in his work *The State and Revolution* written shortly before the Revolution.

Pasternak's humanism was more of a feminine nature: passive and suffering. In this respect he was the exact opposite of Mayakovsky and Gorky. Thus he was never able to appreciate the humanism of revolution as such.

He was ideologically unprepared to understand the principal aims of the revolution, and he wrote a novel permeated with the pathos of Christianity. It contains poetry too, whose authorship is attributed to the novel's hero, Dr. Yuri Zhivago, who has suffered all the misadventures, political and personal, of the revolutionary years. The poetry is written mainly on New Testament themes.

Lev Tolstoi's "non-resistance to evil" idea also figures in Pasternak's novel, but it is, alas, presented in a jumble with contrived scenes of "Bolshevik atrocities" in the manner of White émigré newspapers of forty years ago.

We quote from his letter dated November 6, 1958, to the editors of *Pravda*: "When I saw the scale which the political campaign around my novel was assuming, I realised that awarding me the prize (the Nobel Prize—K.Z.) was a political step which resulted in these monstrous consequences, and I declined it of my own free will without pressure from anyone.

"In my letter to N. S. Khrushchov I wrote that I was bound to Russia by ties of birth, life and work, and that it was unthinkable for me to leave it, and live in exile in a strange land." Further on

116

he says: "... according to the conclusions drawn from the critical analysis of my novel it appears that I support the following erroneous views in my novel. Allegedly, I declare that any revolution is an historically unlawful thing, that the October Revolution was just such an unlawful event, that it brought grief to Russia and led the Russian successive intelligentsia to ruin.

"It is obvious that I cannot endorse such declarations, exaggerated to the absurd. Still, my work which was awarded the Nobel Prize provided the pretext for such a regrettable interpretation, and this is the reason why I declined the prize.

"If the publication of the book had been suspended, which I asked my publisher in Italy to do (in the other countries it was put out without my knowledge), I would probably have managed to amend it, at least in part. But the book has been printed and it is too late to talk about it now."

Pasternak had his novel published abroad, thereby evoking the indignation of the Soviet public.

J. B. Priestley told me that many people in the West took it as an act of courage on Pasternak's part. I do not agree. More likely, Pasternak did not quite realise what he was doing, because if he had really wanted to openly challenge Soviet public opinion he would not have declined the Nobel Prize or shown remorse, but would have left the Soviet Union.

I have had to dwell on this story longer than it deserves. But what with the radio and the newspapers coming out in millions of copies, the political struggle between the two worlds may represent even a modest violet hiding in the shade of tall, forest grass as a sort of rocket shooting up into the sky.

Pasternak himself deplored the consequences resulting from the publication of his novel. The pressure which allegedly was brought to bear on him had nothing to do with this: Pasternak was too big a man to be influenced in his opinions and actions by such a despicable thing as cowardice. I knew this remarkable man and poet too well to think so ill of him. His poetry and his life taken together make a wonderful chapter in the literature of our age.

Some of the pages in this chapter will perhaps be forgotten and the generations to come will neither understand nor appreciate them. But the fragrance of Pasternak's poetry, his genius will be remembered for a long time to come.

Chapter 12

Fedin

Konstantin Fedin. 1925.

The qualities I find most appealing in Fedin as both a person and a writer are his chastity, seriousness and honesty. What is chastity in a writer? It is the quality which guides him in his approach to his theme, to his material, and his interpretation of it. A superficial talent simplifies his task and rounds off the corners. But a genuine artist who is honest with himself and has a strong sense of responsibility never tackles any of life's problems head-on. A genuine artist is always a researcher at heart. He does not draw hasty conclusions because he knows that life may prove him wrong. He is motivated by his fidelity to truth and his respect for people.

In one of his articles Fedin said that he did not think it right to make any changes, from positions of today, in what he wrote twenty or thirty years ago. In 1947, when the Sovietsky Pisatel Publishing House announced its intention to re-publish the best works of Soviet writers, some of the authors (Seifulina, Shaginyan and Selvinsky among them) made fundamental changes in their books written in the 1920s. They gave a new interpretation to events and the actions of their heroes. Selvinsky, for instance, when revising his *Ulalayevshchina* weeded out his glamourised attitude to anarchic free-living, and produced what amounted to a completely new book. Alexei Tolstoi was forever changing his novels. His *Black Gold* was re-made into *Emigrés*, and the result was two different books on the same subject. Leonov re-wrote his novel *The Thief* (1927) and even gave it a different ideological message.

Konstantin Fedin is a writer of a different mould. His moral tact and his tendency to regard life in its philosophical aspect seem to protect him from the poet's susceptibility to romantic infatuations with life's ever new and inimitable colours and sounds.

I am far from saying that Fedin became the man we know today all at once. He went through the same, complex ideological evolution as all the other Soviet writers. And in a way, Fedin is a living embodiment of the history of Soviet literature.

But there was in him a sort of axis which controlled the evolutionary process in his case: first—his loyalty to the ideals of a revolutionary transformation of the world on principles of humaneness and justice; and second—his moral integrity. There was also one other circumstance which was very fortunate for Fedin, and this was his friendship with Maxim Gorky. Young Fedin's very first literary ventures endeared him to Gorky who thereafter treated him with big-brotherly affection, telling him about his plans, his thoughts on Soviet and world literature, and his more general philosophical reflections. The whole of that first generation of Soviet writers owes a great deal to Gorky. None of my contemporaries that I know of were ever denied his attention, kindness and helpful criticism. Yet, I dare say, he was fondest of all of Fedin, liking him especially for his seriousness and honesty.

Konstantin Fedin was born in 1892, and grew up in Saratov in an intellectual milieu to which his parents belonged. His mother came from a family with revolutionary traditions. Fedin was educated at the Commercial Institute in Moscow. He was in Germany when World War I broke out, and was interned there. On his return to Russia—already Soviet Russia—in 1918, he first worked on a newspaper in Syzran, then in 1920 went to Petrograd at the invitation of Gorky who wanted to meet this budding writer who had sent him one of his first stories to read ("Garden"). This is what Fedin himself has said about his first collection of short stories *Waste Plot*: "I was for many years especially attached to the little man who is the hero of *Waste Plot*. I had to unburden myself of this load which had weighed down on me for ten whole years. It was the fruit of my life in the old literature, the fruit of my isolated, shut-in school years, and my secret dream.... My prose lagged behind my development as a whole and my state of mind. This, I believe, is a purely psychological matter. On the other hand, it was not until 1922-1924 that I felt I had stored up enough means to seriously tackle modern (and extremely complicated) material; I could not have coped with it before, but now I could take it up in earnest."

Fedin's first large novel *Towns and Years* (1924), which brought him wide renown both in Russia and abroad, is a highly original work. First of all, in composition and form. The plot develops in reverse, as it were, from the end to the beginning. The scene is set in Germany in 1915-1916 during World War I, and in Soviet Russia. In parts the story is autobiographical, and Fedin is describing his personal impressions. The two central characters are Andrei Startsov and Kurt Van. Andrei is the sort of man who shrinks at the touch like a mimosa leaf. He is kind-hearted and soft. He lives by love, but his love is shallow. First he loves Marie Urbach, then Rita. Actually, he betrays everyone. His antithesis is the Bolshevik Kurt Van, the embodiment of abstract hatred. Fedin sees everything in its philosophical aspect, but somehow removed from reality. Startsov, the "kind soul", saves Markgraf Schenau–an enemy of the revolution. Kurt kills Andrei. The author concludes the novel with these words: "We look back over the road we have travelled, a road of cruelty and love, a road spattered with blood and bright with flowers. He traversed that road without smearing himself with a drop of blood, without crushing a single flower. Oh, if only he had taken upon himself one spot of blood, no more, or crushed one, if only one flower! Maybe then our pity for him would have grown into love, and we would not have let him die so painfully and so wretchedly."

In this novel, crowds of people, incidental and major characters, pass in review before the reader. There are scenes of war and of Russia rearing up in revolution. There are personal tragedies, love stories, lyrical passages, and philosophical reflections.

Perhaps Fedin did not succeed in revealing the psychology of the new hero–a Communist–as fully as Fadeyev was to do in *The Rout* three years later, or as Furmanov had done earlier in *Chapayev*.

But, on the other hand, he displayed great perspicacity in rendering the anti-human essence of the German Philistine, the German Burgher, the ugly cruelty and the profoundly amoral militarist psychology of the so-called "average German", with all of which we were to become so well acquainted later, in the war with nazi Germany. In *Towns and Years* Fedin describes how a German doctor tests new anaesthetics on Russian prisoners of war. One of his victims is Fyodor Lependin, a private. This is a very likeable character, a hard-working, good-natured Russian peasant with a poetic soul (reminding us of Tolstoi's Karatayev in *War and Peace*). In prisoner-of-war camp Lependin has both his legs sawn off. And then, when he comes home to Starye Ruchyi, he is hanged on an apple tree (the apple trees he had dreamed about while in prison) by the mutinous German prisoners-of-war led by the same Schenau whom Startsov had once rescued. Some of Lependin's fellow villagers also joined the mutineers.

The novel certainly abounds in human tragedies. It is a romantic novel in mood. Yet at the same time it is a work of philosophical reflections on who is to blame for all that has happened, what must a person do, and which road to take.

Thus, the essential nature of Fedin's talent had already become crystallised as long as forty years ago. The direction in which he conducted his artistic seekings is very typical for a Soviet writer. From Fedin's novels you can easily trace how the method of socialist realism took shape, why Soviet literature did not take the Bergson road of analysis (like James Joyce or Marcel Proust), or become absorbed in the irrational world of Freud. Revolutionary reality attracted the writer like an irresistible magnet, commanding attention and forcing him to face it squarely. Alexei Tolstoi wrote in 1925 (a few years after his return to the U.S.S.R.): "The time has come to study the Revolution and for the artist to become an historian and thinker." This is why the "existentionalist" approach (in the manner of, say, Camus) proved unsuitable to Soviet writers. With both Freudians and existentialists a man becomes a kind of "drifting personality", a unit deprived of will carried along in a stream of life's senseless incidents (someone like Meursault in Camus' *l'Etranger*).

Soviet literature takes the very opposite approach to life. It does not go out "in search of lost time" like Proust ("A la recherche du temps perdu") but tries to trace the interaction of time and man, philosophising on the problem of time and man generally. Soviet writers—Serafimovich, Furmanov, Fedin, Fadeyev, Leonov, Alexei Tolstoi, Sholokhov, Pogodin, Paustovsky and others—use factual material taken from life in the post-revolutionary period to show how the concept of good and evil is cultivated, how people develop their sense of friendship, their awareness of the interrelation between the individual and society, the meaning of life's purpose and the importance of will power. Moreover, they show the standpoint from which the new Soviet man cognizes reality.

Fedin's portrayal of man in interaction with his time, is the main feature of his artistic method which characterises him as a socialist realist. Among his writings of the 1920s there are many short stories describing the developments in the life of the peasantry after the Revolution (*Transvaal, Peasants* and *Morning in Vyazhnoye*). His novel *Brothers* (1928) deals with the ideological seekings of the intellectuals. The scene is set in Volga country and then further East–in Uralsk. It is the story of two brothers, Nikita and Rostislav Karev. Nikita is a composer who wants to find his place among the workers of the new world and participate in the Revolution with his symphonies. But psychologically he is still closer to Startsov; he is unlucky in life and love, and part of his soul is steeped in Dostoyevskian morbidness. As a matter of fact, this morbidness inherited from Dostoyevsky (the sorry cripple in *Brothers* for whom Varenka, the beautiful daughter of a wealthy merchant, has a perverse attachment could well be the twin of Smerdyakov in Dostoyevsky's *Brothers Karamazov*) was also common to Leonov and several other Soviet writers. In the 1920s, however, Dostoyevsky was taken one-sidedly and admired mainly for his irrational contradictions, which still appeal to his existentionalist admirers in the West. But the greatness of Dostoyevsky's genius lies in something else–in his infinite compassion for the humiliated and the insulted, and in his superb ability to show the dialectics of the workings of the human soul. An example of this was well presented by E. Golosovker in his book *Dostoyevsky and Kant* where he makes a subtle analysis of Dostoyevsky's polemic with Kant's theory of antinomies, in defence of feeling.

From Fedin's novels we can trace how gradually the images of the leading forces of the Revolution became more full-bodied in Soviet literature, and how much more philosophically profound the criticism of features of the old way of life became. The evolution of Fedin's communist characters mirrors his own ideological and artistic development. This makes a most interesting theme, and we could quite well review the entire history of Soviet literature from this angle. Its achievements must be put down, in large measure, to the philosophical and psychological study it has made of those social forces which guided Soviet life along the road of communism. How were these forces to be represented? What kind of men were they? At first they were represented schematically, this scheme merely showing the role played by the commissar as a military and political leader. Fadeyev, as I have mentioned earlier, was the first writer to make a profound psychological and ethical study of a Communist (*The Rout*). Fedin in his trilogy *Early Joys* (1943-1945), *No Ordinary Summer* and *Conflagration* (1963) gave a many-sided and in many ways novel rendering of Communists, revealing their human strengths and weaknesses. His main heroes, both Communists, are Pyotr Ragozin and Kirill Izvekov. They have a different background: Ragozin comes from a working-class family and Izvekov from a family of intellectuals. The two characters develop gradually against a vast panorama of Russian life, involving a great number of people from different social strata, and covering a period of many years—from before the Revolution to the war against Hitler's Germany. Fedin modelled his heroes on the Leninist type of revolutionary. His Ragozin has suffered the hardships of persecution and tsarist prison for his political views and has been tempered in class struggle; he is a man of high principles, he can be both hard and gentle and has the capacity to love and hate. Fedin writes: "Ragozin's rule to make immediate but never hasty decisions justified itself once more."

Lenin's notions of revolutionary militancy and the Communist's urge to transform the world were not abstract concepts. In his own character these traits were combined with an ability to appraise the historical situation soberly and realistically. He criticised hastiness because it showed a non-realistic approach to reality. It is therefore significant that in the character of Ragozin, a Russian revolutionary, Fedin stressed such positive qualities as speed without haste in his well-considered actions and decisions.

We find these same qualities in Kirill Izvekov, but they are given a different colouring in view of this man's more complex nature.

Fedin's novels of the nineteen-twenties and nineteen-thirties, such as *The Abduction of Europa* and *Sanatorium Arktur,* his short stories, his plays, and his trilogy (1943-1963) give us a large portrait gallery of Soviet people. His interpretation of the representatives of different classes and social strata—the peasantry, the working class, the intelligentsia and the bourgeoisie—was beneficially influenced by those ideological and social changes which took place in Russia, transforming it from a poor and semi-illiterate country into a spiritually close-knit and politically monolithic society with a rapidly developing economy. Fedin himself matured ideologically in the process. After the war he became a prominent figure in the country's public life, and was elected head of the multinational Union of Soviet Writers, a post held before him by Gorky and then Fadeyev.

In his trilogy Fedin once again showed his masterly ability to paint a psychological portrait and his profound knowledge of the intellectual milieu (the image of the playwright Pastukhov proves this).

Fedin may be called a writer of ideas and reality. In the latter sense he is also a historian of Soviet society. At the same time, the philosophical, ideological aspect in which he examines historical events and people has lent a certain coolness to his manner of narration. It is the coolness of a researcher, although the material which he is examining should scorch the reader. The leisurely pace at which his narrative flows also tends to make his style somewhat axiomatic. There is no suspense in his plot development. He does not build his stories on adventure or emotional tragedy (like Dostoyevsky), and his plots, though based on dramatic events, do not carry the reader away. He prefers to render the epic of life, and in some of his books (for instance, *The Abduction of Europa)* he speaks out as a political writer who investigates through his artistic imagery the main conflicts of the age between capitalism and communism. Still, politics in its pure state is not Fedin's province. With his lyrical digressions and his detailed description of the times and the people, he invites the reader to pore over these pages of life and not leaf through them casually.

Fedin himself, an artist and a thinker, has read the history of our turbulent times very carefully and without haste; he thought over each page and, protecting himself from the fire of the events by reflecting on them coldly, described them in a manner that appears over-complicated in a desire to make the honesty of his statements convincing to the reader. The most winning thing about Fedin, I think, is his honest approach and his moral certainty of the truthfulness of all he writes.

Chapter 13

The 1930s. The Modern Hero. Nikolai Ostrovsky

Nikolai Ostrovsky. 1934.

Events of such magnitude were taking place in the country that under their impact the entire character of Soviet literature changed practically overnight, although fighting was still going strong among the RAPP (Russian Association of Proletarian Writers) members and themes of the NEP period were still alive. Probably never in world literature did a mere two or three years work such a profound change. The launching of the first five-year plan in 1928 was an enormously thrilling experience. The general enthusiasm swept up literature too, and took its mind off itself, so to speak. Ilya Ehrenburg wrote in his short novel *On the Second Day*: "That was the year when the country started up with a jolt. Engines screamed from the strain of pulling heavy trains. Overnight, as if by magic, the railway platforms became piled with mountains of bundles, baskets and bales—a motley heap of belongings, all crawling with lice. Settled life had come to an end. People had started up, they were on the go, and nothing could stop them now."

Something similar was happening in literature. Something gave it a jolt and set it in motion. The motley baggage of the NEP period (like Panteleimon Romanov's novel *Comrade Kislyakov*), all that reflected the commonplaceness of life or described the psychological broodings of the intellectuals, lost its glamour in the new atmosphere and was replaced, with lightning speed, with themes of the socialist offensive which stirred minds and fired them with genuine poetic inspiration. That period marked the beginning of a rapid decline in such specifically intellectualist themes as Pasternak's "But what about that thing that in my chest I treasure, the diehardness, the hardest one to die?", characteristic of the preceding stage in Soviet literature.

This change of theme showed first of all that the intellectuals, the writers among them, were attaining ideological maturity and whatever vacillation there may have been was definitely over. These years marked a new stage in the development of Soviet literature. Whereas in the NEP period many writers still found no answer to the question: where does the revolution go from here?—and consequently peopled their books with heroes who (in various different guises) embodied retreat, the answer had now become self-evident. The struggle between socialist and capitalist elements that had gone on within the revolutionary process, making it a two-way, contradictory process was at an end. There was no longer any doubt: the country was heading for socialism, advancing with the irresistible force of an avalanche. "The Great Turning Point" had been reached. Writers were now anxious not to miss anything of these unique historical events, not to be found lacking at the time of this great assault, as Leonov later described it in his novel *Skutarevsky*. The question now was how to reach the "fighting front" first and see its heroes. Reality drew literature to it with the force of its romantic attraction. Everything appeared in a new, historic light—absolutely everything, people and things which only the day before had seemed to symbolise poverty, backwardness and everything that went with the "old Russia", evoking irony or pity. Valentin Katayev exclaimed in his novel *Time, Forward!* (1933): "Are not the kerchief and cheap slippers of a girl from the Komsomol, the singlet of a shock-worker, the challenge banner of a shock brigade, a children's poster adorned with the painting of a turtle or a steam engine, and ragged canvas trousers a thousand times more precious to us than Danton's brown dress-coat, Demoulins' overturned chair, or a Phrygian cap. . . ."

In those years there was already a relatively large number of established and budding writers working in Soviet literature. All of them, let alone the non-proletarian writers who had reason to feel behind the times, were drawn into the powerful current of the country's life. One of the RAPP groupings called "Zakal" (Hardening) came out against Fadeyev, who was then writing his *The Last of the Udeghes*, because they believed that the main distinction of proletarian art was its efficiency in portraying the daily changing forms of reality, and that Fadeyev, at the rate at which he was writing, was in danger of "sleeping through socialism". Alexander Bezymensky proclaimed the slogan:

Forget about losing a couple of rhymes,
Just see that you don't fall behind the times.

Mikhail Sholokhov, who took a hand in accomplishing the collectivisation of farming in his home village of Vyeshenskaya, put aside the third part of *And Quiet Flows the Don* on which he was then working, and (in 1930) while the impressions were fresh in his mind began to write his *Virgin Soil Upturned*. But people had such a heightened awareness of the importance of the very latest achievements, that Sholokhov, too, no sooner had he finished this book felt that he had fallen behind the times again. He wrote: "The dilemma which confronted me was how to keep pace with the key problems of the day. Here you would be writing about the setting up of collective farms, and the question at issue would already be work-day units. Events outgrow and outpace people, and this is what makes our task so difficult."

Hundreds of writers gave their whole attention to the most burning problems of the day. Writers adopted a style which was a mixture of *rapportage* and a romantic idiom, suited for conveying the general mood of exultation. Critics began to speak of "neo-romanticism" which resembled the pathos of the Proletkult poetry during the Civil War. Military metaphors were used quite naturally in numerous novels, essays and poems, by everyone from Gladkov to Ilyin, and from Leonov to Mayakovsky. Boris Agapov who renounced his constructivist poetry to become an essayist in the great army of fighters for socialism, wrote: "Actually, it was the front. In mud and cold men dug the trenches for the foundations, adjusted and re-loaded their weapons, the concrete mixers, and startled everyone with the machine-gun rattle of their drop hammers. They lived the life of the army (people from Perekhodnikov's Commune)—the bugle at the break of dawn, then a roll

Nikolai Tikhonov. 1949.

call, and off to the front. It was the second revolutionary generation going to war, this time in a smoke screen of cement dust. The excavator-tanks cleared the way for them, the concrete guns covered their advance with artillery fire, later reinforcing with cement the trenches they had seized. Lucky were the men who had the courage not to take cover in the rear, who threw themselves into the most difficult battle then being fought in the country, who all their lives will carry this memory in their hearts, treasuring it like a medal, a memory which will never let them slip or take to flight" (from "Technical Stories").

The changes which the first five-year plan wrought in literature were manifold and profound. Four features stood out against the general background. The first, which I have already mentioned, was the switch over to new themes dealing with production and construction. The second was a heightened interest in history. The third was the spread of the essay genre. And the fourth—the availability of more material than could possibly be digested.

The first feature has a direct bearing on that unique form of Soviet literary life, engendered by the first five-year plan, known as the writers' brigades. As early as 1923, a group of writers visited the collective farms and then described what was happening in the countryside. It was much later, however, that the practice of organising such trips for on-the-spot reports became adopted on a really large scale. In 1930, a team of six well-known writers—Nikolai Tikhonov, Leonid Leonov, Vladimir Lugovskoi, Vsevolod Ivanov, Pyotr Pavlenko and Grigory Sannikov—went to Turkmenistan at the invitation of the Turkmenian Government. Most of them left unfinished manuscripts on their desks in Moscow, books dealing mainly with the past. The task set before them was of immediate, vital importance: through the medium of their own particular artistic means and methods they were to portray the new, Soviet Turkmenistan in literature. Socialist realism was the method that naturally suggested itself to the writers. They chose several themes—cotton, collective farms, irrigation, Party work, the Komsomol, the Red Army, the status of Turkmenian women, and nomads—and divided them up among themselves. The original intention was to produce a single book which would give the reader a complete picture of Turkmenistan. Nikolai Tikhonov later wrote: "We did not manage to put it all into one book. We wrote ten instead. Vsevolod Ivanov wrote *The Stories of Team Leader Sinitsin* and a play *Naib-Khan's Compromise*; Leonid Leonov—a short novel *Saranchuki*; Vladimir Lugovskoi—two volumes of verse (one entitled *To the Bolsheviks of the Desert and the Spring*); Pyotr Pavlenko—the novel *Desert* and a book of essays under the title *A Journey to Turkmenistan*; Grigory Sannikov—a poem about cotton; and I myself wrote a book of stories under the title *Nomads* and a book of poems *Yurga* which is included in Volume 2 of my collected verse."

These books provide interesting material for literary research. It transpired, for instance, that the power of belles lettres traditions was still rather strong, and so was the influence of long-established forms and techniques firmly linked with old themes and viewpoints. The new content tended to clash with these techniques and was at odds with them: this applies in particular to the aestheticism of Pavlenko's style in *Desert*, and Vsevolod Ivanov's adventure-story plot and ironic tone in *The Stories of Team Leader Sinitsin*. But on the whole the trip was a great success, especially if we regard it from the writers' point of view. They made progress in mastering the method of socialist realism, gained a better understanding of reality, and had the useful experience of working on set themes. Each felt the richer for this experience. The best stories giving the most realistic picture of Turkmenistan in that period were Tikhonov's *Nomads* (which was about the socialist changes in the life of Turkmenia's nomadic tribes—the Belujas and the Djemshids, and about life on the collective farms in the mountains) and Leonov's *Saranchuki* (about an invasion of hordes of locusts and how the people dealt with it). The poetry of Tikhonov and Lugovskoi, the former full of quiet courage, and the latter emotionally lyrical, is also interesting.

All these examples shed some light on a problem which worried many people, namely the problem of "planned" literature. There is a widespread view in some Western circles that socialist realism is, in effect, the dictate of the Party ordering the authors what to write and in what spirit.

As I have already said, Lenin did not refuse to give the artists counsel on behalf of the ruling party, but his own point of view was that fiction was a delicate business and thus could not be influenced directly and, even less so, in a rough, heavy-handed manner.

After the decision on the Proletkults, the Central Committee of the Communist Party held two more discussions on the state of Soviet literature and the course of its development, and adopted pertinent decisions.

The resolution adopted in July 1925 allowed the literary groupings and trends freedom of competition in the matter of form, and stipulated that in the meantime the Party would help the writers to make the transition to socialist ideology in their work. By 1930 this transition could be regarded as accomplished on the whole, and the Central Committee adopted a new decision on the need to set up a Union of Soviet Writers. Since then all Soviet writers have been united by this organisation. The existing literary groupings, among them the All-Union Association of Proletarian Writers which claimed supremacy over the rest, folded up. All of them were disbanded by the Central Committee's decision adopted on April 23, 1932. Eventually, the Union grew into a regular association administered by members of the writers' unions in the national republics and regions. In 1965, the Union of Soviet Writers had more than six thousand members.

In October 1932, that is several months after a committee had been elected to organise the first congress of Soviet writers, a meeting was held in Gorky's house which was attended by Stalin and other Party and Government leaders. I was present at that meeting and was one of the speakers there. It was then that Stalin gave the Soviet writers' artistic method the definition of socialist realism. Actually he merely formulated what was already in the air, and the combination of the two words—realism and socialist—had already appeared in the press. What it meant was that if a writer was depicting life truthfully he could not ignore the historical forces which guided this life to socialism, in other words, he could not ignore the role of the workers, Communists, peasants and intellectuals in re-building Russia on new principles. A few years ago I had a conversation on the subject with Bruno Romani, a correspondent of the Italian newspaper *Messaggero*.

"Do you mean to say that what socialist realism actually demands of a writer is an honest attitude to reality?" he asked me.

"Yes," I replied. "I mean just that."

In one of his articles Gorky wrote that the new realism was compounded of facts from the new socialist experience. Every unbiassed writer, seeing the new life about him and wanting to describe it truthfully, will inevitably encounter the heroism of the masses. And this heroism is naturally reflected in literature. Consequently, not simply production relations but human relations become established in the process.

In a recent conversation with a certain well-known English writer I heard the following argument from him: "But a writer is always a bit of a rebel, he has to be a rebel, that's what keeps him going."

"Yes, of course," I replied, "but the question is what he is rebelling against. Mayakovsky was a rebel too. I'll give you an example which may perhaps sound too elementary to you: when a man is building a house it is senseless to take up arms because rubble is still heaped round the unfinished building and some parts of it are shrouded in lime dust. The thing to do is look at the blueprints, and try to appreciate the man's efforts and the purpose of these efforts."

"Your example certainly is elementary. The writer's business is to teach the man how to live in this house and to take a look into his soul."

"I quite agree with you there," I said. "But when we look into the soul of this man, this maker and builder, let us not sow seeds of senseless rebellion in it, or seeds of despondency and unbelief in the job he has undertaken."

In the June 30, 1962 issue of the American magazine *Saturday Review* there was an article by Malcolm Bradbury, a British scholar, entitled "The Taste for Anarchy", in which he said that

"... the very word 'civilised' seems to have taken on rather an unpleasant ring in England today. It offends in two ways. To some people it is associated with dilettantism and privilege; to others, it refers simply to what is separate and remote, to the things of high culture, which as a society the English are inclined to avoid in favour of things more accessible and less demanding."

This reaction to civilisation characterises the sentiments of people in the capitalist world in general, and not just in England, where J. B. Priestley, for instance, spoke out against the radio, television, and other mass means of brainwashing. In Italy, the late Angioletti, the first chairman of the European Community of Writers, voiced a protest against vulgar TV programmes. Jet planes, cars, refrigerators and the rest are all very well, but some are afraid that machinery is getting out of man's control and is beginning to exert too much pressure on the mind. H. G. Wells had spoken of this years ago in his novel *Mind at the End of Its Tether*. It is perhaps worth quoting him. "Man must go steeply up or down and the odds seem to be all in favour of his going down and out. If he goes up, then so great is the adaptation demanded of him that he must cease to be a man. Ordinary man is at the end of his tether."

These words were written under the impression of those gigantic stresses to which modern civilisation was subjecting the physiology and psychology of men in every sphere without exception: technology, science, public life, the exchange of information which has assumed a fantastic scale, and so on. A person begins to feel that he is in a room that he has cluttered with countless objects and devices, all useful in themselves but depriving him of space, freedom and air. And so he conceives a "taste for anarchy"; he wants to chuck out all this stuff and go back to nature. Now and again some group of young people does just that. A few years ago a group of young Americans left home to settle in the Galapagos Islands to relish the delights of a primitive life. They even had all their teeth pulled out and had dentures made instead since there would be no dentists on a desert island.

I shall not go any deeper into the outlook for man's relationship with the civilisation and machinery which he himself has created. One thing must be pointed out, though: these "stresses" have brought home to all the ideas developed by modern cybernetics and the teaching of Pavlov that psychology governs physiology and, by millions of contacts with the physical and social world, it also guides man. So no matter how much we may repel, however much we may cultivate a taste for anarchy, we know now from the findings of modern science that man is a planned and governed creature, and not simply the one who does the planning and the governing. This refers to all the spheres of human activity. The resultant force of freedom or lack of freedom is in the hands of those who have discovered the laws of history and who understand the course of its development.

It is sometimes said in the West that literary freedom ended in the U.S.S.R. in the nineteen-thirties, and literature began to be planned "from above" by the Party. I would put it differently—the planning of literature "from below" became intensified. Life itself had changed, carrying people along, in the same way that a strong wind fills out the sails of boats standing at anchor and carries them away into the open sea. To millions of people, the literary intelligentsia among them, the labour heroism displayed in fulfilling the first five-year plan was like that clean, strong wind. Many writers began to understand the erroneousness of their stand and some (like Pilnyak, Panteleimon Romanov, the LEF, the constructivists, and others) made public statements to this effect.

It was not the dictates of the Central Committee which "planned" literature, or in other words guided it in its choice of themes and expressive means, and controlled its spirit and its moods. It was by the inspired, heroic atmosphere reigning in the first five-year plan period that literature was influenced, governed and planned. The Party expresses what the people feel, and in this lies the strength of what is known as Party guidance. The Party calls on the writers to speak of what the people want to hear about, to respond to the people's spiritual needs.

The extremely tense atmosphere of the nineteen-thirties (we must remember that the Soviet Union had to step up industrial construction if only because Hitler had already come to power in Germany) shaped its own talents of a heroic cast.

The first of these talents to be dwelt upon is Nikolai Ostrovsky.

Ostrovsky entered the literary scene with his more or less autobiographical novel *How the Steel Was Tempered* (1932-1934)—one of those remarkable human documents that shed light on whole historical epochs.

I would include it among the most interesting books ever written. The title *How the Steel Was Tempered* is symbolic. It is the story of how a man was hardened to become as strong as steel. Apart from its artistic merits, the book is important for its historical truth, as proved by the life of the author himself.

Nikolai Ostrovsky (1904-1937) was born into a working-class family in a small Ukrainian town. He was one of the first boys there to join the Komsomol. At 15 he ran away from home to the Civil War front and fought in the ranks of the legendary Kotovsky brigade. Next he joined Budyonny's First Cavalry, and it was there that the character of this courageous, strong-minded boy of 16 began to be tempered. He was seriously wounded, which resulted in the

133

loss of his right eye, and was demobilised. Yet he still tried by every possible means to participate in the struggle for communism. There is an episode in the novel in which he describes how he chopped wood in the forest with a Komsomol team. A wet, heavy snow was falling, they had no boots, no place to sleep, nothing to eat, and it seemed that human strength could not endure all the misfortunes which befell him. But he found the strength. It gushed forth from an inexhaustible source: his enthusiasm and his boundless faith in communism.

Ostrovsky fell ill with a rare disease—ankylose polyarthritis, which takes the form of a gradual stiffening of the joints and general paralysis. At the age of 22 he was completely bed-ridden.

I met him in Moscow when he had already finished writing *How the Steel Was Tempered*, which I was editing. He lay stretched out on his bed, blind, and only able to move his fingers. He had a mobile device supporting his outstretched arm, with the aid of which he could trace out letters slowly and painstakingly. He still had a ringing voice. It sounded unexpectedly young and strong coming from this crippled, emaciated body.

In his remarkable book Ostrovsky told the story of his life. It is not merely a tale of struggle, but also a story of love. It presents the spiritual landscape, the spiritual panorama of a hero of our time. Ostrovsky says that life is only given to a person once, and he must live it in such a way as not to burn with shame for his past. He must live intensely in a constant endeavour to achieve mankind's great aims.

There is an irresistible moral appeal in this book, just as there was in Ostrovsky himself. This appeal is compounded of more than just courage and fortitude. More important is that fine human quality of stubborn refusal to be beaten by physical handicaps, the fighting spirit that endeavours to overcome adversity, whatever the odds. There are many examples of people like this in many lands, people like the American girl Helen Keller who was blind and deaf from infancy, yet became a writer, or the Soviet mathematician L. Pontryagin who has been blind from birth and is now a member of the Academy of Sciences. Ostrovsky's moral triumph over his physical handicaps is a manifestation of this quality, and is thus just one of the links in the chain of his heroic life.

This is what Alexander Fadeyev wrote to Ostrovsky about the hero of *How the Steel Was Tempered*, Pavel Korchagin: "I think that in the whole of Soviet literature there has not yet been a character as true-to-life and as enchanting in his goodness."

Ostrovsky once said to me: "A man becomes a real man if he is dedicated to some real idea, because then he lives as an integrated whole and not in parts."

I think that Pavel Korchagin is probably the most heroic character in Russian literature, crowning a whole gallery of heroes like Rakhmetov in Chernyshevsky's *What Should Be Done?*, Pavel Vlasov in Gorky's *Mother*, Commissar Klychkov from Furmanov's *Chapayev*, and Levinson from Fadeyev's *The Rout*.

Ostrovsky's hero shines like a star above the heroes of subsequent years, among them the main character in Kazakevich's *The Star*. Pavel Korchagin is the elder brother of Meresyev in Boris Polevoi's *Story of the Real Man*. He is the elder brother and guiding star of the heroes of the last war, of those who carried through the first five-year plans, who built Komsomolsk-on-the-Amur, who searched for diamonds in the taiga, who reclaimed the steppes and developed the virgin lands, and who manned the first space ships. We have a perfect right to call all these people heroes. They differ from the ancient heroes described by Homer, Pindar and Lucretius. Nor are they like the hero in whom Carlyle saw the basis of human development. They are even less like Nietzsche's superman. The super-tasks which the Soviet hero has to solve link him as an individual with the collective, with the people. If this hero were deprived of his aim—communism, if he were denied contact with the collective, he would fade out like a lamp that has been switched off.

Romain Rolland understood this very well, as we can see from a letter to Ostrovsky in which he wrote: "You make one whole with your great resurrected and liberated people, you are linked with its enormous triumph and its irrepressible energy. You are in it, and it is in you."

Speaking of writers of the heroic cast who best represent the literary atmosphere of the nineteen-thirties, I would mention Arkady Gaidar (Arkady Petrovich Golikov, 1904-1941) second to Ostrovsky. Even his early life story bears comparison to Ostrovsky's. In 1917, Gaidar was a thirteen-year-old pupil at an Arzamas school. At 14 he joined the Red Army. At 15 he was already in command of a company, and at 17 of a special regiment assigned to fight counter-revolutionary bands. He fought in battles on the approaches to Kiev, in the Caucasus, on the Polish front, and in Tambov country against Antonov's counter-revolutionary bands. He used to say that he loved the Red Army and meant to remain in the service all his life. At the beginning of World War II, Gaidar found himself in enemy encirclement, but he fought his way out and, refusing to be evacuated to the rear, joined the partisans and died a hero's death in a battle in the Ukraine on October 26, 1941. He was buried next to the Ukrainian national poet Taras Shevchenko, on the high bank of the Dnieper.

At a meeting of the Central Committee of the Komsomol Gaidar said: "Let people think one day to come that we called ourselves children's writers out of cunning, because actually we were training a strong Red-starred guard." Gaidar wrote about youngsters, but his books, especially his *School*, are read by young and old alike. The idea behind all his plots is to help shape strong characters with

Arkady Gaidar with his son Timur. 1939.

a clearly defined purpose in life. His heroes are complex natures. Not infrequently they find themselves in opposition to their environment. And sometimes they have to suffer defeat.

In his story *The Fate of a Drummer* Gaidar wrote: " 'Stand up straight, drummer,' the same voice kept telling me. 'Stand up straight before it's too late.' I opened my eyes and reached for my revolver. And as I closed my fingers round it everything became very, very quiet. The air itself grew still. And suddenly I heard a clear, strong sound, as if someone had touched a long, melodious string and, glad that someone had touched it at last, the string quivered and sang, astonishing the whole world with the amazing purity of its tone."

These words make a fitting epigraph for the whole of Gaidar's work. The appeal of his stories lies in their amazing moral purity. When you read Gaidar you want to straighten up morally. Nikolai Ostrovsky made you feel like that too. I remember when I spoke with him I felt ashamed for human infirmity.

One of Gaidar's best books was the story *Timur and His Squad* which came out just before the war. Timur was a youngster who might well have been the younger brother of Pavel Korchagin from *How the Steel Was Tempered* and of Oleg Koshevoi from Fadeyev's *The Young Guard*. He organised his friends to help the families of soldiers and to try and reform the local hooligans. Timur is a romantic hero, but he is the kind you believe in, even though the author may have exaggerated his virtues somewhat.

Gaidar experimented with new artistic means, combining realistic techniques with romantic fancy. In this respect he borrowed a great deal from Gorky.

Another writer of the same heroic cast was the playwright Vsevolod Vishnevsky (1900-1951) who also emerged upon the literary scene in the nineteen-thirties. "I am a soldier-writer," he used to say about himself. He also left home when he was fourteen years old and enlisted as a ship's boy in the Baltic fleet. His plays *The First Cavalry Army* and, even more so, *An Optimistic Tragedy* are infused with extraordinary pathos, drawn from the crucible of history itself. The narrator in *An Optimistic Tragedy* says:

"Welcome, new generation. The fighters did not demand that you should be sad after their death. In none of you did the bloodstream stop because several armies of men were buried in the ground during the Civil War. Life does not die. People are able to laugh and eat at the graves of their dear ones. And it's just fine that they are! 'Be kinder,' the soldiers said, dying. 'Chin up, Revolution!' The regiment is addressing this to posterity, you see. You do not have to hold a wake. The regiment invites you to think in silence and try to understand what is the true meaning of struggle and death to us."

I heard Vishnevsky speak at meetings many times, and I was invariably astonished at the spell-binding, hypnotising power of his voice. During the war, his radio broadcasts and his personal appearances in the city squares of besieged Leningrad where he spoke under fire, played an enormous role in boosting the population's morale.

He was one of those people to whom one can apply the expression: "he blazed like a torch". No wonder he was so attached to Mayakovsky. He saw the tragic in life, but he realised that the heroic in people was what led history forward.

Vsevolod Vishnevsky. 1936.

I have mentioned just three writers, but I believe they are so typical for their time that readers will be able to understand those new features and moods which distinguished Soviet literature of the nineteen-thirties.

The nineteen-thirties saw the emergence of a new generation of writers. It was in those years in fact that we really came to know Sholokhov, the plays of Nikolai Pogodin, the poetry of Alexei Surkov and Konstantin Simonov, the novels of Panferov who specialised in portraying the development of the Soviet village, and the works of many other poets and prose writers. It was also then that Ilya Ehrenburg gave up writing his ironically sentimental pamphlet-novels, and produced his *On the Second Day* and *Without Drawing Breath* filled with the pathos of the times. Writers signed up as volunteers to fight Franco's fascism in Spain. But probably the most important phenomenon of the time was the new attitude to the hero, a new approach to the problem of the hero.

In order not to bewilder the reader with too many names, I shall dwell in greater detail on this essential problem–the problem of the new hero. What is he like, this man who has to make new history? Is he simply a man who exists, or is he a teleological man pursuing a definite aim? What are the forces that shape the purposeless and the purposeful man? Where does freedom end and non-freedom begin? Why do men acquire either a taste for anarchy or a taste for purpose? These were the problems which Russian life and literature had to solve.

The greatness of the cause itself makes the essence of Soviet heroism. In characterising Chapayev, Furmanov stresses that he did not possess any extraordinary, superhuman qualities which gave a man the undying glory of a "hero"; his qualities were very ordinary and human; he lacked many valuable qualities altogether, but the ones he did have were amazingly strong, vigorous, and clearly defined. The same description could equally well apply to Pavel Korchagin from Ostrovsky's *How the Steel Was Tempered*, or Surkov from Fadeyev's *The Last of the Udeghes*. Chapayev, Furmanov says, was given the aura of a *bogatyr* by the legends woven round him by his officers, his men, and the local peasants. He became a folk hero like Svyatogor or Mikula Selyaninovich. But a folk hero is always democratic, he always stands up for the people and embodies the people's finest qualities.

A folk *bogatyr* has something out of the ordinary too, for he performs feats which are beyond the power of ordinary mortals. This extraordinariness, however, is diametrically opposed to the exclusiveness of Nietzsche's superman, that bourgeois hero who is a being apart, who alienates ordinary men and dominates their lives for his own ends.

The most important thing in the evolution of the hero in Soviet literature is that the features which set this hero apart from the masses lose their prominence and it is the typical qualities common to socialist society, to the people as a whole, that are emphasised. It is not the hero who has been reduced to the size of the "little man", but on the contrary the "little man" who has risen to the stature of a hero. In the early years the shock-workers or the Bolsheviks–men who embodied the heroic in life–were as yet in the minority, they stood out as exceptional phenomena amid the mass of people still obsessed, to a large extent, by private-property interests.

This change had to find its reflection in literature. In the following years the prevailing motif in the work of Soviet writers was to become the mass heroism displayed by the people in their labour. Life itself set literature the task of portraying the new character of the people shaped in the struggle for socialism.

Russian 19th-century classics invariably turned to the theme: what is a Russian, and what is the Russian national character? Just as invariably the conclusion they arrived at was that for all the splendid qualities of the Russian character its most salient features were passivity, anarchy, the inevitable Russian "leave it to luck" and "everything will work out somehow." Lev Tolstoi's Platon Karatayev, Turgenev's Kalinich, Goncharov's Oblomov, and Korolenko's Tyulin are akin to one another in their attitude to life: they regard it as fate which they must humbly accept in order to feel the poetry of being. Oblomov is a nobleman and landowner, while Tyulin is a peasant ferryman, and yet, apart from the infinite indolence and indifference to their condition which they share, they have many excellent qualities in common as well, such as tolerance, humaneness, a readiness to help, and a poetic perception of life and nature. Oblomov is by no means a "negative" character. By and large, this mechanical classification of characters into "positive" and "negative" is inapplicable to great artists. A great writer always represents the human in its concrete, temporal, historical form. If he wants to give a truthful picture of reality he cannot help noticing that it is the backward social forms and relations (feudal and capitalist) which are to blame for the ugliness in man, and that it is natural for man to aspire to rise above his social position.

For Tolstoi, Anna Karenina was a "positive" type of Russian woman, just as Tatyana in *Eugene Onegin* was for Pushkin. The national Russian character at its best shows through their gentlewomen's qualities, breaking through to the surface, as it were. Gorky also portrays many of his characters—merchants and capitalists like Artamonov, Yegor Bulychev and Vassa Zheleznova—in precisely the same way: not simply as money-makers, but also as victims of power and wealth.

The old-world serenity of the background against which Korolenko paints his Tyulin (in *The River Splashes*) enhances the appeal of this melancholy hero of the old patriarchic Russia. It is a hot summer's day. It has been raining hard in the upper reaches of this broad river, and now it splashes and plays as it swells with more and more water pouring into it. Tyulin's philosophic composure is unperturbed, and he merely acknowledges the requests of the passengers he takes across and the rising water which washes boats ashore. And life passes him by. "Dear Tyulin," Korolenko concludes his story on this good-natured exclamation. "Dear, gay, naughty, playful Vetluga! Where and when have I seen you before?"

In the old days the Russian writers often came across such attractive, placid scenes, and there was always a great temptation to interpret them as symbolic of the Russian people's nature. There are countless examples of such interpretations in pre-revolutionary Russian literature, where attempts were even made to make religious contemplation a central feature of the Russian national character. Dostoyevsky wrote to Maikov in 1870: "I will confess it to you alone, Apollon Nikolayevich: I want to make Tikhon Zadonsky the main character in my second story, under another name, of course. Who knows, maybe I shall succeed in drawing an imposing, virtuous, saintly figure. How do we now: maybe it is Tikhon who is that positive Russian type which our literature is trying to find." And Pyotr Kropotkin said about *Oblomovshchina*—the passivity and indolence personified by Oblomov, the main character in Goncharov's famous novel of the same name—that the whole of Russian life, the whole of Russian history bore traces of this disease. But was it in fact a disease? Kropotkin, the anarchist, and author of *Mutual Assistance*, spoke of it with sympathy: "The absence of *aggressive* virtues, non-resistance and passive obedience, all these traits of character are in large measure common to the Russian race."

But all those traits (sluggishness, in the first place) which were from time immemorial attributed to the Russian race simply had their roots in the underdevelopment of the production forces and social relations, and in the slave labour system. The indolence of the Tyulins was merely their way of responding to the futility and indifference with which they were surrounded from infancy, for such was the Russian reality of the time. Behind this form of unresistance lay enormous untapped reserves of creative energy. It is an interesting thing that in folklore this Oblomov-like character never appears as the hero. The people had a better opinion of themselves, because in actual fact they were always rising in rebellion and seeking revolutionary ways of resolving life's contradictions. Ilya Muromets, the *bogatyr* who "did nothing but sit" until he was 33 years old, was in fact rallying his strength for his future exploits.

For obvious reasons, the Oblomov trait in the national character did not find a broad, generalised reflection in Soviet literature. *Oblomovshchina*, the symbol of inactivity, is entirely foreign to the very nature of revolution. And the first thing the people did in the revolution was shake themselves free of Tyulin's indifference to the world about him. *Oblomovshchina* became a term used to characterise those who resisted the new and were hostile to the revolution. This will be found in a number of novels (Gladkov's *Energy*, Ilyin's *The Great Conveyor* and others). Contrarily, such Stolz[1] qualities as energy and initiative became the principal features of the people's, or more precisely, the peasant's character. Energy, passion and dedication are the chief characteristics of, say, Kirill Zhdarkin (the peasant hero of *Bruski*–Panferov's four-part novel about the Russian peasantry in the Revolution), that antipode of Tyulin. A decisive turn was taken in the shaping of the Russian national character; the process went according to a reversed pattern, as it were, and followed the finest folk traditions.

The evolution of the type of activity, the type of revolutionary protest, and the type of work effort was a more complicated process. Old Russian literature sought traits of the national character in this evolution as well. Acquisitive activity in pursuit of private-owner-ship interests was absolutely incompatible with the notion of the type of activity common to millions of people, and so the question was posed differently: what national traits did the Russians lend their activity in general, be it commerce or revolution? V. Rozanov, an interpreter of Russian life and one of these would-be philos-ophers, wrote: "Let us take capital and capitalism, and we shall see that even our methods of accumulation are profoundly different from those practised in the West. Our masses are poor and clumsy in self-enrichment, even when they desire it very badly. Our rich man is an extraordinary character: 'He clips his coupons'. And once again we observe a disinclination to bustle and a love of tranquility common to river pilots and roofers."

As examples of the "active" Russian character the literature of the past gave us, first of all, the image of a daredevil, and descrip-tions of dashing escapades, wild abandon, Russian generosity and broad-mindedness, unrestricted by any reasonable limits and ending in self-sacrifice and self-destruction. Dostoyevsky in his *A Writer's Diary* (1873), telling about a man who displayed Russian daring when he made up his mind to "fire at the Communion cup", says: "We have before us two national types which are extremely representative of the Russian people as a whole. In the first place, it is a forgetfulness of all measure in everything. It is an inner need to go too far, to taste the thrill of walking to the edge of a precipice, hanging over the side, peering into the depths, and in some cases, far from infrequent, plunging down madly, head first. It is an inner need to deny, sometimes felt by the most undenying and worshipful people, a need to deny the most undeniable and revered, to deny everything, the thing held most sacred in one's heart, one's most

---

[1] Oblomov's foil and antithesis in Goncharov's novel, a somewhat idealised image of a businessman.–*Ed.*

perfect ideal, the sacrament of the whole nation in its entirety, before which one has just stood in adoration and which has suddenly become an unbearable burden. What is most amazing is the hastiness, the impulsiveness with which a Russian sometimes hurries to declare himself in specific moments of his own or the nation's life, to declare himself in either the good or the despicable. There is no holding him sometimes. When it comes to love, drink, dissipation, hurt pride or envy, a Russian is capable of almost utter self-abandon, he is prepared to sever all ties, to renounce everything: his family, his conventions, and God, once he is caught up in this whirlwind, a whirlwind of convulsive and instant self-negation and self-destruction, so common to the Russian national character at certain fateful moments of life."

Yet all these features, discerned by genius and shaped into a single image, do not reflect the essence of the Russian national character as a whole. It is but a temporal form in which the inexhaustible creative powers of the people manifest themselves, a form created for the same reasons as *Oblomovshchina*, not common to all and not imperative, though widespread. Chaadayev in *Philosophical Letters* (1823) said: "What all of us lack is some sort of solidness, method, or logic." Under capitalism the Russian people could not have cultivated this solidness, or this logic in their creative self-expression. Only a proletarian socialist revolution could have developed this new kind of creative behaviour in people, a fact which has been extensively shown in Soviet literature, but nowhere as compellingly and clearly as in Furmanov's *Chapayev*. Much of what Dostoyevsky has noted was also common to Chapayev: the inner need to go too far in anger, in joy or in dedication to the common cause, the impulsive desire to declare himself, to exaggerate a little, to brag and even to get caught in the "whirlwind of convulsive and instant self-negation." Thus, after a slight quarrel with the division commissar, Chapayev decides to hand in a report requesting to be "removed from office". Furmanov remarks: "The strange thing is that Chapayev did not seem to treasure his division at all, and yet it comprised all those heroic regiments with which he was so close. The main trait of his character took the upper hand here: this trait was to sacrifice the dearest thing he had without a moment's consideration or hesitation, at the slightest, even a trifling, provocation."

Such inconsistent and erratic behaviour, and this "absence of method or logic", reflected the undeveloped state of Russia's social life. At the same time, circumscribed though this form may be, Chapayev is ebullient with a powerful creative urge, he is full of revolutionary protest, he displays genuine heroism in revolutionary struggle, and Russian revolutionary enthusiasm. Socialism, or rather the proletarian revolution, separates this heroic self-expression from its anarchic form and thus reveals the human meaning of heroism, strengthens the hero's sense of dignity, his faith in himself and his desire to live, and restores this man to his original self. "And another thing," Chapayev says to his commissar, "the higher I rise, the more I treasure life. You develop such conceit, you know: you're no louse, you say to yourself, you're a real man, damn you, and you want to live properly, the real life. It's not that I'm turning coward, I've got more sense, that's all."

Under socialism the Russian national character is being purged of these traits forever. This purging process has been reflected by many socialist realist writers—Fadeyev, Sholokhov, Furmanov and Makarenko among them. The Revolution has corrected the legends about the moral qualities of the Russian national character. The Russian people's attitude to work has also changed. Russian literature from Saltykov-Shchedrin to Gorky has variously represented, besides the indolence known as *Oblomovshchina*, the headlong rush into frenzied work without method or constancy, its romantically impulsive character, and the infatuation with the exciting scale of the job undertaken with complete disregard for the details, the purpose and the results.

The Russian national character has changed considerably since the Revolution. And so have all the above-mentioned traits which for decades and even centuries have been attributed to the Russian people, and which have been described by 19th-century writers like Turgenev, Tolstoi, Dostoyevsky and Chekhov. The process of transformation was particularly intensified in the 1930s, and this found its due reflection in Soviet literature.

Malcolm Bradbury, whom I have mentioned earlier, wrote in an article that people in England (and in other old civilised countries as well) were developing a taste for anarchy and were dissatisfied with the modern civilisation created by capitalism. He refers to Matthew Arnold's *Culture and Anarchy*. The institutions of civilisation do not live up to their purpose. What is more, they restrict the freedom of the individual and exert increasingly strong pressure on him, depriving him of perspective. That is why, Bradbury thinks, people—meaning above all scholars and intellectuals—begin to remember a duty to anarchy. This is reflected in literature. Irresponsible, spontaneous, unreasonable actions, motivated not by the interests of society but more often than not by ultra-individualistic and sexual desires, are given prominence. This is particularly apparent in many French novels, in the books of Françoise Sagan, for instance. Even if her heroes do agree to submit to the influence of the codes of society and established morals, they show no more grace than a ship which is obliged to drift because it has lost control and gone off course. In a sense it is a drifting society, and literature reflects this state of drifting which results from the anarchy of the capitalist method of production and the anarchy of sex. The strong influence exercised by Freud on the literatures of Italy, Britain and France for several decades now is self-evident.

In Russia we observe an entirely different picture which, I repeat, unfolded most impressively in the late nineteen-thirties when society was mobilised for concerted endeavour. Admittedly this mobilisation had its negative side too, for it was after 1935 that the oppressive consequences of the Stalin personality cult began to manifest themselves with particular force. But it must not be imagined that the practice of extolling official well-being or fanatical heroism characterised the whole of the literature of that period. It was in those years that Ilf and Petrov entered the scene with a new kind of satire, quite different from that of Zoshchenko. Ilf and Petrov also levelled their satire at the Philistinism which existed then and has partly survived to our day, but the whole idea of the Golden Calf raises the problem to a different, I should say, a historical plane. This idea is that there's no room for millionaires in the Soviet Union, money won't buy them anything, there's nowhere for them to make a splurge, no chance to paint the town red. By developing this idea in the scenes with Koreiko, a millionaire by chance, the authors are able to show Soviet life from a peculiar angle. Their main barbs are aimed against red-tape which was so hateful to Lenin who regarded it as one of the most dangerous practices for the socialist system.

Thus the nineteen-thirties, just as the nineteen-twenties, advanced their own special problems which were reflected in the literature of the time. The positive aspects of that period recorded by literature included the changes which had come into the national Russian character: better organisation, self-discipline and efficiency. The shady side was the way the Stalin personality cult exerted its pressure on literature, particularly in the years just before World War II. This pressure was very hard indeed.

But for all that, it was not the personality cult which "planned" literature, but the heroic labour exploits of the masses who carried through the five-year plans. "Man is Created Here" (from Goethe's *Faust*) are the words chosen by Fyodor Gladkov as an epigraph for his novel *Energy* describing the construction of the hydroelectric power station on the Dnieper. It was indeed in the great effort of construction, in the process of life as it produced new forms that a new type of man and a new national character were created.

Chapter 14

The War Against Fascism
and Soviet Literature

From the point of view of actual development and the range of problems covered, the war against Hitler Germany brought literature nothing essentially new in the ideological sense, but it did bring out more clearly certain latent features and accentuated its achievements.

The total mobilisation of society in wartime was fully justified. The people of their own accord made heroic, supreme efforts to destroy the aggressor, liberate their country and defend the gains of the Revolution. Naturally enough all this was reflected in literature. It became especially clear in the war years that Soviet writers were ideologically united, that the interests of the people were their own, and that they were prepared to defend their country against the enemy not only with their talent but with their lives. Suffice it to say that more than a third of the membership of the Union of Soviet Writers, irrespective of age, went off to the front as privates, officers, political officers and war correspondents. Of the 900 who were at the front, 345 died in battle. Among them were such well-known writers as Arkady Gaidar, Yuri Krymov, author of *Tanker Derbent*, and Yevgeny Petrov, essayist and satirist. Ten writers received the title of Hero of the Soviet Union.

Life in the trenches among the soldiers gave writers a deeper insight into the heart of the people, inspiring them to produce outstanding works. It was in field conditions that Alexander Tvardovsky conceived his *Vasily Terkin* which has become a national poem in the true sense of the word. It was published in the front-line papers, and people learnt it by heart. The image of the jolly, brave and modest peasant, Private Vasily Terkin, might well have been created by the soldiers themselves, and they loved him like a living person.

Another of Tvardovsky's poems, called *A House by the Roadside*, has always had a tremendously powerful impact on my imagination by virtue of its tragedy and truth. In this house a soldier left his wife and baby, and while he was away fighting a second child was born to his wife in a German prison camp.

It was at the war that Nikolai Tikhonov, Konstantin Simonov, Alexei Surkov, Mikhail Svetlov, Alexander Prokofiev, Ilya Selvinsky and Mikhail Isakovsky wrote their memorable poetry.

When the American exhibition was on in Moscow in 1959, one of the lady guides came up to Alexei Surkov and asked: "It was you, wasn't it, to whom Simonov dedicated his poem *Remember, Alyosha...*?" This poem, like Isakovsky's *Katyusha* and other songs have virtually flown across the ocean—ample proof that they came straight from the heart.

Literature was enriched during the war by the essays of Vasily Grossman and Pyotr Pavlenko, by Alexei Tolstoi's *Ivan the Terrible*, Vadim Kozhevnikov's stories, and the contributions of many, many other authors.

Sholokhov, Fadeyev and Korneichuk were all at the front. Even Pasternak, a poet who appeared to keep so well away from any kind of storms, even he felt an inner urge to go to the front. In a book of poetry he gave me he wrote that he would never be able to forget the people he met there and the hearty welcome he was given in General Gorbatov's units.

No man or woman in the country could have remained on the sidelines or failed to appreciate the historical significance of the struggle.

Vera Inber, a woman getting on in years, remained in besieged Leningrad with her husband who was in charge of a hospital, and attended literary meetings regularly, undaunted by enemy bombardment. In *The Pulkovo Meridian* she describes life in the besieged city in tragic and heroic pictures. The poem is inspired by the idea of humanism, and in it Vera Inber says:

> *We're humanists.*
> > *And we,*
> *The scores and hundreds of us,*
> *In Leningrad's alerted darkness,*
> *Felt suddenly that we were huge.*
> *We were a force.*
> *The glory of the people we were with*
> *Was deathless.*
> *So never mind the night.*
> *No matter that we cannot see as yet*
> *The face of Victory, her features.*
> *The rays of her gold crown*
> *Are rising in the sky already....*

The two literary genres which flourished equally in wartime were publicist articles and lyric poetry. Worthy of special mention are those poets who lived and wrote in besieged Leningrad: above all Olga Bergoltz for her tragic lyricism, and Alexander Prokofiev for the lyrical evocativeness of his Motherland images in *Russia*. This poem is like a song, or rather a stream of songs flowing into one another.

In his report "The 25th Birthday of Soviet Literature" addressed to the general meeting of the Academy of Sciences in November 1942, Alexei Tolstoi said that the remarkable thing about Soviet literature was that it did not confine itself to the "slit of a trench". In other words, it did not confine itself exclusively to propaganda, calling on the population and the soldiers to perform their patriotic duty. Far from it. Under the stress of war, literature could not hold back its tears, which were perhaps more bitter than those shed in the nineteen-thirties. Lyricism softened it, emotions became more expansive and free, and literature rang with passionate humanism. In this sense, Soviet literature sharply differed from the literature of fascist Germany where the utterings of Goebbels were repeated in variations in hundreds of books. Soviet literature made a stand against fascism with the whole of its ideological essence.

Some gifted writers who seemed to find themselves anew in the war theme came to the fore during the war years and immediately afterwards. The first to spring to mind is Konstantin Simonov. His *Days and Nights,* a novel about the defence of Stalingrad, was one of the most widely read books at the time and was immediately translated into all the world's major languages. The author, who in this novel "handled hot material coolly", found for it a unique narrative tone (stemming from Lev Tolstoi to a certain extent) which has both the austerity of a formal account and the throbbing pathos of the underlying drama.

Thereafter, Konstantin Simonov devoted all his prose to the theme of war. His latest novels *The Living and the Dead* and *Men Are Not Born Soldiers* are a chronicle of human destinies in those years. They are fine novels and extremely popular with Soviet readers.

Vasily Grossman in his story *The People Are Immortal* (1942) takes a different approach to the war theme. The story can be called a tragic legend in prose. This is how he tells it:

"Soldiers were dying. Who will tell others about their feat? Only the quickly skimming clouds saw how private Ryabokon fought to his last bullet, how political officer Yeretik, after shooting ten Germans, blew himself up with a hand already turning cold; how Glushkov, surrounded by the enemy, went on firing until he drew his last breath; how machine-gunners Glagolev and Kordakhin, bleeding to death, went on squeezing the trigger while there was strength in their stiffening fingers, and while their failing vision could discern the enemy in the hot, thickening haze.

"Great is the nation whose sons die with honour and dignity on its boundless fields of battle. The sky and the stars know about them, the earth has heard their last sighs, the unreaped rye and the roadside trees have witnessed their heroism."

Later Vasily Grossman was to abandon this emotional style. But in the wartime it was very widespread, and is to be found in Leonid Leonov's *The Battle for Velikoshumsk*, Leonid Sobolev's *The Soul of a Seaman*, Nikolai Tikhonov's *Leningrad Stories*, Alexei Tolstoi's *Ivan Sudarev's Stories*, Boris Gorbatov's *The Unconquered*, and other romantically dramatic works.

We find quite a different style in Alexander Bek's *Volokolamsk Highway*. In this book he exposes the cruel logic of battle and the preparation for battle. Momysh-Uly, the hero of the story, says indignantly to the political officer: "Why do you speak in those ready-made phrases, Dordia? Not steel alone, but words too, even the holiest words, get worn down and begin to 'skid' like a gear with blunted teeth if you don't give them a fresh edge."

Alexander Bek does not make his heroes hold lengthy discourses or digress from the matter in hand. He shows the implacable ruthlessness of battle. If a man is making ready to kill another man, he must be suitably prepared for it. No need to describe any scenic beauty then, or the pathos of heroism. "Do not expect me to describe the scenery, for I don't know whether the view spreading out before us was beautiful or not. The surface of the sluggish, narrow Ruza was like a dark mirror, and on it sprawled some large, artificial-looking leaves on which white water lilies no doubt grew in summer. Maybe it was beautiful, but I made a mental note: it's a rotten little river, it's shallow and easy for the enemy to ford."

Bek describes the everyday prose of the heroic life of General Panfilov and his men, but all their actions are ruled by the war's implacably frightening logic which determines the soldier's every step.

The spokesman for this logic is Momysh-Uly. I do not know what to call this story—heroic or tragic. It is somewhat reminiscent of Simonov's *Days and Nights*, yet it goes much further. The principal hero is the logic of circumstances or the mechanism which determines human actions. Bek has taken the war—the most brutal of all possible situations, where the human in men clashes with that which denies all that is human. Here heroism becomes the fuel which gives the human stream the power to move across a mine field.

Alexander Bek's *Volokolamsk Highway* is one of those books which make you ponder on the cruelty of human reason when, in an attempt to find the ultimate truth, it rips away life's last, protective veil.

These two trends—one addressed to the senses and inviting a romantically emotional response, and the other relentlessly demanding that we should know the naked truth—were further developed in a whole series of books written after the war. Among those writers who followed the first trend was Boris Polevoi, the author of *The Story of a Real Man*. The second trend is represented by such well-known writers as Victor Nekrasov and Vera Panova who elect to underplay the drama in their narrative, describing the obverse side of events involving the destinies of rank-and-file people.

Emanuel Kazakevich's story *The Star* whose heroes are scouts (joining the army as a volunteer, Kazakevich himself was a scout in the last war) abounds in extremely tense situations, but the dramatic narrative is mellowed by the author's gentle lyricism which somehow reconciles you to the relentless logic of war. What is a scout? A man who "no longer belongs to himself, nor to his commanders, nor even to his memories". "He is as nameless as a bird in the woods. He could easily forego articulate speech and just imitate the whistling of birds to give signals to his comrades. He grows into the fields, the forests and the gullies, he becomes the spirit of these parts—a dangerous, watchful spirit, nursing one thought alone in his head: how to carry out his task."

The question confronting literature after the war was whether socialist realism, that is realism based on the socialist experience, would develop the tendency to analyse and reveal the psychology and characters of men, in other words encourage realism's aptitude for investigation, which presupposes the showing of life's contradictions as well, or whether the emotional would prevail and preoccupation with the romantic and the heroic would more or less eclipse the desire, natural to all genuine art, to render life the way it is.

The war years showed that literature had good use for such genres as lyricism and even simple songs which, it transpired, also contained something that cemented people together. They also showed that humanism, which was clearly the general principle of wartime literature, could be quite lawfully rendered in a new manner, as witness the books of Victor Nekrasov and Vera Panova.

Chapter 15

Poets. The Problem
of the Generations

Poetry undoubtedly has less influence on the minds of men than do the teachings of philosophers or religious thinkers who find millions of followers. Among the ten books which have exerted the strongest influence on mankind William Durant (the author of a many-volume history of civilisation) named Marx's *Capital*[1] along with Confucius, Rousseau and Darwin. Durant did not include a single work of fiction in the ten books.

Be that as it may, the Russian poetry of the last fifty years certainly ranks among the world's best and most original. It is, of course, rather difficult for a foreigner who does not know Russian to judge, because poetry always stands to lose in translation. If I were asked what distinguishes modern Russian poetry, I would say: a wealth of talents, and the boldness and keenness of their quests.

Poetry attains great heights when it flies on wings of music and politics. The word politics will sound shockingly straight-forward to some people. But it is after all the poet's political attitude that does and should express with the greatest philosophical accuracy how harmoniously his awareness of the times is blended in his soul with music.

In any case, the aim which Soviet poets have pursued during the last four or five decades has been to embrace politics so that the poetry of words should express the poetry of life.

In this chapter I propose to examine the present state of poetry in the U.S.S.R. We shall of necessity have to confine ourselves to the major trends and poets. But before we go any further, let us go back a little way and, if only very briefly, review the past.

---

[1] In 1955, Raymond Queneau polled the French writers and all of them named *Capital* as one of the ten best books in the world. It is also interesting to note that next to Paul Valery's book of essays, Casanova's *Memoirs* and Prosper Merimée's novels, the books named included Tolstoi's *War and Peace*, Dostoyevsky's *Brothers Karamazov, Idiot, The Possessed*, and *Crime and Punishment*, and Gogol's *Dead Souls*.

Where and how did those trends which we witness today originate?

Soviet literature took shape under the impact of revolutionary ideas and images. Mayakovsky wrote in 1917:

> *Today we re-examine what the worlds are based on.*
> *Today we make life over to the smallest button on its*
> *clothes. . . .*

In the period immediately preceding the Revolution of 1917 the predominant position in Russian poetry was held by the symbolists, headed by Bryusov and Blok, and the acmeists, led by Gumilev.

Blok is a poet of unrest. His refined lyricism which finds a way to the innermost recesses of the human soul and subtly grasps its passing moods, is at the same time imbued with a sense of history. Blok's poetry speaks of the frustration of thraldom—inhuman, ugly and brutal. He longs for romantic beauty in art. He called the old world a frightening world. There were some who thought it a paradox that Blok of all people should welcome the Bolsheviks as a purifying force. But in fact there was nothing paradoxical about it. Withdrawing from the frightening world of the past, Blok bravely stepped into the purifying fire of the Revolution. *The Twelve*, in which he rendered with amazing genius the "revolutionary music" of the epoch, was translated into many European languages as early as 1918-19.

Valery Bryusov, the recognised head of Russian symbolism, was a poet of an entirely different order. A scholar and erudite, with an expert knowledge of thoughts and feelings, who devoted his poems to all sorts of human emotions, to all ages and nations, he too accepted the socialist revolution. His poem about Lenin is infused with a patriot's pride in his country's revolutionary boldness.

However, the poets of the older generation could not reflect that new quality which came into Russian life or become the spokesmen for the people who rallied to the colours of the Leninist Party. Unlike the symbolists, Nikolai Gumilev—head of the acmeists, an advocate of Russian expansion which made one think of Rudyard Kipling, and a master of chiselled verse in which life sparkles with the heady excitement of wine—turned sharply away from the people in those stormy revolutionary years. More than that, this excellent poet took part in a counter-revolutionary plot and, like Chenier, paid for it with his life.

Of the older generation only one, a former futurist, was destined to become a poet of the new, revolutionary Russia. This was Vladimir Mayakovsky who was born to address crowds of people in the city squares with his thunderous voice. All that went before the

Revolution was mere experimenting. But now Mayakovsky was able to exclaim:

> *Higher,*
> > *hold higher,*
> > > *those rows of heads!*
> *A new Great Flood we are going to spread*
> *And wash all the world and the cities clean. . . .*

There are people who never cease to grow in stature and importance. Mayakovsky was one of them. Poets like him are born in a nation only once in perhaps a hundred years. Personally, I consider him the most important Russian poet since Pushkin. Certainly, he is the most original. In my opinion no poet since Mayakovsky has been able to express the spirit of revolutionary renovation with anything like his wealth of intonations and his profound human understanding. The remarkable thing is that this spirit is apparent not just from the content of his poetry but from his very choice of words, his rhythms and the pace of his verses.

Reading Mayakovsky will enable people in the years to come to inwardly experience what was experienced by the men who accomplished the October Revolution, and to appreciate the emotions of their revolutionary ancestors who laid the foundation stones of the edifice of the new world. Mayakovsky died in 1930, and it was precisely in the 1930s that he was so badly needed.

Civic poetry, that is poetry which expresses people's social interests, has existed for thousands of years. It can be traced back to the grain carriers' songs that have been preserved on papyrus found in the tombs of the Pharaohs. The existence of civic poetry is only natural, for as Aristotle said "man is a social animal". In different social formations and in different eras, civic poetry, of course, had its own specific themes and content. Mayakovsky did not simply fill his poetry with the new content of our time—the struggle for communism. He produced a new type of poetry in which politics, being the main sphere of the people's interests, was the loudest motif of all. The reason is obvious: in a formerly backward country political slogans were a most effective means of revolutionary propaganda.

In the West the word "propaganda" is not infrequently used with a derogatory connotation. As if propaganda is not the truth, or is anyway only a part-truth posing as the whole truth. But if we analyse the meaning of the word etymologically, we shall find that propaganda (that is, an organised and deliberate propagation of particular ideas) is an inherent feature of any work of art, as I have already said earlier. Some works are more objective and many-sided and the propaganda in them is less overt. But a writer of stature is always a ruler of men's minds. He teaches men how to live, and propagates his ideas.

This striving to teach and propagate a particular range of ideas is more typical for Soviet literature than any other. Mayakovsky was a propagandist of communism, and he did not hesitate to declare with a polemic challenge that he was prepared to place his pen in the service of the present hour, of the present reality, and, consequently, the Soviet Government and the Communist Party who championed it. "In the service", mind you.

I could name many, many other poets who in their various styles extolled the proletarian revolution and contributed to the political struggle for communism. One of them was Demyan Bedny who was especially popular in the Civil War years. His fables and satirical feuilletons were always topical and enjoyed enormous success with the Red Army.

A contrast to this overtly political type of poetry was offered by the pre-revolutionary poets to whom all these new moods were strange. I have already mentioned their names, with Boris Pasternak topping the list.

I suppose some people will ask: "So history is a macro-world, and the human Self is a micro-world?" But let us not play a game of words. For all its seeming cleverness, it is pointless to counterpose all the possible extremes. It was Hegel who showed how the conflict of metaphysical theses is solved dialectically. In life, the transformation of one category into another is as natural as the transformation of rain into rivers and lakes, and the transformation of rivers and lakes into clouds. The beginning of Soviet poetry, we see, was marked by splits, extremes and more divergency of opinion.

I do not intend to dwell on everything that happened in Russian poetry in the course of fifty years. I am not writing a history of Soviet poetry. All I want to do is throw a bit of light on the picture it presents today. We find that the two trends—purely civic poetry and pure lyricism, remain. But the quarrel between them has long since lost the edge it had for Mayakovsky and Anna Akhmatova forty years ago. Critics gave up their dogmatic counter-posing of these two extreme varieties of poetry way back in the nineteen-thirties. They no longer treat "pure lyricism" with scathing irony for lagging behind life. Nor do they extoll civic poetry as the one and only type, excluding all others. True, the two types are still counterposed every now and again. Once in *Pravda* I read a poem by Yaroslav Smelyakov (one of the poets who entered the scene in the nineteen-thirties) called *Speaking of Poetry.* Imitating Mayakovsky's *In Full Voice,* Smelyakov also speaks of his poetry as "coarse", proudly comparing his "coarseness" to the "rubbish" of "intimate verses".

In general, the tendencies and preferences have, naturally, re-mained. But the extremes have disappeared. Why, you will ask? For the very simple reason that the Soviet people themselves, the country and the way of life have changed beyond recognition. The very look of the towns has changed after the cultural revolution and as a result of what has been achieved in the different spheres of activity. Today, millions of people in the Soviet Union are able to understand the structure of Shostakovich's symphonies, and have their own enlightened opinion on the different trends in art, while the intellectuals look upon differential calculus as a matter of routine.

In my own (I stress, my own) opinion, it is the young people who set the pattern in Soviet poetry today. They have brought into it a breadth of interests and the boldness of experiment just as Mayakovsky did in his time.

Far be it from me to imply that the poets of the older generation –Nikolai Tikhonov, Alexei Surkov, Ilya Selvinsky, Alexander Prokofyev, Nikolai Aseyev, Mikhail Isakovsky and Semyon Kirsanov–have already had their say. Readers by no means expect them to leave the stage as actors who have said their piece and still linger on. All these poets are unique talents. In a text book on Soviet literature their work would make whole chapters. They are read today, and their songs (for instance, Mikhail Isakovsky's) are lasting favourites. Some of Isakovsky's poetic formulas have become popular sayings.

Alexei Surkov is perhaps the most consistent and militant cham-pion of civic poetry. But it must be admitted that the civic poems of this outstanding public figure lack, what I would call, purely artistic energy. A singer of revolutionary struggle, Surkov uses a conventional approach to problems of form. But for all that, he has a certain originality as a soldier-poet who can never get away from the smell of smoke and the taste of iron when assessing people and events.

The romantic militancy of the epoch also coloured the early poetry of Nikolai Tikhonov, but it was interpreted in the manner of the acmeist school. He then went through a phase of formalistic experi-mentation. Still, even now it is the romance of the times which lends power to his poetry, although it is regrettably inhibited by a certain inner chilliness.

Of the poets who have been writing for almost half a century now and who are past sixty, the most striking figure is Ilya Selvin-sky, whose talent is amazing in range and sheer force. He is a sort of Gargantua of Soviet poetry. In his vast output he proves himself a virtuoso of form. He is the author of several books of verse, a number of large epic canvases (*Ulalayevshchina, Pushtorg, The Arctic* and others), and many tragedies in verse. Once, in 1930, Selvinsky wrote and published the *Elektrozavodskaya Gazeta*. In the nineteen-twenties he headed the school of constructivism and challenged Mayakovsky's thesis:

> *Scribbling love songs for you*
> > *would suit me as well,*
> *Even better—*
> > *for pleasure and purse.*
> *But I,*
> > *I'd trample,*
> > > *my voice to quell*
> *On the throat of my own verse*

with his own thesis of a man "in full flower" (in the spirit of Feuerbach). However, Selvinsky eventually admitted that in the epoch of acute class struggle it was premature of him to promote the idea of a man in full flower, thus recognising that Mayakovsky had been right after all.

A person who lives a life of many and varied interests, and enjoys an encyclopaedic abundance of thoughts and feelings and infinite freedom, cannot be considered an abstraction. Such an ideal cannot be opposed to the historical man whose behaviour is not guided simply by anarchic self-indulgence but also by historical responsibility.

It has become a commonplace to say that we live in a changing world. People in all countries say this because the development of history is increasing its pace in a truly geometric progression. But in no other country, perhaps, are these changes as visible and tangible as in the U.S.S.R. At least to people who took part in or simply witnessed the Socialist Revolution of 1917 in Russia, the world they live in now seems entirely new. And not just because there are cars instead of horses in the streets of Moscow, or because gaslight has been replaced with electricity, but because the very rhythm of life has changed. For poets who belong to Selvinsky's generation, like Pavel Antokolsky or Vera Inber, all this necessitated an ideological and artistic re-adjustment. The poets of their generation, therefore, had to catch up with the times and not simply portray them; they had to re-adjust themselves and create at the same time.

Of this middle generation emerging in the nineteen-thirties, I would name Konstantin Simonov as the most striking figure; certainly, the most widely popular. His creative energy as a poet, playwright, novelist, war correspondent and social leader, is extraordinary. Everything about his talent has an enormous appeal: his devotion to communist ideas, his industriousness, the range of his impressions, his keen powers of observation, his steadiness and his speed (although the last does him more harm than good). He has the wholesomeness, the energy and the self-reliance which make the very essence of the new generation of Soviet intellectuals, of Soviet people whose character has been shaped wholly in our epoch.

All this in itself might have provided material for poetry. But Simonov's lyric poetry does not reflect even a tenth part of his personality with its wide and varied range of emotions and impulses. It's a strange thing, but there is no romance in his lyric poetry, no communication with the great wide world, no call.

I wonder why. Certainly it is not due to lack of talent. I think, it is probably because he takes a one-sided view of lyric poetry and does not feel the need for this sort of complete lyrical self-revelation. As I see it, it is a case of journalism inhibiting lyricism.

The impact of Simonov's poetry comes from the vividness of his descriptions and his tenacious grip on concrete details. He has travelled a lot and seen a lot, and so the range of his themes and observations is naturally very wide. (*Visiting Bernard Shaw* is, perhaps, one of his best poems). Simonov is keenly sensitive to the social or political pulse of life. This ability to feel the throbbing nerve of life is another reason for his popularity. The success of some of his poems written in the first years of war, for instance *Wait For Me*, was truly sensational. Like Alexei Surkov, though in a different manner, Simonov also revealed himself most fully, both as a novelist and as a poet, in the war theme. Each of these writers has contributed his heroic chapter to Soviet poetry.

The influence which the war against nazi Germany had on the spiritual development of people in general made itself felt in the poetry of practically every country in Europe, especially England, France and Italy. Soviet poetry, like literature as a whole, was affected too. The course of the war showed that Soviet people were fighting in defence of humanity, for the welfare of man. Alexei Tolstoi expressed this well when he said that the war against Hitler's Germany was not so much a war of machines as a war of moral categories. The war did not restrict Russian literature to the propaganda of war feats and war aims, but on the contrary stimulated the revelation of human, moral categories.

Pride of place among that middle generation of poets who emerged from the trials of war as ideologically mature artists with a great store of human experience, undoubtedly goes to Alexander Tvardovsky. There is a seed of rationalism in his poetry too. Perhaps, it would be more correct to say that he likes to reason things out, and in his poetry thought has the upper hand over emotion, leading it along, so to speak. This is why the composition of his verses and poems is so clear and logically consistent. Hence, too, his predilection for classical forms and folk traditions. Tvardovsky is amazingly sensitive to the life of the ordinary people, the Russian peasants, the collective farmers, the stove makers, the soldiers: in short, the

Alexander Tvardovsky. 1958.

Russian Ivan. He portrays all these different people with epic breadth against the background of the Revolution and the war. The rural sources which fed his poetry are evident in everything: in his idiom, and his liking for popular sayings, proverbs and aphorisms which all belong to the speech of country folk. Two Russian poetic traditions seem to have converged in Tvardovsky. One stemming from Nekrasov, the sorrowful folk bard, and the other from Pushkin, the sanguine lover of life.

The great dramatic power and epic sweep with which Sholokhov portrayed the Russian people at the most crucial moments in their history (the years of the Civil War and the collectivisation of farming) is fully matched by Alexander Tvardovsky. His poems *The Land of Muravia* (about collectivisation), *Vasily Terkin* (a Russian soldier in the war against fascism) and *A House by the Roadside* can be ranked with the classics of Russian literature.

That, at any rate, is how Soviet readers look upon these poems. Vasily Terkin has become a living person loved by everybody. His prototypes are discovered everywhere, in all the services, and among the collective farmers where prototypes of Davidov (the hero of Sholokhov's *Virgin Soil Upturned*) are also frequently to be found.

Tvardovsky's poem *Space Beyond Space* gives a panoramic view of life in the Soviet Union today. There are descriptions of Siberia and the construction of the giant hydroelectric power station on the Angara, there are encounters with people released from concentration camp, and reflections on Stalin, his place in history and the attitude to him today. Travel impressions link the separate episodes into a whole, and running through the poem—through the encounters with people, recollections, lyrical digressions, bitter memories, and descriptions of the modern scene—are the author's thoughts on the destinies of the people advancing towards their historical goal, undaunted by the hardships encountered along the roads they have to travel.

His partiality to village imagery and themes is less in evidence here than in his other poems. The horizons are much broader. But the texture of the poetry is not evenly woven throughout, and to my mind the composition is somewhat prolix.

Tvardovsky's poetry is very democratic. He is a poet of the masses, of the "vast human ocean". But he does not simply sail about this ocean in a little fishing boat, singing a song and thrilling to the lashing winds and storms. He reflects on fairways, ships and captains. You are aware of his intellect all the time, and you do not always know what you were more captivated by: his intellect and the keenness of his observations, or that inexpressible impulse of his poetic soul which moves you so in Yesenin.

Critics have a way of linking together the names of Isakovsky, Surkov, Tvardovsky and sometimes even Alexander Prokofyev (the song-like pattern of whose poetry has roots in folklore) as poets belonging to the same trend. I do not think this is really justified. They may have something in common—indeed they all come of peasant stock and have the same political affiliations: but there the

159

likeness ends. They are quite different as poets. Mikhail Isakovsky writes lyric songs, Surkov writes political verses, and Tvardovsky has established himself as an epic poet.

This somehow brings us to Stepan Shchipachev who really belongs to the older generation of writers. He also comes of peasant stock, but he is the exact opposite of Tvardovsky in the very nature of his talent and, consequently, in his choice of genre. There is no global philosophy or propaganda in Shchipachev's poetry. His field is "pure lyricism". And he must be given his due for cultivating a style of his own and giving his work the stamp of individuality. Even at the time when political themes predominated in Soviet literature he had the boldness to take up the "eternal themes" to try and find his new hero in them. And find him he did. His lyrical hero is a man of impeccable honour, dignified and reserved, and with a strong sense of responsibility to society and history.

His best poetry is dedicated to the "eternal theme" of love. The history of poetry from Catullus and Horace to Shakespeare and Ronsard (to say nothing of the twentieth-century decadent poets) has long since sanctified love's madness and frenzy. All the world's witches and poets have brewed their bit of love potion. But Shchipachev offers us a sobering drink. There must be restraint and fidelity in love. He does not mean faithfulness to marriage vows, but rather an emotional integrity.

Shchipachev is popular with Soviet readers. His love poems, whatever one may think of their artistic merits, will be found to play a role of fundamental importance in shaping the new socialist ethics, a process from which the development of Soviet lyric poetry is inseparable.

Shchipachev's hero is more inclined to observe than to experience, to reflect rather than to succumb to emotion. In his love poems he portrays the signs of love, its spiritual anatomy, so to speak, and only in a smaller measure the feeling of love. His favourite form is therefore contemplative, reflective poetry divided into stanzas.

It is a curious thing that Shchipachev assumes the role of mentor or judge when he describes the world of emotions; he is more apt to analyse and evaluate these emotions than fall under their spell like Verlaine or Yesenin. Apparently rationalism, which we find in the work of many Soviet poets, is something of a disease of the age. The correct way of thinking becomes more important than genuine feeling. I wonder if this is why Shchipachev's poetry has a steadying rather than a stirring effect. It keeps the reader to a single straight and narrow path instead of leading him into the great wide world. And in spite of what the author says about it being ill-suited to a poet to moralise, very many of his poems have "the moral-to-this-story" ending just the same. It is this that lends a fable-like tone to his stanzas and elegies, and this also explains his penchant for Oriental, especially classic Persian, lyricism which is mainly based on parables.

Leonid Martynov is quite another matter. He, too, belongs to the older generation. It does happen to some poets that for one reason or another they do not become widely known until quite late in their career. This was the case with Martynov. He first

Nikolai Zabolotsky. 1937.

appeared on the literary scene as an author of lengthy poems written in the colourful style of Russian fairy tales (for instance, his *Poem About Uvenkai*). Later, the fairy-tale idea became the prism through which he viewed the surrounding world. Such is Martynov today.

He brings out the poetic quality of poetry as such, the contours of the world are slightly out of true in his poems, and there is in them that madness of first creation when everything begins anew and moves from its accustomed place.

In a cycle of poems called *The Shore* he has trees wandering about the earth, and strange, homeless people walking down the street with the classically "wild" look in their eyes. There have to be ghouls and goblins, of course, like in all Russian fairy-tales, but ahead lies a radiant, colourful world, and good will naturally triumphs over evil, for this is Russia. There is something of Vasnetsov in Martynov's word-painting of Russia, and the intonation of a folk storyteller achieved by doubling the lines, by repetitions and a play of rhymes. But while escaping rationalism Martynov often falls into the other extreme. It's what the ancients called Pythic murmuring.

Horace was quite right when he said in his *Letter to the Pisos* that an honest and knowing man would notice the weaknesses in poetry and would want an expression to be clarified if he thought it vague. I must admit that the image of an incomprehensible "mad" poet, described by Horace, evokes as little admiration in me as it did in him. Maybe Orpheus was able to hypnotise beasts and "wild men" with his music, but those who deserve the name of man want there to be some thought behind the poet's words as well.

Nikolai Zabolotsky died in October 1958, and so, strictly speaking, cannot be regarded as one of the poets of today. But for me he still remains the most gifted and profound of modern Russian poets. There is a classical balance of thought and emotion in his poetry. Whereas Martynov left the open epic plains to plunge deeper and deeper into the fairy-tale forest of his imagery, Zabolotsky began with poetic fancy and gradually achieved clarity. His poetry contains a philosophical thought which runs through the swarm of his romantic dreams, blending with them perfectly and therefore unobtrusively. Once Zabolotsky said to me that the most important thing for a poet to have is his own special angle of vision. And in the "chaste depths of poetry" he discovers what others would never have discerned.

It is difficult to describe the range of Zabolotsky's themes. Whatever he writes about—a plain little girl, an old actress, flying cranes, the taiga, cities, steppeland or the leaves of an eucalyptus tree—he reveals to us a beautiful new world which, however, is filled with hidden anxiety (unlike Shchipachev). Zabolotsky does not preach or teach, he simply tells us of his discoveries and makes us think. Here is an instance: when daylight fades into the grey of evening and the sunset sky begins to play "like a colossal moving atom" an image of another man emerges: he stands at the other end of the Universe, in the garden, in the dark, and also gazes at the stars. "Why do I, at my journey's end, trouble his spirit with my unsubstantial dream," the poet says.

Like Tyutchev, Nikolai Zabolotsky alarms your imagination. His language is rather old-fashioned. Unlike Kirsanov he does not strive to dazzle you with his verbal fireworks. There are people of whom one says: when you're in their company it is best to say nothing and think. In a way this applies to Zabolotsky.

I have named those poets who have left a strong impression on me. My choice may be called subjective, of course. But one can hardly avoid subjectivity in such matters. Literary criticism is not a pharmacy where substances are weighed on precision scales to within a fraction of a gram. People do not use the pharmacist's method to weigh their likes or dislikes. You may like a poem or you may not. Some you like better, others less. And if I were to introduce a dozen more names, it would not make the general picture any clearer. In every country there are thousands of people writing poetry. In the U.S.S.R. at any rate two or three books of verse come out every day, and only counting Russian poetry at that.

Poetry is the first step in the art of handling words. A youth's first love brings him to Euterpe. But "poetry-making is audacious work," wrote Goethe. Many are invited but few are chosen at the feast of Apollo. Every one of Euterpe's suitors tries to stretch Odysseus's bow, but it is not given to all. An Odysseus or a Telemachus is born in poetry but rarely. And then, not every poetic arrow is capable of piercing the heart of every reader. Some like involved poetry, others prefer clarity. Alexander Tvardovsky, that paladin of logical clarity, once said that in his opinion good poetry with a profound content could be re-told in prose just as well. That, he believes, is a sign of excellence which lies only in content. I, too, like clear, transparent verse, but this thesis of Tvardovsky's does not appeal to me. In poetry, its logical content must always be rendered through the prism of music. Hence the fancifulness of its moves. Pushkin once said: "Poetry, bless it, must be a little silly." Some poets took these words, said more in fun, quite seriously and began to imitate the chirping of birds or the muttering of a Pythian oracle in their poems. But poetry that is too, too clever, turns the tables on the poet himself: he simply loses his readers.

Genuine poetry is always rooted in real life. Its arguments, demands and interests communicated through poetic images stir our hearts much more deeply than mere verbal abstractions, or the capricious movements of emotional clouds passing through a man's soul.

The importance played in modern Soviet poetry by the young

poets who entered the scene in the post-war period must be put down to their strong sense of personal involvement in all that is happening today. Poets of this generation suffered the hardships of war in childhood or adolescence. Their very psychology is deeply imprinted with the awareness of the changes which took place in the Soviet Union, especially after the war. By changes, I partly mean the tremendous leap made in economic development and the much improved conditions of life generally. But more than anything else, I mean the changes connected with the elimination of the consequences of the Stalin personality cult and the spiritual growth of the new young intelligentsia.

What qualities are typical of the new generation of intellectuals, the young specialists in particular who are engaged in developing Soviet science and technology? For one thing, their solid grounding in the most revolutionary spheres of modern culture: physics of elementary particles, physics of solid bodies, mathematics, polimers, electronics, cybernetics, and so forth. Moreover, the character of their work requires of this generation a better knowledge of foreign languages and foreign literature than their fathers had. There are more than a million of these thirty-year-old intellectuals. It is a generation mainly characterised by its uninhibited spiritual breadth and its creative energy in striving for the final goal of communism.

Antagonistic observers in the West, in both Europe and the United States, are attempting to prove that Soviet writers, to their great joy, are renouncing propagandist literature and heading in the direction of "pure lyricism" and "art for art's sake". I'm afraid I shall have to disillusion these experts and observers (like George Gibian, author of *Interval of Freedom* published in the U.S.A.). The new generation is not turning away from Soviet reality. On the contrary, it is completely immersed with all its thoughts and interests in the present-day life of the country. There is no longer any conflict between politics and one's inner world, between the private and the social, between civic poetry and "pure lyricism". This generation is full of heroic communist militancy, there are no bogies to fetter its spirit, and like Mayakovsky it wants to clear the road to communism of all that has become petrified and obsolete.

Those who want to understand the nature of events in the U.S.S.R. must ponder on the words: a great renovation. A renovation for the sake of what? For the sake of the "human man" (to use Marx's expression). In other words, for the sake of harmoniously developed man, a man whose nature, shedding animal instincts, would unfold in all its human beauty. But there is a historical logic of its own in mankind's advance towards these new forms of social existence. And before gaining boundless freedom some of freedom's gifts have to be temporarily declined in the struggle for it. In a socialist state, the enforced retreat to coercion is, however, accompanied by constant spurts into the future, into that realm of freedom. As Mayakovsky said:

> The barriers down
> > and the enemy routed,
> The battle pain over,
> > and time to rejoice,
> We'll get them to bring all the ornaments out
> And spread there before you—
> > just pick your choice!

The new and the old still exist side by side. And the struggle for the new is at the same time a struggle against the old.

Revolutionary development by its very nature cannot go at an even pace, like traffic along an autostrada. In the nineteen-thirties, the element of criticism and satire was muted in Soviet poetry. Nowadays it is naturally more pronounced, and altogether it must be said that portraying life in all its aspects has become typical for all Soviet poetry. Therefore the attempts of some bourgeois critics (in the U.S.A. and England especially) to dig out, like raisins from a bun, those stories and poems which "have no politics" seem very naive to me. What they are looking for is evidence of the young Soviet writers' withdrawal from the ideals of communism. Their efforts must be attributed to naivety or a very superficial knowledge of the subject. Wishful thinking, is more like it.

In actual fact we see quite a different picture: a naturally extended range of literary themes, a deeper probing into the inner world of Soviet people, and a more pronounced element of criticism as a means of struggle for genuine communism. All these features are expressed obviously enough in the poetry of Yevgeny Yevtushenko.

Yevtushenko is a prolific poet, and new books of verse come from his pen every year or two. He is popular with the young people who regard him, not without reason, as the spokesman for their moods and thoughts. He was only 12 when the war broke out, and by the time he was 22 his poetry had begun to appear in the literary magazines. In Yevtushenko I do not see any artistic discoveries, as we find in Mayakovsky, nor that startling depth of emotion and thought which makes you pause and ponder over Zabolotsky's lines.

Yevtushenko's poetry is narrative in manner. His longer works (for instance, the poem Bratsk) leave an impression of being somewhat drawn out, and some of his verses actually show the untidiness suggestive of being written in a hurry.

But what one cannot deny him is his creative energy and his

165

passionate responsiveness to all that happens around him: Yevtushenko strikes at many nerves at once, hitting the right keys of a huge keyboard. There is everything in his poetry: traits of the new in Soviet reality; intimate verses, risque to the point of bad taste; outline portraits of contemporaries; lyrical confessions, and so on. It is as though he is speaking in the voices of many different people, always in a hurry, excitedly plunging into polemics, or anxious to share his overwhelming impressions.

Yevtushenko is the medium for the Soviet crowd. His wholesale address is his weakness because he is not always able to tell a hero from a Philistine. Yet it is also his strength. And, perhaps, the poems written in the first person singular are not his best. The story of Narcissus shows how harmful excessive self-interest can be. In my opinion, Yevtushenko is at his most powerful when he paints word-portraits of people. His portrait gallery of Soviet people includes a woman crane operator, a factory girl, a pensioner, a student, a bad character, an industrial worker, and many, many others, painted with great expressiveness. Not infrequently Yevtushenko presents his hero polemically: a lad whom everyone called a teddyboy, a nihilist and upon whom his own father frowned, dies rescuing a drowning friend. It turns out that he was a good, clean man, capable of rising to heroism. The moral of the story is: don't judge by appearances.

Yevtushenko's poetry demonstrates a complete fusion of the lyrical and the civic. Writing civic poetry is a demanding task, he rightly says. He goes on:

> *There's no coercion to it,*
> *It's voluntary war.*
> *A depth of understanding,*
> *And honour, above all.*

Yevtushenko, like Andrei Voznesensky, Bella Akhmadulina, Svetlana Yevseyeva and others (but Yevtushenko, first and foremost) brought a new content into Soviet poetry, a new way of looking at the surrounding world. Yevtushenko and Voznesensky make everything that came before them look old-fashioned, just as life itself makes the forms which rightly belong to a past stage appear old-fashioned.

A great deal is written about Yevtushenko, and he is often criticised. He offends the hypocrites and the bigots (a breed that has naturally not become quite extinct yet). But actually he invites fair criticism as well. For one thing, he tackles acute political themes although he is not really up in politics.

His *Autobiography* published in the French magazine *l'Express* in February-April 1963 contains (in the second part especially) the flavour of a false political sensation. Moreover, in this autobiography of an "early matured man" (as it was called in the magazine) Yevtushenko assumed the rather unattractive pose of a heroic champion of truth who is extremely pleased with himself.

After the Twentieth Party Congress (in February 1956) much in the development of the Soviet Union in the economic, scientific and spiritual spheres acquired a truly revolutionary character, making headway at a greatly accelerated pace. One of the manifestations of this revolutionary growth is the craving for creative freedom, the desire to venture along unchartered roads. The idea of pioneering the virgin lands in Siberia appealed to some young people, others wanted to conquer outer space, and still others went into poetry, through the medium of which they strove to convey all this process and capture the rapid passage of time. Never mind that the result sometimes lacked maturity, accuracy and polish (as was the case with Yevtushenko). It was anyway a sign of the new times.

Although the form is entirely different, the same pulse of blossoming creative energy beats in the poetry of Andrei Voznesensky (who studied for an architect), of the same generation of young poets. The reckless, uncontrollable boldness of his comparisons and emotions is amazing. Take his *Goya*. The poetry is difficult to translate because it is constructed on the phonetic repetition of the sounds "S" and "R" at the beginning of successive sentences and the effect they create of rolling one over the other.

Unlike Yevtushenko who puts the accent on political content, Voznesensky is most concerned with form. But this by no means involves the simple jingling of sounds or formalistic experimentation which Selvinsky was so fond of in his youth, as indeed were many other poets besides: Marina Tsvetayeva, Semyon Kirsanov, the French dadaists, etc. I do not think it would be fair to call this formalism.

All that I have written earlier about this generation—the coevals of the first spaceman—is there in Voznesensky's poetry. As he himself has said:

> *A spark of experiment, a spark of risk,*
> *A spark of Olympian spirit.*
> *A heart you can kindle, a stove just as well,*
> *Or maybe the world, and burn it to hell.*

Who does he write about? A woman cashier, an artist, a student, a miner, a pilot, commuters, war invalids, architects.... But his statements are never point-blank. He believes in going the roundabout way: he prefers to draw a parabola rather than a safe circle. Every poet, if he is a genuine poet, wants first of all to break free of the conventional linguistic and rhythmical fetters and speak out in his own manner. Velimir Khlebnikov (his influence is also very evident in Voznesensky's work) said about himself:

> *I'm a star rider,*
> *I'm Gul-Mullah's trumpet. . . .*

Voznesensky, too, is a star rider. But to leap as high as the stars a man needs more than strong muscles. We are delighted, and not just surprised, when a man with well-developed leg muscles jumps more than his own height. The bar is placed at the 2m 28cm mark. And the whole world is astonished, although actually there is nothing more to it than strong muscles and training. A person just happens to be born with strong legs. Anatole France devoted a good half of his article about Stendhal to the man's leg muscles. Andrei Voznesensky is a Valery Brumel of Soviet poetry. Considering that Brumel's jump acquired such political importance that the athlete was invited to speak at a peace congress, attended by professors and metropolitans, it is not surprising that Voznesensky's leap had also evoked a world-wide response. He placed the bar of formal innovation higher than anyone else. In his imagination he leapt as high as the stars, and some of his verses (for instance, from the poem *Triangular Pear*, 1963) are astonishing for their unpredictable and impulsive flights of fancy.

> *My self-portrait. Neon retorts.*
> *The Airoport.*
> *Apostle guarding the heavenly fort.*
> *Duralumin windows rumbling and grumbling,*
> *Like an X-Ray of the soul.*
> *How strange, when the sky is reflected in you,*
> *In smouldering routes to fantastic towns. . . .*

However, in his experimenting with Russian poetry Voznesensky showed that he had a greater aptitude for playing with words, metaphors and rhythms, than for communicating thought. The strongest quality of his talent is the ability to record life's fleeting impressions in verse form. More often than not his metaphors are of a visual nature. Compared to the older generation–Zabolotsky, Tvardovsky and Selvinsky, with their atmosphere of tense meditation on life, and even to his coeval Yevgeny Vinokurov–Voznesensky's lyricism seems like a sparkling fireworks display, and no more. I subscribe to what Vinokurov said at the international meeting of poets in the summer of 1963. "In poetry, thought means most to me. Music in poetry is very important, but then how great, how infinite is meaning–word, *logos*, that is the beginning of all beginnings. Thought does not age.... And poetry is the supreme act of thought." Further on he said: "It is a fallacy to treat poetry like some sport. The real quest is going on not in the sphere of poetry-making technique where progress is measured in milimetres, but in the sphere of meaning, of psychology, where a distance of hundreds of thousands of kilometres may be covered in one spurt. Genuine innovation goes along a vertical line, into the depths."

Yevgeny Vinokurov, who published several books of verse after the war, attracted notice because his poetry is so humane and morally sound. In his last book *The Human Face* he wants to tell people to be human: if you will only be that you will be able to find your place in communist construction.

Voznesensky is more artistic, more gifted than Vinokurov. But Vinokurov has more depth. Voznesensky's dashing raids in poetry and his game of ideological bravado, both in his writings and in his public appearances (abroad especially), have evoked sharp criticism in the press. This criticism was not long in bearing fruit. Voznesensky decided to turn to serious themes. He wrote a poem about Lenin demonstrating the great wealth of his talent which he used to squander on trifles. His metaphors remained as fresh as ever and his poetic moves as unpredictable. But in this poem, where thought assumed the reins of power, his talent unfolded in all its vividness and fullness. A part of this poem entitled "Longjumeau" was printed in *Pravda* (October 13, 1963). It deals with the years Lenin spent in France, and the period of his work at the Party school at Longjumeau near Paris.

> *Lenin's as simple as matter. As complex too.*
> *Our people aren't saps to be fed from a spoon.*
> *They're not simply cogs, they're thinkers.*
> *He loved your meetings, Ivans and Dmitries,*
> *He infected you with his philosophy's pathos*
> *And himself got charged by the masses.*

I cannot possibly make a full survey of the numerous works of our gifted young poets in this book, nor does space permit me to even name them all. What I must do is examine briefly the new phenomena in our poetry. The appearance of a book like Bella Akhmadullina's *Taut Wire* simply cannot go unmentioned. It is a book of poetry by an intelligent, subtle, observant and very modern author. Or take the poetry of Svetlana Yevseyeva. This young poetess (like Rimma Kazakova) has fortitude and no sugariness.

Svetlana Yevseyeva belongs to the generation which grew up in the war. She writes:

> *In our tumbledown, ancient house,*
> *Full of families without men. . . .*

And then: *You will stand at the door and wonder.*

> *No, the master won't answer your ring.*
> *I remember no home with some menfolk*
> *To be doing such everyday things. . . .*

She writes of fishermen's wives who are always waiting for their men to come back, and their ears are like sea-shells filled with the sound of the sea. Svetlana says that spring is "when a sparrow swings on a still-bare branch". She tells us about herself in her charming poem *Summer*: "I am the crowd in the street. . . . In the metro I fancy I'm the marble, accustomed to light." Her heroine dreams of lofty things, but at the same time she is thinking that the hostel superintendent must not forget to issue the camel wool blankets.

In her *Orina*, a modern ballad, she says:

> *I milked the cows and cleaned the shed,*
> *And went to the village fair*
> *To buy myself beads of a brilliant red,*
> *And combs for my greasy hair. . . .*

Svetlana Yevseyeva draws an impressive picture of a woman construction worker who mixes concrete as though she were mixing dough in the great industrial kitchen of our age, and who, in her own kitchen at home, places the bread to bake in the oven as though she were performing an ancient rite.

In conclusion I shall say a few words about the problem of the generations, as it is called. The first thing I would like to point out is that there is simply no such problem in the Soviet Union that needs solving either now or later. What started the talk about the supposed existence of this problem was the arrogant declaration made by some of the young poets and film directors that they and none other—not their elder brothers and fathers—were called upon to create an authentically communist culture, uninhibited by dogmatism and survivals of the past epoch. Comments like the following appeared in the foreign press: "Today, in October 1962, it can be stated that the young generation is making its famous break-through." The author of this article in the Swedish bourgeois newspaper *Stockholm Tidningen* went on to say that: "Looking through the cuttings from foreign newspapers about Yevtushenko's recent visit to England, one discovers the frequently repeated headline: 'Yevtushenko–the Soviet Union's Angry Young Man.' Actually, he is his generation's official agent.... I believe he was one of the pioneers in the 'angry' movement in the Soviet Union, but he is no longer the only one. There are angrier and possibly even abler young men in the U.S.S.R."

This problem in Soviet literature gained a measure of acuteness when some of our young, immature poets began to lose their sense of the radical ideological distinction between socialist and bourgeois art. The Party and Soviet public opinion could not, of course, disregard these instances of forgetfulness on the part of our poets of the basic principles of Soviet literature–loyalty to the interests of the Party and the people. But speaking of the period following the Twentieth Congress of the C.P.S.U. which abounded in events, new names and literary works, I must say that the problem of fathers and sons which had engendered contradictory rumours in the foreign press was by no means the most important problem of the time. The central issue was still socialist realism. What then did those years add to the development of this artistic method?

I have already said that after 1956-57 our young writers revealed a craving for innovation and creative freedom. This self-assertion of the younger generation found the strongest reflection in the work of the poets. The new wave rose high and broke the dams here and there. These ideological mistakes are often attributable to haste and brimming energy seeking for an outlet.

Communist construction is in full sway everywhere in the country. New factories and buildings are springing up. Electric power is transmitted along endless humming wires to all the corners of the vast land. Blast furnaces send up a great red glow into the sky, and ripe wheat rustles in the steppelands.... And in the morning, when the sun rises in the east, we hear the sound of thousands of wings. They are the wings of poetry. They soar into the sky and fly towards what we Soviet people call our tomorrow–towards communism.

Chapter 16

Pogodin and Other Dramatists

It was not long after the Revolution that mass spectacles with thousands of people taking part were staged in Leningrad on the Field of Mars. Only a few of the scripts have been preserved, among them Alexander Neverov's *Civil War* (1920) and Artyom Vesyoly's *We* (1921). Finally, in the 1920s, the first plays on Soviet themes were staged by the former imperial theatres and the Moscow Art Theatre, directed at the time by Stanislavsky and Nemirovich-Danchenko.

Several plays by Anatoly Lunacharsky, People's Commissar for Education, were also staged. Lunacharsky was a remarkable literary critic, and an expert on art and the history of Russian and West-European literature. He was also a poet and playwright, and his *Oliver Cromwell* (1920), *Tommaso Campanella* (1922) and *The Chancellor and the Plumber* were probably the first plays by a Soviet author to bring into the old theatre the romance of the Revolution. Still, Lunacharsky's plays did not run for long. And not just because the demand was for more topical plays (his were all historical), but also because the author was more of a philosopher and journalist than an artist and psychologist. He called one of his collections of plays and essays *Ideas in Masks*. Genuine dramaturgy (that is, realist and not symbolic) demands that ideas be rendered through the medium of human characters. Marx once said about Schiller (in a letter to Lassalle) that his heroes were more like a speaking trumpet for ideas than living characters. The same could be said of Lunacharsky as a dramatist.

The first play in which the new revolutionary reality was revealed through human characters was probably Konstantin Trenev's (1878-1945) *Lyubov Yarovaya* (1926). An ex-teacher, Trenev made his heroine, Lyubov Yarovaya, a teacher too, and in her, to use his own words, "embodied the attitude of a writer and citizen to the Revolution". Yarovaya's past emerges from the dialogue, and we learn how this woman, once far removed from politics, came to be a fighter for the Revolution. Her life is linked with Pavel Koshkin, a Bolshevik and politician with a gift for organisation. Nikolai Pogodin was quite right when he said in 1946 that: "The most precious thing about this play was the author's discovery of a new gold mine in theatrical art. And it was made clear to us playwrights that the image of the new, positive hero was going to be acclaimed most highly by Soviet audiences."

And indeed, the sailor Shvandya, Lyubov Yarovaya, Koshkin, and the Chairman of the Uyezd Committee (in Bill-Byelotserkovsky's *Assault*) became the new popular heroes in Soviet literature. They were a far cry from Pilnyak's "leather jackets" and

Konstantin Trenev. 1938.

Ehrenburg's "improved communist models of men". They were real people. Trenev's *Lyubov Yarovaya* and Bill-Byelotserkovsky's *Assault* introduced the heroico-revolutionary trend into the Soviet theatre. Thus, it was as far back as the middle of the nineteen-twenties that the genre which, in my opinion, was eventually to determine the character of Soviet dramaturgy was conceived. In Mayakovsky's plays *The Bathhouse* and *The Bedbug* these elements of revolutionary heroism were combined with mordant satire. But this satire itself drew its truth, its inspiration and its critical trenchancy from the heroic ideals of the Revolution.

I dare say my choice of a playwright for the title of this chapter may seem subjective. But in my opinion it is Nikolai Pogodin's plays that embody most fully and clearly the distinctive features peculiar to Soviet dramaturgy.

Many plays by Leonid Leonov, Vseveold Ivanov, Vladimir Kirshon, Alexander Afinogenov, Boris Lavrenev, Boris Romashov, and also Victor Rosov and other moderns, won lasting popularity with audiences and enjoyed long runs. The individual artistic personalities of these dramatists have an important bearing on their plays. Thus Leonid Leonov combines philosophy with psychology, while Boris Lavrenev brings out the romance in political themes. The most striking feature of Pogodin's and Vsevolod Vishnevsky's plays is the keenness with which they probe life and plunge into the fire of human emotions.

These playwrights are in love with the heroism of socialist construction, and this infatuation sharpened their revolutionary vision and their keenness in discerning the new in life. But this infatuation had both its strong and weak sides. The weakness lay in the too romantic attitude to the heroes of the Revolution which, in some plays, actually pushed the struggle and the contradictions into the background. In his article "On Plays" (1933) Gorky wrote: "We are living in a profoundly and totally dramatic epoch without precedent, an epoch of tensely dramatic processes of destruction and creation."

In Pogodin's plays we can trace the gradual development of this sense of drama and a more profound understanding of the social and psychological conflicts of our time.

Nikolai Pogodin (1900-1962) was born into a peasant family and grew up in the Don region. As a boy he worked in a metal workshop and then at a bookbinder's. He started out as a journalist in 1920. He received his literary training during his ten years' work on various newspapers, including *Pravda* which printed over two hundred of his articles and reports. Pogodin travelled widely in Central Siberia, Central Asia and the Volga country on newspaper assignments until 1930 when he changed over to play-writing. He wrote more than thirty plays, including both light-weight, ephemeral comedies and serious works of lasting popularity, such as his plays about Lenin. Pogodin is informative and interesting both in his accomplishments and his weaknesses. He was a citizen and writer of the nineteen-thirties, a man who belonged to the period of the

174

first five-year plans and the first socialist achievements. He depicted in his plays the people he had written about in his newspaper articles, people he had met in Siberia and in the coal fields of the Donbass where the mines were being restored at the time. His heroes were workers and peasants engaged in carrying out the first five-year plans. This was Russia awakening from its Asiatic slumber, a new Russia whose slogan was to "catch up and overtake" the Western countries. In Pogodin's first plays (*Tempo, Poem of the Hatchet, My Friend* and others) the dialogue has the liveliness of an on-the-spot reportage. The heroes—commissars, seasonal workers and sharp-tongued young women—argue hotly and laugh noisily. These are not psychological dramas after Ibsen. The stage is crowded with people, a kaleidoscope of characters who come and go. And one has the feeling that the author himself is somewhere in their midst, a man in love with his countrymen, ignorant and illiterate. The tempo at which the workers go at the job is not given a psychological explanation, but the whole play breathes enthusiasm, excitement, good fun and affection. This is the new Russia on the first stage of her ascent to the peaks of the future communist society.

Pogodin's plays are polyphonic and, like Vsevolod Vishnevsky's, involve a large caste of dramatis personae. He tends to divide his material into episodes rather than acts (like in classical plays).

In his *Poem of the Hatchet* one of the heroes says: "What is a hatchet? It's a piece of steel. And what is steel? It's the country's metallurgical problem." In *Tempo, Poem of the Hatchet, After the Ball, My Friend, Aristocrats, Silver Hollow* and other plays written by Pogodin in the nineteen-thirties, the scene is set in factory workshops, at collective farms and production meetings. He based his plots on problems which actually faced the country at the time. Pogodin's plays abound in contrasts. He uses the fabric of the everydays to bring out the drama of his plots. The tension of the atmosphere is rendered through dialogue. And that is why I think that Pogodin's plays express with the greatest eloquence those new features in the turbulent, heroic and dramatic life of the Soviet people in those years when the first five-year plans were launched and afterwards, in the post-war years, features which have come to stay in the Soviet theatre.

In the *Poem of the Hatchet* one of the characters, Party Committee Secretary Barguzin, says to the director of the plant: "We've got to fight. I thought it all over last night. Yes, we're going to fight a war for our hatchet, for our metal, for our industry. Your newspaper's not called right. You ought to call it 'Battle'. No, not that. 'Attack'. Yes, 'Attack'. "

Pogodin renders the strenuous effort of the workers and their sheer heroism with great sensitivity. Now one and now another face stands out from the crowd for a minute, and all of them are portrayed with understanding and affection. It does not surprise us that quite often his positive heroes are given comedy roles to play. In his notes to the play *Poem of the Hatchet* he says about one of the female leads: "Anka rushes about the empty workshop. Her hair is dishevelled and her cheeks are flaming. She is in love, and it is only thus, in this wild display of joy, strength and passion, only in this vigorous movement that she can express her emotion. The very air and the walls seem to hum in answer."

Indeed, the air in Pogodin's plays really does seem to hum in answer to the hum of activity where a new world was being built.

The Aristocrats which tells the story of criminals in a prison camp was originally called *A Human Rhapsody*. Pogodin is truly a rhapsodist who sees the heroic in all that is human. When you read his plays you seem to be drawn into his motley crowd of characters, you actually seem to hear the people talking in different voices, singing and shouting, and you feel life itself gushing forth from the pages of the book.

Of course his plays do have their faults. They are perhaps too romanticised, and too descriptive. But these shortcomings are redeemed by his awareness of the new in Russian life, by his ability to characterise a person in two or three sentences, and to convey the meaning of the Soviet people's heroic efforts and aims.

Last but not least, Pogodin was one of the first Soviet playwrights to succeed in rendering a life-like image of Lenin. In *The Man with a Rifle* (1937) Lenin is shown as an organiser and leader of the 1917 October Revolution. The title of the play was taken from one of Lenin's speeches where he mentioned hearing an elderly woman who was travelling in the same train with him say that a man with a rifle was no one to fear any more, because this soldier was one of themselves now, another working man. In the play this soldier is Shadrin. The following episode takes place at the Smolny a few days after the Revolution: Shadrin, who does not know that the man in front of him is Lenin, addresses him in all simplicity: "Know where could I get some tea?" To which Lenin replies: "Homesick for tea, eh?" Lenin starts a conversation with Shadrin, asking him about the situation at the front and the morale of the soldiers, and by drawing him out compels the man to ponder on things and arrive at some conclusions for himself. This dialogue is very human and lively. In 1942, I saw this play put on for the collective farmers in a village in Uzbekistan. The Uzbek peasants, accustomed to folklore of the feudal times, were extremely shocked that Lenin was presented not as a giant with his head touching the clouds but as a short, bald-headed man wearing an ordinary suit and speaking informally with a soldier. But that was a long time ago. Realist art has now reached the peoples of the Soviet East as well.

In *Kremlin Chimes*, the second play of the series, Pogodin shows Lenin in another historical period when, the Civil War over, the work of restoring and building up the economy was begun under his guidance. In this play the author holds an indirect polemic with H.G. Wells who called Lenin the "Kremlin dreamer". Yes, he was a dreamer, Pogodin says. But a man must dream! The future must be envisaged in dreams before it can be built. The point is *how* to dream. Lenin was a realistic dreamer. Whereas in the first play he was shown in conversation with Shadrin, a common soldier, in *Kremlin Chimes* (first edition 1940, second edition 1955) much space is devoted to the theme of the intelligentsia embodied in the image of Zabelin, a power engineer. In this play Pogodin initiates us into the inner world of Lenin, the genius and creator.

The third part of the trilogy, *The Third Pathétique* (1958), deals with the last period in Lenin's life, and has as its theme Lenin's humanism and faith in the people. Although it ends with Lenin's death, the play is a hymn to the living Lenin. Pogodin's lyricism has a very powerful impact in this play, which expresses his admiration for those splendid new features in the life of mankind that are linked with the name of Lenin.

Another dramatist of impressive stature was Vsevolod Vishnevsky, who started the new type of heroic drama. His output was much smaller than Pogodin's. Only two plays, *The First Cavalry Army* and *An Optimistic Tragedy*, have won lasting popularity and continue to be staged to this day.

Vishnevsky, however, was not just a playwright, he is also known for his war diaries and his memorable war-time speeches. I often remember him as one of the most colourful personalities of my day. Like a torch lit by the October Revolution and the Civil War, he burnt with the fire of the struggle between the two worlds and burnt out in the war against nazi Germany. He remained in Leningrad throughout the siege, and indeed throughout the war. In a speech that was broadcast and televised, Fidel Castro said, on return from the Soviet Union that he could not forget that there were more than 600,000 people buried in the Piskarevskoye Memorial Cemetery in Leningrad who had died from hunger and the bombing during the siege. In their dying hour, these people heard the voice of Vsevolod Vishnevsky in almost daily radio broadcasts. I find a certain resemblance between Vsevolod Vishnevsky and Fidel Castro in temperament and revolutionary ardour.

In 1936 Vishnevsky said: "You want to know what I'd like to do in art? What themes stir me most? The theme of war, and the tragic in life, tragic, that is, in my optimistic view of it. I can neither see nor understand life without tragedy. It's the theme I'm going to work on, developing it beyond the limits of a straight war theme."

A soldier in the Red Army, Vishnevsky belonged completely to the masses. And indeed he began his career with mass spectacles. In 1921, he wrote a play called *The Trial of the Kronstadt Mutineers*, which was put on by sailors at the Seamen's Club in Novorossiisk. The performance lasted eight hours, the sailors taking turns to go on stage or sit out in the hall.

After reading his *First Cavalry Army* Mayakovsky said to Vsevolod Vishnevsky that the play was a continuation of his own line. The drama, the exaggeration, the scale and the extravaganza are all there in Mayakovsky's *Mystery Bouffe*, *The Bedbug* and *The Bathhouse*. And Vishnevsky's diaries, published after his death, are full of recollections of Mayakovsky.

What would you call *An Optimistic Tragedy*? It is a hymn to the Revolution and to seamen (to quote Vishnevsky). It is at the same time an epic and a tragedy. A woman commissar comes to grips with a company of sailors who had turned anarchist, and wins. Vishnevsky pitches death against laughter, brutality against lofty romance. His plays may be called unique political symphonies reproducing life's many and different voices.

Like Pogodin, Vsevolod Vishnevsky did make mistakes in some of his plays. Pogodin, in his play about the three students going out as pioneers to the virgin lands, ignored the heroic element entirely, while Vishnevsky paid excessive tribute to the cult of Stalin's personality in his screenplay *Unforgettable 1919*. But I shall always regard Vsevolod Vishnevsky as one of the most remarkable artists born of the socialist revolution.

There is one other trend in Soviet dramaturgy which is allied with the traditions of Chekhov's psychological drama and Gorky's intellectual drama. Of Pogodin one may say that to a certain extent he believed in following the Gorky tradition. In the plays of Alexander Afinogenov, on the other hand, one may discern features of the Ibsen and the Chekhov traditions. His *The Crank*, *Fear*, *The Remote Past*, *Mashenka* and *On the Eve* all have a small number of dramatis personae. The scene is not set in workshops, nor do his characters speak at mass meetings; more often than not they are shown in a family circle. His plays are not broken up into numerous episodes but are divided into the conventional three or four acts. They are as lyrical as Chekhov's, and yet they are full of suspense and sharp conflicts.

Afinogenov's plays (like Pogodin's trilogy about Lenin) have been produced by the Moscow Art Theatre. The players endowed the main characters—engineers, old intellectuals, veteran revolutionaries, romantic young girls and war widows—with the gentle charm which distinguishes the idiom of the author. Alexander Afinogenov died on October 29, 1941, at the age of 37, when a nazi plane dropped a bomb on the building of the Central Committee of the Communist Party where he happened to be at the time.

I would not make so bold as to assert that all the modern Soviet plays on modern themes appearing on the stage provide the actors with suitable material for really challenging interpretations. Be that as it may, Soviet plays do show a sensitive response to all that is new and typical in the life of our society. Such, for instance, is Alexander Korneichuk's *Wings* which speaks of trust in man as one of the basic principles of our morality; and such are Stein's *Personal Record* and *Astoria Hotel*. In some plays—for example in Victor Rosov's *Good Luck* and A. Volodin's *Factory Girl*—we observe a tendency to leave out heroism altogether (which had become a sort of canon) and to portray Soviet life in a more down-to-earth manner.

Unquestionably, the overwhelming tendency to interpret life only in its heroic, romantic aspect characteristic of the period of the Stalin personality cult produced a one-sided picture and blurred the lively struggle going on between the existing historical contradictions. But the other extreme, the deliberate evasion of heroism, must inevitably lead to "earthing" the people who are building up a new world. Gorky was quite right when he said that our age is dramatic in every respect, that it is an age abounding in conflicts. And yet characters shaped in conditions of truly Shakespearian contrasts are not so easy to portray. In this respect Soviet dramatists have to be pathfinders.

Chapter 17

Leonov

Leonid Leonov. 1948.

Bending low over a small table, Leonov is scraping something with a file, carefully and painstakingly, while I loll on the sofa in the next room with a book. This is his dining room and at the same time his cactus garden. Leonov has the finest collection of cacti in the U.S.S.R. and he is very proud of the fact. The setting sun draws a radiant outline of the thick-lipped, hairy monsters.

Leonov comes in to show me the thing he has just finished making: this is a birch burl from which he has carved a vague, mysterious face.

"Not bad, eh?" he says. "How do you like my echini? This fat one with the prickles pointing in every direction I got from Germany a short while ago. It's the rarest thing in Moscow. None of the botanical gardens has one." After a thoughtful pause, he adds: "Can anyone understand the nature of such lines, their laws?"

Over the top of my book I watch Leonov hanging his wood carving on the wall. . . .

He remained young-looking for a long time: a broad-shouldered chap with a healthy Russian face and a shock of brown hair. Now that he is past sixty, he has grown a moustache. Some pretty tough material has gone into the making of him. He wrinkles his eyes up a little as he looks from under his overhanging brows. This is how a peasant looks from his window at a stranger coming down the village street: it is not exactly a cunning look, but rather a measuring glance to decide what sort of man he is.

Leonov is clever with his hands, he loves making things and wants to get to the bottom of everything by himself. He has the hands of a working man, the skin on the fingers is rough and hard to clean. In the summertime, which he spends at his Peredelkino home, he is always pottering with his green "pets", transplanting them from place to place. When he was younger he was fond of singing in the company of friends. He would put his whole heart into those little-known folk ballads and thieves' songs, and then kiss his listeners. But he was always very sober.

For a long time he had some sort of Brazilian liana standing in a pot under a glass bell on his desk—a feeble dwarf with thin little leaves, pining away in the Moscow flat. Leonov liked to finger those leaves before getting down to work. He would have a neat stack of paper before him which he would cover with a very neat writing, as fine and minute as those tiny leaves.

Leonov is a hard-working man. For more than forty years now, since 1922 when his first book came out, he has begun his day by sitting down at this desk to write, study and read: to learn English and the art of writing, and to read about everything under the sun, from his own profession to cybernetics.

He has a new book out nearly every year. And every new work seems more talented than the last. The whole fifty-year history of the Soviet Union is reflected in them as truthfully as the banks of a river are reflected in its clear waters.

Leonid Maximovich Leonov (b. 1899) was born into the family of a little-known writer. He began with romance, playing a game of words and rendering folk tales and legends. This had its social sense. In the years immediately following the Revolution the small, puny character who eventually walked through many of Leonov's books had not yet taken shape.

His first stories: *Buryga, Yegorushka's Death, Tuatamur, Exit Ham, Halil, The Petushikhino Breakthrough* and *The End of the Little Man* all came out within a single year–a most impressive harvest.

Buryga is a sort of fairy tale, an intricate wood carving, a rendering of a superstition, a game played with bookish words, a drawing of the old-world village.

Halil is a Persian qasida, *Exit Ham* is a stylised Biblical novelette, and *Tuatamur* is also a stylised, dramatic story about the sinister Mongol, not as contrived as Kazimir Edshmidt's but done in the same literary traditions.

Yegorushka's Death is a fantastic tale about a Pomor. *The Petushikhino Breakthrough* describes post-revolutionary events in an old moss-grown village beside an ancient monastery. *The End of the Little Man* is a shriek of the old intelligentsia appalled by the Revolution. Professor Likharev, a paleonthologist, who is the principal character of this story, cannot accept the Revolution because he sees in it a return to pre-historic times, and goes mad.

In early Leonov we see two features common to a large number of authors writing in the nineteen-twenties. First, on the surface, is his romantically elevated, intricate style. Below the surface, there lies his individualistic concern for the right to live of every man, even the most insignificant. It is the theme of Pushkin's *Bronze Horseman.* To put it in other words: the rights of an individual do not always correspond to the interests of the state. It may be a new, revolutionary state, but it is still a state, and therefore practices coercion.

In *Kovyakin's Notes* (1924) the hero of the story says: "The more individuals there are the worse it is. Each individual demands his drop of blood. And to my mind, a drop of human blood is worth more than any individual with all his innards."

One is reminded of Dostoyevsky's words that all the efforts to remake the world are not worth a single tear shed by a ruined girl.

"Look out, don't touch me," cries the little man. He runs, getting in the way of history which, like the raging Neva in Pushkin's *Bronze Horseman,* sweeps the solitary people away.

As a writer Leonid Leonov has travelled from the psychological blind alleys of a suffering and pettily individualistic little man to where the streets are seething with life, where men are busy building a new world, where people and things clash, and the struggle is going on in the open. At times the struggle grows fierce, a fight to the death for the interests of the working people.

The new character in Leonov's books, even when he did make his appearance, did not assert himself at once. *The Badgers* (1924), Leonov's first novel, deals with the main theme of the time—the struggle for socialism. The world is rent in two. The story tells of two brothers—Semyon and Anton, both of them peasants. Semyon joins an anti-Soviet band and hides out in the forest, burrowing into the ground like a badger. His brother Anton is a Communist, and a commissar. Anton comes out the winner, scoring a moral and, what is more important, a spiritual victory. His is the rightful cause. The conflict between town and village is rendered by Leonov as a conflict between the rural private-ownership mentality of the "badgers" and the straightness of the victorious urban proletariat.

In Leonov's next works—the play *Untilovsk* (1926), the novels *Thief* (1927), *A Provincial Story* (1927), and *Extraordinary Stories About Peasants* (1927-1928)—we see that the struggle is by no means over, and that inwardly, philosophically and creatively the rebellious petty-bourgeois individual now posing as a "little man", now hiding behind the gorgeous samite of legend, now donning a sumptuous literary attire, has not yet been completely vanquished.

However, the achievements of the first five-year plan which so aggravated the class struggle in the country—or rather the struggle itself—brought clarity and ideological freshness into all these apparently eternal, Dostoyevsky-like themes. At the time it was still difficult to sum up all those enormous historical upheavals and their effect on the work of Soviet writers. But one thing can be said now: the effect was much greater than might appear on the surface. The events which took place in the U.S.S.R. in those years led not only to an acceleration in the rate of socialist construction and a fresh upsurge of energy in the working class, but also to an acceleration of the "psychological and ideological processes" in the minds of men under the influence of the time's tremendous social tensions. Like in a vessel filled with liquid warmed up from below, some particles floated to the surface, others sank to the bottom, more and more quickly. Deep-lying concepts that once seemed fundamental and immutable, were shaken up and ejected, while much which had hitherto gone either unappreciated or unnoticed now emerged. This explains what in Leonov's work may, on the surface of it, appear an unreasonable ideological zigzag, a "misappropriation" of yet unripe creative thoughts, whereas in actual fact it is all perfectly justified.

The novel *The River Sott* (1929) and the short story *Saranchuki* (1930) placed Leonov among the leading writers of revolutionary Soviet Russia. He says in *The River Sott*: "The village split, and from that cleft a new human growth appeared, pushing it wider and wider apart."

In a sense, the Sott symbolises socialist construction as a whole, but as seen by an onlooker, someone who is not yet directly involved in it. The scene is set in the back of beyond, where there is nothing but forest and marshes and the only habitation is an ancient monastery with its collection of weird human freaks. This is a corner of "picturesque" Russia with its bears, pre-Petrine beards, snows, vodka, and the "Slav soul". Advancing on it is an army of Bolshevik builders, headed by Uvadyev, a man cast in "red iron". They have arrived to build a paper mill on the bank of the Sott River. The tremendous psychological, social and ideological turmoil caused by the arrival of socialism in this world is splendidly presented by Leonov. The characters—peasants, engineers and monks—are not so much painted with a brush as meticulously carved out of wood. The central figure is the communist worker, a symbol of inflexible strength, whom the author compels us to believe in and respect.

Ideologically, however, this book is not without its faults. In certain instances Leonov does not yet see the world exactly as the Communists do. But what matters far more is that he does see and appreciate the main thing in the great struggle for communism, and does not simply recreate the atmosphere but actually takes part in the struggle himself.

For their artistic merits, *The Badgers*, *The River Sott* and *Saranchuki* are certainly Leonov's best books.

Leonov is extremely quick in his choice of themes, and every turn of history is immediately reflected by him. For instance, the contradictions of the NEP period were reflected in the novel *Thief* (1927) which, by the way, was thoroughly revised by the author a few years ago; he turned to the theme of rural backwardness in *Extraordinary Stories About Peasants*, the theme of industrialisation in *The River Sott*; the participation of the pre-revolutionary intelligentsia in socialist construction in the novel *Skutarevsky* (1932); and, last but not least, the victories scored by socialism in the second five-year plan period in *The Way to the Ocean* (1935), a novel which reaches far into the future, to battles for world socialism, and which has for one of its heroes the figure of a Bolshevik, a leader in every respect.

Leonov has written a number of plays on the war theme—*Invasion*, *Lenushka* and others. The latest of his major works, the novel *Russian Forest*, gives a comprehensive picture of Russian life from before the Revolution to long after the Second World War.

Still, it would be wrong to suppose that Leonov is led by his theme, as is the case with many writers of the descriptive genre. No, Leonov is less given to descriptions and does not stick closely to his theme as much as other writers. On the contrary, he is more given to thinking. His books are perhaps the most intellectual in modern Soviet literature. But the intellectual nature of his writing, always based on philosophical thought and the study of human relations, is to a certain extent screened by the fancifulness of his plots, and the intricacy of his somewhat rhetorical style.

Leonov could be called a labyrinthologist. His talent acquires a peculiar brilliance when he describes scenes or phenomena that remind us of those labyrinths of the human spirit through which walked a man with the tortured expression of a convict and the psychological chisel of a ruthless and brilliant artist—Dostoyevsky. Leonov is in his element when he plunges into the elements, if you'll excuse the pun. His manner of writing—and this refers in equal measure to his novels and his publicistic writings—is so rhetorical and even high-flown that at times it may tire the reader. It must be said frankly that Leonov is not easy to read at one go. Every theme and even a phrase just begun becomes immediately overgrown with incidental images and metaphors which snowball into something extremely involved. For instance, we do not have simply a train crash but: "the twisted frames of the coaches, twined together by the terrible force of the impact, made the base of this barbaric altar. The sacrifice on this altar was still smoking. . . . The creeping red of tragedy cast a miserly film over it all." And so on. (From *The Way to the Ocean*.) The plot develops slowly, with dozens of *motifs*, complementing the main theme or leading away from it, pouring into it as it flows on. All these ornaments are painted with skill, excellent taste and sincerity. It is not the psychological ornamentation of Marcel Proust. Leonov's ornamentation overflows with his uncontainable sense of colour, smell, shading and line. Sometimes his intricate carving of word patterns makes one think that he simply takes delight in the game he is playing with the Russian language, just like the Chinese craftsmen love the superhumanly patient work of carving a nest of lacy blackwood balls, an amazing feat of manual skill.

In those places where the canvas allows, Leonov weaves his words to form pictures with exquisite artistry, and we no longer find his style rhetorical. This is, for instance, how in *The River Sott* he describes the dark, impenetrable world of the monks, which is a symbol counterposed to the new world: "Seated along the low, windowless timber wall were about twelve old men, the leaders and rocks of this human desert. The souls of all of them were distorted in some way, which was what had driven them here. Susanna looked in amazement at the men's noses with the distended nostrils, at their heavy-lobed ears, their eyes that either blazed with fire or were so icy that they could quench the fire in the eyes of the others, their huge scorbutic mouths, rent by a silent scream, their swollen hands, or again hands so eloquent in their thinness that they may have been purposely moulded thus by an ironic artist."

As a painter of psychological portraits Leonov succeeds best with people whose souls have their blind alleys and labyrinths. Take his novel *Thief* for example. Leonov gives a brilliant picture of Moscow in the NEP period, or rather of Moscow's underworld: drink-ruined circus acrobats, thiefs, prostitutes, speculators, shady dealers and people "with no fixed occupation". The hero of the novel Dmitry Vekshin is an ex-Communist, who has rolled downhill and become a thief, and yet has retained a peculiar pathos of "truth" even in the "lower depths" of life. Firsov, a writer, tells Vekshin that a certain "high-standing" person has advised him to describe the whales and not bother with the small fry. But Firsov does not heed this advice because he is fascinated by the labyrinths of the human mind which he investigates in these people of the lower depths, among the "anarchy of the conquered". And then Firsov says: "But what if I am too curious, what if I want to discover everything about a person, down to his most deeply hidden roots? What if every person appears to me to have a pimple, and what if it is these pimples that I am curious about . . . what then?"

In early Leonov this curiosity about "human pimples" was closely bound up with his "little man" *motifs*. Little by little these *motifs* were pushed into the background by the new Soviet themes and new material with which the "little man", with his inferiority complex and spiritual tangles, came into inevitable conflict. Already in *Skutarevsky* and *The Way to the Ocean* he has become a character of secondary importance. But though relegated to his true place in society, he is still able to take revenge on the author by influencing the character of his word-painting which, being excessively concerned with "pimples" renders the form superior to the content.

However, it would be a mistake to let Leonov's rhetorical or complicated style obstruct our view of his deep reflections on certain themes of lasting importance. For instance, the philosophy of Vissarion, a monk in *The River Sott*, is echoed in the views of a large number of apocalyptic philosophers in the West today with their technophobia (see Hubscher's *Denker unserer Zeit* for instance). Vissarion says: "The world is on the decline, such as has never been known yet, it is based on hatred and vengeance, its laws are made for scoundrels, its machines are for the debilitated, its art is for the insane. . . . Civilisation is the road, degeneration is the finish. I am unwell, my words will run together. . .but try to understand me. It is not thought, not ideas that shape the mind, but things. It is not God who robbed mankind, but things—the evil master of the world."

In the novel *The Russian Forest*, Leonov has created such impressive characters as Vikhrov, his daughter Polya, and Professor Gratsiansky.

Polya Vikhrova, a Moscow student, represents the new Soviet intelligentsia whose interests are centred on ethical problems. The basic idea of the novel is the power of life, and the forest itself is a symbol of this life, a source of water, a source of beauty. Vikhrov whom the author calls a "deputy of the forests" is actually a messenger of life.

Gratsiansky, on the contrary, is irritated by everything that shines with cleanliness, life and light. It is not surprising that he thrusts a stick into a forest spring which for Vikhrov is a symbol of the forest's primordial purity. Gratsiansky is a complex character, and we can divine that he serves as a vehicle for Leonov's polemicising with his former idol Dostoyevsky. The debate on the future of the Russian forest is a debate on the future between Vikhrov and Gratsiansky. The latter appears to be bound by invisible threads to Vissarion Bulanin who dreamed of a naked man on a naked earth. Gratsiansky also wants to denude the Russian rivers, to clear away the forests and deprive them of their life-giving source. Vissarion is a former White officer who has put on the guise of a monk. Gratsiansky has a Nietzschean, even a fascist psychology, but he appears in the guise of a Soviet man, a professor.

I think that in his novels—as huge as cathedrals and as full of tiny cogs and wheels as a watch—Leonov does finally find his way to the essential problems of our day: to problems of life and death, the roads of history, the role of technical progress, and mankind's prospects for the future. He clothes his thoughts in forms which do not always allow one to see it at first glance. His novels, like some homes, are overcrowded with furniture so that it is often not easy to find one's way about them. Maybe living in them is not always easy either. But even if a desk is piled high with books one can still find whatever it is one is looking for, provided one is prepared to search. It is the same with Leonov. In his novels, sooner than anywhere else, we can find the thing that interests all of us: searching thought.

Chapter 18

Ehrenburg

Ilya Ehrenburg. 1943

Ilya Ehrenburg was known all over the world, both as a writer and as a member of the World Peace Council. Ehrenburg's popularity as a writer and a public figure became especially widespread during the Second World War and in the post-war years when the struggle for peace was launched in view of the contradictions arising between the capitalist and socialist camps. Ehrenburg's trenchant and brilliant pamphlets against the war-mongers and in defense of peace appeared in the press in European countries and in the United States.

I find it difficult to write about Ehrenburg. It is difficult because in order to evaluate the aesthetic worth of his writings (the same is more or less true of any writer) one must be able not to let oneself be influenced by the topicality of his newspaper work. And in the case of Ehrenburg it is not easy to do.

Although Ehrenburg himself as a poet, novelist and publicist, liked to stress that he was purely an artist, and that his tastes were personal and subjective, in actual fact there was no clear dividing-line between Ehrenburg the artist and Ehrenburg the politician. Sometimes he was simply the politician, travelling about the world with purely political assignments, delivering speeches, awarding medals and prizes, and so forth. These days, of course, every artist is a politician. But there is a difference between a political and an artistic perception of life.

Ehrenburg was a very unusual personality. This thin, stooping man with a disgruntled and frequently squeamish expression, had the highly vulnerable heart of a poet: a poet, moreover, inclined to sentimentality.

As an artist Ehrenburg overlooked none of the themes that were "in the air", so to speak, at any particular time. World War I, the economic dislocation and rehabilitation of Europe, the socialist revolution, the crisis and the contradictions of capitalism, technical progress, the economic rise of the U.S.A., imperialism, the New Economic Policy, the war against Hitler Germany and fascism, the campaign for peace—these and dozens of other topical themes were treated in turn in his novels, articles and short stories: whatever was of current importance. The sequence of themes is interesting in itself, because it reflects the psychological evolution of a man who, finding himself in the thick of the battle between socialism and capitalism, sought refuge first in "the small man's right to personal happiness", then in eternal cultural values, and so on.

Ehrenburg is a writer of the subjective cast; that is, he is concerned first and foremost with his own personal attitude to reality, an attitude which acquires objectivity only in the characters of his different books. This style became shaped as a means of embodying *motifs* of a cultured individual's "independence", denied him by the cruel world, and also *motifs* of sentimental humanism which used irony as a protective screen.

Ehrenburg (1891-1968) entered the literary scene in the period between the two Russian revolutions. He left Russia in 1908 on account of his connection with the revolutionary movement and his position of social outcast which was the lot of the Jews under tsarism. He made his home in Paris where he lived in the international milieu of anarchically inclined bohemians. It was then that those sentimental Chaplinesque little-man *motifs* began to develop in his poetry. However, there is no need to go into Ehrenburg's biography here since he himself has told his life story in the two volumes of autobiographical notes entitled *People, Years, Life* (1961-1965).

The fifteen or so books of verse published by Ehrenburg in the period from 1911 to 1921, both abroad and in the U.S.S.R., passed unnoticed. He first commanded attention with his book *The Countenance of War* (1920), a pamphlet against the First World War. Fame came to him after the publication of his novel *The Extraordinary Adventures of Julio Jurenito and His Pupils*, written in Belgium in 1921, of which Lenin spoke with approval. The strongest side of Ehrenburg's talent–his satirical criticism of capitalism–is displayed here in all its brilliance. However, it must be said, that this criticism was made from the standpoint of anarchist nihilism. The hero of the novel is a "great agent provocateur", a "man without convictions", a wanderer of the world who preaches a sort of religion of "wise nihilism" to a handful of pupils (the author himself among them), all of different nationalities and social standing who symbolically represent the main trends of culture. What is there for a man to believe in? One of Julio Jurenito's favourite pupils is a Negro named Aishi, who fought in the French army. He used to go round pulling out the teeth of dead German soldiers and made a necklace of them which he hung on the "Champion of Civilisation" statue, for doing which the University of Lisbon awarded him the title of Doctor. The idea of the novel is that all is false, shameless and cynical in this falsest of worlds, and its motto is: do in Rome as the Romans do. *Julio Jurenito* was written in war-ravaged Europe, in an atmosphere of bourgeois cynicism and disillusionment with all moral values. The "teacher" and his pupils also make a trip to Soviet Russia. But here, too, the "teacher" sees nothing except the "exotic novelty" of the Soviet scene. And Julio Jurenito decides to put an end to his senseless existence, choosing a most original method: he puts on new boots and starts down the main street of Konotop, a small town in the Ukraine, counting on these boots to tempt the bandits with whom the country was teeming. The stratagem works, and bandits kill this great agent provocateur, the "midwife of history".

Julio Jurenito will probably remain the most vivid illustration, not just in Russian but in the whole of European literature, of the post-war sentiments of the harassed western intelligentsia. In his book there is everything: sophistication, cynicism, trenchant satire, sentimental lyricism, and the gay abandon of despair. All this combined makes a brilliant firework of paradoxes, subtle observations of the life of the European bourgeoisie, and sarcastic details. It may be called a confession, a pamphlet, a grotesque, or a poem.

After *Julio Jurenito* Ehrenburg devoted himself entirely to prose. He followed a road entirely his own, for he became a writer of two worlds: the world of capitalism and the world of socialism, the West and Russia. He dropped the sounding line of his sentimental humanism into the two worlds in turn, and summed up the results in his numerous novels and stories. The ideas which guided him. in reproducing his impressions and the method of his approach did not allow him to discern the positive forces of history, the prospects of the future and, consequently, the roads to socialism. Therefore, Ehrenburg's earlier books about life in the Soviet Union in 1922-1927, give us a critical reflection of reality, rather than reality itself, in the mirror of his Chaplinesque sentimentalism.

A suitable epigraph to all these books—*The Life and Death of Nikolai Kurbov, Mercure de Russe, Thirteen Pipes, The Shark, In Protochny Street* (1926), *The Love of Jeanne Ney* and *The Stormy Life of Lazik Reutschwanz*—would be the following words from *The Life and Death of Nikolai Kurbov*: "People can only be people. The chickens also want to live." The theme of these novels and stories is the preponderance of such "eternal" personal emotions as love, sorrow, tenderness, self-preservation, and so on, over the abstract algebra of the Revolution and the state. The thing to do is live while one can, eat warm and fragrant bread, curl up near the purring stove, and make love (*Nikolai Kurbov*). With Ehrenburg all these *motifs* were tinged with lyrical regret over the "failure" of the revolution, a beautiful human Utopia for which the author was full of subjective sympathy.

His books about the world of capitalism, written at the same time, were entirely different in tone. In *Julio Jurenito, Trust D.E.*, and *How Europe Came to Ruin* (1923) the author's satirical indictment of the whole capitalist system and his Werther-like distress in the world of machines goes hand in hand with his admiration for the technical culture of the West. This technical culture grows into a sort of new aesthetic basis of the world. "And so, a new style has been created by science and industry and only Russia is an instance of many absurdities," he wrote in *And Still It Revolves* (1921).

Gradually Ehrenburg's criticism of the world order began to rise above subjectivism, his pamphlets developed into essays, and facts became all-important. This change came about when he took up journalism. His collections of articles about Europe (*The Stamp of the Times, The Overdue Denouement* and others) and his books about Ivar Kreuger and Tomáš Baťa give a brilliant picture of social and cultural life in the principal countries of Central Europe, and the ugliness and contradictions of the capitalist system.

However, Ehrenburg did not find the correct attitude to western culture at once. In *White Coal, or Werther's Tears* he is full of admiration for technical constructivism and also goes to the other extreme (like Duhamel) renouncing machines and protesting against industry in general. He says: "I believe the second Great Flood is in preparation—machine madness, a crusade of maniquins. . . technical progress is growing with every passing day. It is this that with the help of the toxins of fatigue and the avalanche of cars is burying human lives. A splendiferous, cruel period of history has begun." And further on he writes: "But the loftiest theme is the despair of man amid aerials and wax automatons."

On the Second Day (1934), a story about the first five-year plan, marked a turning point in Ehrenburg's work and is one of his most realistic books. The first victories of socialism overcame his mistrust and nihilism and enabled him to see the new forces of history. The result was his artistic conversion to the new world. Three themes are intertwined in this novel: the creation of the socialist world, the destinies of culture, and the struggle against nihilism.

In my opinion, *On the Second Day* and *Without Pausing for Breath* are not among Ehrenburg's best, even though I did praise them once in print. I think most highly of his books written in the 1940s and 1950s.

One of these novels is *The Fall of Paris*, which deals with the period in World War II when the nazis were advancing on the French capital. Ehrenburg convincingly proves that the fall of Paris began much earlier, when the inclination of the French political leaders to capitulate was made evident at Munich.

The novel *In Storm* made a particularly big splash and has been translated into twenty foreign languages. It is a story about the French Resistance and the people (like Madeau, and Sambo, an artist) who came to join the movement.

The Decuman Wave gives a sweeping panoramic picture of what happened after the war and is dedicated to the struggle for world peace. In this novel, as in many of his others, there is a great procession of characters, the action keeps shifting from one country to another, and there are no lengthy descriptions of events or emotions. The pace is rapid, the style is laconic, the tone changes abruptly from irony to satire, and the psychology of the heroes is often rendered by reportorial means. Ehrenburg's heroes are forever talking politics and solving political problems. As a writer, he could be called a sort of "sign of the times".

Ehrenburg's wartime publicistic writings had the most powerful impact on readers and enjoyed the most outstanding popularity. His articles had the impact of artillery fire. Their aphoristic style, based on short sentences and contrasts, left a lasting impression. Ehrenburg's humaneness was compellingly eloquent. His message, addressed to the noblest feelings in men, made them stronger in spirit. His words resounded in the heart of every Soviet reader like the ashes of Klaas knocking in the heart of Eulenspiegel.

In his memoirs *People, Years, Life*, Ehrenburg speaks of Isaac Babel, Boris Pasternak and many other Soviet writers whose names until then had been kept in the coulisse. These memoirs, however, have been criticised for presenting a "twilight" view of literature and the age, and giving a most subjective portrayal of the writers.

Admittedly, Ehrenburg's books arouse different feelings in different people, in the sense that not every reader can accept his manner of writing and especially the arrogance of his tone. The impression one gets from his memoirs is that he never failed to gain the upper hand and was always proved right. True, Ehrenburg does admit that he made some ideological mistakes, but he mentions this rather casually and not from the position of a historical analysis.

But let us forgive him his faults which are common human failings, present to a greater or lesser degree in all men. Be that as it may, I know no other writer in Soviet literature—or in any other European literature either, for that matter—who can equal Ehrenburg for the compelling power of his publicistic talent. And this power he always used for the good of people of all races and nationalities.

Chapter 19

Paustovsky

Konstantin Paustovsky. 1952.

Paustovsky seems to look straight into his readers' eyes with tenderness and human understanding. All his books radiate goodness and beauty to which he was so sensitive. The antipode of Osborne with his *Look Back in Anger*, Paustovsky seems to say to the reader: "Look back in joy and kindness", for the world about us is good.

In his books an author always gives an answer to the questions posed him by the age he lives in. As Walt Whitman said, the poet is the man who gives the answers. The character of these answers is very largely determined by the writer's talent, wisdom and feeling. These answers may appear to be completely unconcerned with the present day. Or again, they may assume mystical forms, don the historical robes of a thousand years ago, or take the guise of fairy tales. An experienced eye, however, will unfailingly discern in the works of an artist some mark connecting him with his age, just as a man always bears on his body the mark of his connection with his mother.

Our epoch of titanic social conflicts, wars, revolutions and astounding technical discoveries places the individual in a peculiar position. His thoughts and feelings cannot keep silent or slumber serenely as though life were a boat rocking gently on the waves as the current slowly carries it downstream. Mayakovsky in one of his poems compared people to boats. Millions and thousands of millions of human destinies are rushing over rocks and rapids in the turbulent current of history. History demands that people should have keen vision, courage, and an understanding of what is going on. But then not everyone is born a fighter. On the contrary, most people instinctively shrink from violence. With some this comes from moral flabbiness and a desire for a placid Philistine existence. A man who has no metal in his character and no ideological backbone is liable to turn into a reptile or a jellyfish.

But there are gentle, lyrical natures who, with their whole being, are drawn to goodness, to pastel shades, who love people and all living things on the good earth. They have a strong sense of honour and a spiritual stability that, whatever anyone says, is always an adornment.

Precisely such was the essence of Paustovsky, the man and the poet. He was indeed a lyric poet in prose. He has shown by what paths a gentle, lyrical soul reaches the road of socialist revolution and how it merges with the ideals of this great revolution. This, in a way, is the philosophical significance of Paustovsky's writings. A contemporary of Alexander Blok, Paustovsky belonged to the romantics and dreamers who wholeheartedly welcomed the storms of our revolutionary age.

Konstantin Paustovsky was born in Moscow on May 31, 1892, into the family of a railway employee. He died in 1968. He spent his childhood in an Ukrainian village and then went to school in Kiev. He studied for two years at Kiev University, after which he transferred to Moscow University, where his studies were interrupted owing to the outbreak of the First World War.

Paustovsky was greatly admired by Maxim Gorky and Romain Rolland, and Lenin's wife, Nadezhda Konstantinovna Krupskaya, praised him for his *Kara-Bugaz*.

A profound sense of responsibility guided Paustovsky throughout his literary career, which began more than fifty years ago. His first story was published in the Kiev magazine *Ogni* (Lights) in 1911 when he was a senior at school. But, as Paustovsky himself said, he immediately realised that he lacked the experience and the knowledge of people necessary for a writer, and so he plunged into life, wandering about Russia, constantly changing jobs.

"It is dangerous for a writer to joke with words," Gogol used to say. And Paustovsky understood this very early in life. His autobiographical work *The Long Ago* ends on the words of the chemist to the youth who has just finished school and wants to become a writer. The young lad is full of romantic hopes in which he is encouraged by the motley society of intellectuals who surround him.

"It's a big thing," the chemist says, "but it calls for a real knowledge of life. Right? And you have very little of it as yet, if any. A writer must understand everything. He must work like a slave and not seek after fame. There's one thing I can tell you–go to people's houses, to fairs, to factories, to the doss-houses. Go everywhere–to theatres, hospitals, mines and prisons. That's right: everywhere. And become steeped in life, the way valerian roots are steeped in alcohol. Let the infusion be strong. And then you'll be able to sell it to people as a miracle-working balsam. In prescribed doses, mind you."

In the story *A Summer in Voronezh* Paustovsky describes a young shepherd boy, Fedya, to whom a writer is a legendary being, indisputably talented in all spheres of life, a sort of wizard who is expected to know everything, see everything, understand everything and do everything excellently. Paustovsky writes: "I did not want to shatter this naïve belief of the village shepherd boy. Maybe because this naïveté concealed the real truth about the genuine craft of a writer–a truth we do not always remember and do not always strive to live up to."

Paustovsky embarked upon life with this definite thought in mind. He wanted to gain personal experience in as many occupations and trades as he could, and so for a time he worked as a tram conductor in Moscow, an orderly on a hospital train during the First World War, an unskilled worker at the metallurgical plant in Yekaterinoslav and then at the turbine works in Taganrog, a sailor, a teacher of Russian literature in a girls' school, and in many other jobs. During the Civil War he joined the ranks to fight Petlyura, and in the years of the Great Patriotic War he was a correspondent on the Southern Front.

Paustovsky had travelled a great deal about the Soviet Union. He had been round the Caspian Sea, in Daghestan, the Caucasus,

Murmansk Region, Karelia, the Crimea, the North Urals, Ryazan Region, and practically everywhere in Central Russia.

It was not until 1926, after the ten-year test which he had set himself, that Paustovsky took up the pen again to devote himself to writing.

At first the world of images which he created was isolated from life and hovered above the real world from which he had emerged. In his early, romantic stories and the novel *Gleaming Clouds* we do not hear the talk typical of Black Sea and Sea of Azov ports, nor do we see any striking pictures from the life of metallurgical workers or seamen. The truth of life and the people's struggle for their happiness were hidden behind the haze of "gleaming clouds", the veil of bookishness and romantic contemplation.

In his book about the artist Levitan, Paustovsky described with great precision and subtlety that peculiar state of mind when a person ceases to be a fighter and becomes merely an observer.

"The twilight hours were especially tormenting. . . . He listened to the singing of a strange woman on the other side of the garden wall, and memorised yet another romance where 'love sobbed'. He wished he could see the woman who sang in such a ringing yet sorrowful voice, he wished he could see the girls who were playing croquet. . . . He wanted to have tea on the verandah, drinking it out of clean glasses, watching the transparent thread of apricot jam slowly trickle down from his spoon and then touching the slice of lemon in his tea with this spoon. He wanted to laugh and make fun, to play catchers, to sing till all hours, to fly round the giants' stride pole, and to listen to the excited whispering of school boys about Garshin whose story *Four Days* had been banned by the censors. He wanted to look into the eyes of the singing woman—when women sing their eyes are always half-closed and full of wistful loveliness."

Socialist reality and Paustovsky's enormous life experience helped him to rise above this romantic contemplation of the world. In his best stories about Soviet people and the beautiful Russian countryside, he showed in bold relief the country's great transformation and painted some memorable portraits of the builders of communist society.

Paustovsky was essentially a lyric poet. Whatever he touched with his pen became drawn into an atmosphere of amazingly gentle lyricism, breathing faith in goodness, and imbued with loving trust in man. In his autobiographical book Paustovsky wrote: "I surmised that good and evil lay side by side in life. Good can often be glimpsed through the thick of lies, misery and sufferings. . . . I tried to find these signs of good everywhere. And I often found them, of course. They can flash out suddenly, like Cinderella's crystal slipper from under her grey, ragged dress, just as her earnest, tender look can flash out in the crowd somewhere."

Paustovsky taught us to see what we often fail to notice in life, and to admire things which do not immediately strike the eye.

In this connection I cannot help remembering the last lines of his story about the Meshchera woods in Ryazan Region. "At first glance, it's a quiet, unpretentious place under a not very bright sky. But the better you come to know it the more you love this ordinary land until it almost wrings your heart. And if I ever have to defend my country I shall know deep down in my heart that I am also defending this piece of land which has taught me to see and understand beauty, however nondescript it may appear—this dreamy, wooded land, as unforgettably beloved as the first love in our life."

This was written two years before the war. In it we see how naturally his lyricism and his feeling for his native soil blended with his love for the whole of the Soviet land.

The book about Levitan ends with the following: "He could not communicate to his paintings even a feeble smile. He was too honest not to see the people's sufferings. He was a poet of the vast, destitute country, a singer of its Nature. . .in this lies the power of his art and the secret of his charm."

Paustovsky adopted Levitan's lyricism, but with him this lyricism, liberated from the thrall of melancholy, acquired new colours and half-tones—joyful, strong and rousing. Yet for all this, we find in Paustovsky another feature, which I personally consider a weakness, and that is his sentimental attitude to suffering. Maxim Gorky was right when he said that suffering must be abhorred as being humiliating to man. Active humanism, endowed with the same responsiveness to suffering as is common to Paustovsky and all Russian literature in general—one has only to think of Tolstoi, Dostoyevsky, Chekhov and Yesenin—is a call to battle for man; it is not an invitation to shed tears of pity. As I see it, this active humanism lies at the basis of the entire progress in the U.S.S.R. Mayakovsky and Alexei Tolstoi have both expressed it very well.

Paustovsky's maturity as a writer and his life experience gradually released him from his bookishness and his romantic contemplation of the world, although I am afraid his perception of the historical struggle continued to show some traces of sentimentality.

He developed his own manner of writing and his own genre, which was also engendered by his lyrical perception of reality. It is a peculiar combination of essay, diary, memoirs and poetry.

Many of Paustovsky's books can be called lyrical diaries of our epoch. Such, for instance, is his story about the construction of the Volga-Don canal, called *The Birth of a Sea*. It is a very informative book, and there are many interesting details which the pen of an artist has made unforgettable for us. But the most precious thing about it is the poetic image of the Soviet land as it becomes transformed the nearer it approaches communism.

Paustovsky belonged to the older generation of writers whose names are well-known to readers and revered by them. A collection of his works in six volumes came out in 1,300,000 copies—a most impressive figure. He published more than 30 books, among them the autobiographical trilogy *The Long Ago, Restless Youth* and *The Beginning of the Unknown Age*, and his book on art called *The Golden Rose*. One of the chapters from *The Long Ago* was printed in the magazine *Vokrug sveta* (Round the World) in 1947, and Ivan Bunin, then living in Paris, happened to read it. Bunin did not know Paustovsky personally, but he wrote him a letter saying how much he had enjoyed reading this story, which he called "The best short story in Russian literature". Needless to say, every opinion is bound to have its share of subjectivity. The fact remains that translations of Paustovsky's books have been published everywhere in Europe.

It is interesting too to note Paustovsky's appraisal of Bunin, that extraordinary master of the Russian language who died abroad, in bitter exile. Paustovsky wrote that the thing he valued most in Bunin was his love "for the beauty and complexity of the world. For the night, for daylight, for the sky, for the endless roar of the ocean, for books, for meditation—in short, for everything about him". In large measure these words are probably applicable to Paustovsky himself. But for Paustovsky, just as for Lev Tolstoi, love meant people first and foremost, and then Motherland—Russia. One of the books in his trilogy ends with the picture of the remnants of the White Army and the bourgeoisie fleeing from Odessa in 1920. Ivan Bunin emigrated with them. Paustovsky, then a newspaper correspondent, stayed in Russia. The sirens of the departing ships sounded to him like a requiem for those people who were abandoning their homeland.

"The ships were vanishing in the mist. The northeastern wind seemed to turn a new page. On this page was to begin the heroic history of Russia—our long-suffering, extraordinary country which we shall love till our dying breath."

The name of Konstantin Paustovsky, a poet of beauty and humanism, has also been inscribed on this clean page in the great book of the new communist mankind.

Chapter 20

Sholokhov

Mikhail Sholokhov. 1952.

What is Sholokhov? It is like asking the skin divers who move about freely on the seabed, what is the sea? On the outside it is a boundless expanse of loudly seething blue waves. Distant horizons, sailing ships, a call to the unknown. But those who open their eyes under water see a strange, mysterious world of slowly swimming fish and fantastic plants, a world that may even seem a bit frightening. So it is with Sholokhov. He is Russia seen both in the movement of her elements and in the collision of her characters.

Sholokhov is not a chronicler of the Don Cossacks. He is a Cossack himself, he writes mainly about Cossacks but in doing so paints a comprehensive picture of Russia.

Hundreds of articles in all the languages, and dozens of books and monographs have been written about Sholokhov. His fascination lies in his marvellous, full-blooded realism, in his ability to bring out the human side of the great theme of our age–the conversion of the bulk of the working people to socialism. Under Sholokhov's pen this theme becomes so strikingly picturesque and dramatic because the heroes are the Don Cossacks whose inherited prejudices connected with their special position as an estate apart in Russian society hampered their historical transition to socialism. This is what Sholokhov writes about in his two major works *And Quiet Flows the Don* and *Virgin Soil Upturned,* moulding his characters with such poetic, Tolstoyan eloquence, and giving such a truthful description of the road they had to travel to arrive at revolution, that his name became known throughout the world.

Mikhail Sholokhov was born in 1905. His father was a clerk, then a cattle dealer, and later manager of a steam mill. The future writer gathered his impressions of the Cossack *kulaks* (rich peasants), officers and the rest of the Cossack élite, at the house of the mill owner (the prototype of Mokhov in *And Quiet Flows the Don*). Sholokhov left school in 1918 when he was thirteen years old. He began to write at the age of eighteen, publishing his stories in Komsomol newspapers and magazines. His first book *Tales of the Don* came out in 1926. He started his *And Quiet Flows the Don* in 1925 (the first and second parts came out in 1928, the third in 1932, and the fourth in 1937-38.) The first part of *Virgin Soil Upturned* was published in 1932, and the second thirty years later.

In *Tales of the Don* and *Azure Steppe* his chief aim was to chronicle the story of the Don Cossacks in the period of the Civil War and the NEP. Actually these books were but an introduction to the monumental epic novel *And Quiet Flows the Don* which embraces a period of several decades and is the first such book about the Cossacks in Russian literature. *And Quiet Flows the Don* is a sort of Cossack encyclopaedia describing the Cossacks' mores and manners, customs and songs, their life in peacetime, their participation in World War I, and their reaction to the Revolution of October 1917 and subsequent events.

It is a panoramic novel, packed with events and characters. The plot centres round the Melekhovs, a family of well-to-do Cossack farmers. The author begins by introducing us to the Cossack world with its tradition-bound way of life. As the plot develops, he takes us into the homes of Cossacks of different social standing: paupers like Mishka Koshevoi, the wealthy mill owner Mokhov, ataman

Korshunov whose daughter Natalya marries Grigory Melekhov, and others. Descriptions of the clothes and household utensils, of mowing, ploughing and fishing, of wedding customs and genre scenes, are the background for Sholokhov's extraordinarily colourful heroes. There is the Melekhov family: Grigory's father, Pantelei Prokofievich, a harsh and quick-tempered man, an old tsarist campaigner and a pillar of Cossack traditions; his mother Ilyinichna; his brother Pyotr—a burly Cossack with a wheat-coloured moustache; and Pyotr's wife, the flirtatious Darya. Then there are the Astakhovs, their next-door neighbours: Stepan and his wife Aksinya, a handsome passionate woman. Aksinya and Grigory fall passionately in love, and in this love both find an outlet for their unconscious protest against the Cossacks' moral and caste prejudices.

Sholokhov shows the collision between humane concepts and the old and obsolete notions of honour, religion, family and social duty, the purpose of the Cossacks' life and the position of women. Grigory's affair with Aksinya, another man's wife, resulting in his leaving home and becoming a hired labourer in the service of a local landowner, was the first jolt that shook his faith in the Cossack moral principles.

Sholokhov draws a fascinating picture of the contradictory relations between his heroes—Grigory, Natalya, Pyotr, Darya and Pantelei Prokofievich. His skilful use of shading enhances the reality of his characters and makes their relations more dramatic. For instance, when Grigory is promoted by the Whites to division commander, his father Pantelei Prokofievich, the head of the family but only a sergeant in rank, feels constrained and "somehow estranged from Grigory".

When the Cossacks enter the war the story spreads beyond the bounds of family relations and acquires vast scope, with new characters appearing against a much broader background. The second part of *And Quiet Flows the Don* gives a detailed account of the military and revolutionary history of the Cossack movement and of the political events in Russia in 1916-18. Sholokhov shows us the most prominent leaders of the counter-revolution: General Kornilov, Alexeyev, the Cossack atamans Kaledin and Bogayevsky, and the revolutionary Cossack leaders Podtyolkov and Krivoshlykov. He describes the story of the Podtyolkov movement, the death of Podtyolkov himself, and the vacillations of the Don Cossacks.

In parts 3 and 4 the plot deals mainly with the course of the Civil War in the Don country (1918-20), and particularly with the upper-Don revolt against Soviet power. Sholokhov has described this last revolt of the Cossacks on the basis of documentary material and the accounts of eyewitnesses, interviewed by him personally. The Melekhovs—father and both sons—play a prominent part in this revolt. Pyotr is killed; Grigory is given command of a regiment and then rises to division commander. Sholokhov shows how Cossack nationalism was unable to withstand the conflict with historical reality, how groundless the Cossacks' fears that "landless, peasant and factory Russia" intended to seize the rich Don territory proved, how their enmity lost intensity and the workingmen's, humane instincts in them gradually took the upper hand and they felt drawn to the opposite—to the Soviets, to Mishka Koshevoi and the Bolsheviks.

The author uses the career of Grigory Melekhov as a means of demonstrating all these dramatic processes. This "wild, handsome Cossack" whom Sholokhov frankly admires at moments, does not quite represent the true destinies of the middle peasants. In tsarist Russia, a man belonging to the middle peasantry could hardly have been promoted to general in the White army. With the Cossacks it was a different matter. But psychologically, Grigory Melekhov is a typical representative of the middle peasantry. With great artistic skill and power of conviction the author sums up the dozens of reasons which guide Grigory in his behaviour, directing him this way and that. When he was in hospital, recuperating after being wounded, Grigory spoke with Garanzha, a revolutionary soldier, who did not mince his words in defining the war: "It's more money for the rich, and a tighter noose round our necks." But when Grigory returned home with a cross of St. George, once again "the subtle poison of flattery, deference and admiration gradually destroyed those seeds of truth planted in his mind by Garanzha. When he left home again, he was not the man who had come there from the front. His Cossack pride, imbibed with his mother's milk, took the upper hand over the great human truth." His emotional development was extremely tortuous. "And because he stood on the dividing line in the struggle between the two worlds, both of which he denounced, a dull, unceasing resentment mounted in his soul." His arrival at the truth was painful, it was indeed born in hard travail. He says to his wife Natalya who calls him to shame for his drinking and his carrying on with merry widows and loose wenches at the other farmsteads: "What shame can there be when our whole life's gone awry.... It's hard.... It's hard, and that's why I try to find forgetfulness in vodka, or some woman, never mind which.... Life's taken a wrong course, and maybe I'm to blame.... I ought to have made peace with the Reds and gone after the Cadets. But how do it? Who'll act as go-between between us and Soviet power? How can we settle our wrongs? Half of the Cossacks are on the other side of the Donets, and the ones who've stayed here have turned savage, they've got their teeth in their land.... Everything's got mixed up in my head, Natasha. The war's taken everything out of me. I seem frightening to my own self now.". .... "My hair's turned grey, I'm losing grip on everything. .... Life has flashed past like summer lightning."

A lyrical *motif* of all-conquering life runs through the whole book—through the history of the Cossacks and the story of Grigory Melekhov who arrives at socialism the hard way, going through the crucible of wars and the sharp contradictions of the epoch. This is the leitmotif of the whole novel. But it sounds most strongly in Sholokhov's description of the steppeland. Knave, a friend of Mishka Koshevoi's, who has been executed by the Whites, is buried in the steppe. Very soon a bustard hen builds a nest on his grave, and life begins to seethe all round again.People are waging their great struggle for happiness on this land, and the land calls them with its beauty and poetry, urging them to win their rightful cause. "Invisible life, fecundated by the Spring, throbbing and pulsating mightily, was unfolding in the steppe: grasses, hidden from the predatory eyes of men, were growing lustily; birds and beasts, big and small, mated in their secret steppeland havens; and the fields bristled with the countless spikes of the new shoots."

This must not be mistaken for the Knut Hamsun pantheistic approach of Nature reconciling people with the power of its beauty which remains utterly indifferent to everything. Sholokhov's landscape lyricism and his hymnal attitude to life and living things are inseparable from his love for the people. The poetry of all that is beautiful and strong (both in the colourful descriptions of the landscape and in the human passions) conveyed by Sholokhov with such truly Tolstoyan evocative power, merely serves to stress the humanity that is the mission of the true Human Being. Since Gorky no Russian author (with the exception of Fadeyev) has written as affectionately as Sholokhov of toilers, and especially of women and the joys and sorrows of motherhood. His rich, strong realism takes the tone of a calmly objective narration. There is nothing frankly tendentious about the novel, but the author's attitude is obvious from the sum of his images, and is as natural as life itself.

Sholokhov revised his *And Quiet Flows the Don* several times. In one of the editions he deleted the more naturalistic scenes and toned down the naturalistic colours of the language, but later he restored it all.

True, there is a certain amount of Zola-ism in Sholokhov's style, and this is perhaps its weakness. I feel that in Sergei Gerasimov's film *And Quiet Flows the Don* this naturalism was unwittingly emphasised and the poetry we read between the lines of the novel has largely been lost.

Sholokhov has his own colours, startlingly bold and truthful. The last book where he describes Grigory Melekhov's experience in

Fomin's insurgent band is fascinating for its psychological revelations. Sholokhov's province in which he really comes into his own is human feelings and relationships. When Aksinya dies, hit by a stray bullet, Grigory lifts his face up to the sky and the sun blinds him, but strangely it looks black to him. A "black sun": I do not know of another image in world literature to equal this in depth and power.

And Quiet Flows the Don (just like Alexei Tolstoi's *The Ordeal* and *Peter the First*) is one of the classics of Soviet literature. It is a tragic epic of the age, a book of love and anger. Reflected in it, like the stormy skies in a broad river, is that period in the history of Russia when human destinies clashed and the beautiful got mixed up with the sordid, all of which taken together carries the reader to distant shores whose outlines have been conjured up by the Revolution in the mind of every Russian. *And Quiet Flows the Don* is a truly great novel of the 20th century, a new *Iliad* of the people and Revolution.

Sholokhov's second great novel, *Virgin Soil Upturned*, deals with the events of the winter of 1929-30, a decisive turning point in the collectivisation of agriculture.

The novel recreates with almost documentary accuracy all the more typical attending circumstances. Although, as in *And Quiet Flows the Don*, the scene is set in a Cossack village (near Veshenskaya once again), the author has pushed into the background all that is typically Cossack in his heroes and has, on the contrary, emphasised features common to the peasantry as a whole. *Virgin Soil Upturned* describes the arrival of Semyon Davydov, a worker from the Leningrad Putilov Plant, one of the twenty-five thousand workers mobilised to help the agricultural districts consolidate the collective-farm system. Sholokhov describes clandestine gatherings of the opposition, the dispossession of the *kulaks*, meetings at the District Party Committees and village Soviets, cases of extremes to which the policy was carried, the collectivisation of all livestock (including chickens), the mutiny of the village wives, the *kulaks'* preparations for a revolt, and the first sowing campaign in that "Bolshevik spring" of 1930.

The main characters of the novel are very typical figures. The two opposite extremes are Davydov, an industrial worker, and Polovtsev, a Cossack captain. Each represents his class, fighting a battle to the death over collectivisation. The story opens with these two men's arrival at the village of Gremyachy Log. Davydov has been sent there by the Party to direct the campaign for collectivisation. Polovtsev arrives secretly and hides out at the home of Ostrovnoi with whom he once served in the same regiment and who, although really a *kulak*, has been clever enough to "play along" with events, and manages to pull the wool over Davydov's eyes so successfully that, completely taken in, he even makes him property manager of the collective farm. The purpose of Polovtsev's coming is to sabotage the work through Ostrovnoi and demoralise the collective farm. The social types of Cossack-peasants are painted with amazing vividness. Razmyotnov, the chairman of the village Soviet, a man of poor peasant origin, is susceptible to bad influence, but the instincts of a working man prove the stronger in him and he becomes Davydov's most reliable right-hand man. Makar Nagulnov, secretary of the village Party cell, is an "extremist" type. He was a partisan in the Civil War, and he says: "We grew attached to the Party not with our learned gristle, like Trotsky, but with our hearts and the blood we shed for the Party." He is like a tense wire, about to snap. Real or imagined enemies make his blood boil. "I've been breathing easier since I heard that all the farmers' property has got to be drawn into collective farms. I've hated it since I was a kid." In Nagulnov this fanatical hatred for property is combined with equally fanatical devotion to the cause of the Revolution. "The whole of me's aimed at a world revolution," he says.

Kondrat Maidannikov is one of the most striking characters in *Virgin Soil Upturned*. He is a middle peasant, and a thrifty farmer. Sholokhov writes: "It was no easy thing for Kondrat to accept the collective farm idea. He wept and bled as he tore the umbilical cord that bound him to his property, to the oxen and his private plot of land." Kondrat comes into the cowshed in the middle of the night to say goodbye to his animals who are to be taken to the collective farm in the morning. It is a moving scene. His oxen, after their morning watering "turned homeward, but Kondrat in a fit of fury rode at them on his horse, barring their way and heading them off to the village Soviet." When Kondrat joined the collective farm he became a zealous, conscientious guardian of its property. Sholokhov uses Maidannikov as an example to show the international revolutionary significance of the collective-farm policy. As soon as he accepted socialism the great wide world unfolded before him. To use the words of Gogol: "Suddenly he could see very far away, to all the corners of the earth." And Sholokhov says: "Kondrat was thinking of the needs of the country, launched on its first five-year plan, he clenched his fists under his homespun coat, and mentally said with hatred to those workers in the West who were not for the Communists: 'You've sold us for a good wage from your masters! You've bartered us for a well-fed life, brothers. . . . Or can't you see from across the frontier how difficult it is for us to raise our economy? Can't you see the need we're suffering, that we're practically barefooted and unclothed, yet we grit our teeth and work. You'll feel ashamed of yourselves afterwards, brothers.' "

Another extremely vivid character and a most humorous one is old Grandad Shchukar.

Yakov Ostrovnoi who lived "a queer, double life" is a very important figure in the enemy camp. He is a clever, energetic manager by nature, but because of his hatred for the collective-farm system and the Bolsheviks, he uses these qualities for slyly calculated sabotage.

The soul of the novel is Semyon Davydov. Like Levinson in Fadeyev's *The Rout* he embodies the historical role of the proletariat in the Revolution. He is an experienced fighter in the class struggle for socialism. He is a friend and teacher of the workers and peasants, and a force as hard and unbending as steel when it comes to dealing with the enemy, the *kulaks*. Davydov is assaulted by some farm women whom the *kulaks* have egged on to loot the public seed stores. During a meeting he calls after the unsuccessful "mutiny", he says to one of the women: "Don't be scared, remove the scarf from your face, no one's going to touch you, even though you did lay me about pretty hard last night. But if you do a bad job of work when we go out to sow tomorrow, I'll give you one hell of a flogging then, so just bear it in mind. And I'm not going to strike you across the shoulder blades, but much lower down so you can't sit on it or lie down, damn you." The very fact that Davydov forgives these deluded women and jokes about it shows how well he understands them and how well he appreciates their kinship to himself and the cause he serves. And yet this same Davydov flies into a rage when Razmyotnov spares the *kulaks* because of their children. "Staring hard into Razmyotnov's face and breathing hard Davydov said: 'So you're sorry for them. . . . And were they sorry for us? Did the tears of our children make the enemy weep? Did they weep over the orphans of the men they'd killed? Did they? My father was discharged from the factory after the strike and exiled to Siberia. . . . Mother was left with the four of us on her hands. . . . She went begging in the streets, my mother did, so we wouldn't die from hunger!' "

Both *Virgin Soil Upturned* and *And Quiet Flows the Don* abound in dramatic episodes (for instance, the murder of a poor peasant by Polovtsev, the dispossession of the *kulaks*, etc.) and some of them are naturalistic in colouring. But in *Virgin Soil Upturned* the leitmotif is the restrained lyrical pathos of man, the pathos of great human ideals. "Gazing about the infinite, newly green steppe Davydov was thinking: 'They're going to be a happy lot. . . . Machines will be doing all the hard work. . . . People will forget the very smell of sweat. . . . I'd like to live till then, dammit.' "

There are some attractive female characters in the novel. One is Lushka, a wild and reckless but intelligent young woman who was

Nagulnov's wife and then became Davydov's mistress. Another is Varya—a particularly charming study of a young girl in love for the first time in her life. The scenes of her laundering Davydov's shirts for him as a surprise, going out to the fields with him, and finally her reaction to his murder, are extremely touching.

Despite some remarkably powerful scenes—such as the dialogue between Davydov and Arzhanov on the way out to the fields—in my opinion the second part of the novel is on the whole not as good as the first. Personally, I get somewhat bored with old Shchukar, the great village wit. If in the first book he helped to tone down the drama of the plot, in the second he no longer serves any such purpose and is rather overdone. Like any buffoonery for the sake of buffoonery his witticisms tend to become tiring. True, in the concluding pages of the novel, this old man appears in a new light and becomes more appealing and understandable.

Virgin Soil Upturned, like the rest of Sholokhov's stories, has a tragic ending. Davydov and Nagulnov are murdered by the enemies of Soviet power. It is the most true-to-life ending, I suppose. In the early nineteen-thirties the champions of the new system of Cossack collective farms still had to wage an armed struggle against their enemies. By the time Sholokhov finished writing this book thirty years later it had already become a historic novel. Davydov and Nagulnov have so endeared themselves to Soviet readers and have become such familiar names that in the Don country today legends are still woven about them and people want to believe that they are alive and still fighting for the Revolution somewhere. I find Nagulnov an especially attractive character. There is a peculiar appeal about this semi-literate man, whose whole being is "aimed at world revolution". He cherishes a beautiful dream and a righteous hatred. He burns with passion for his idea. He is a living embodiment of that enormous tension which gripped the souls of the Russians in those years. The image of Nagulnov makes it psychologically understandable why those people went to the taiga, to the end of the world to build new towns, meanwhile living in snow-drifted tents, and stoically weathering all the hardships and the superhuman strain. Nagulnov is clearly the predecessor of those Soviet men who in the Great Patriotic War blocked the embrasures of pill boxes with their bodies and rammed enemy planes, braving certain death.

In this novel, which is perhaps less integrated and lyrical than *And Quiet Flows the Don*, Sholokhov has brought out many essential features common to Russians of the Soviet epoch.

Sholokhov writes slowly. He is still working on his last novel *They Fought For Their Country* about the Great Patriotic War against nazi Germany. I shall not hazard any guesses about the reason. It may be that Sholokhov is finding it too painful to go back in mind to those atrocities which the nazis had perpetrated on our soil. Or maybe the characters of this new book have not yet taken final shape. Many episodes from this future novel have already been published and even brought out in book form, and they speak of the unwaning power of Sholokhov's talent.

This is especially true of his short story *The Fate of a Man*, which like *And Quiet Flows the Don* and *Virgin Soil Upturned* has been made into a film. This is the story of a soldier who is taken prisoner by the Germans, escapes, and comes home to find that the war has deprived him of everything—his family has been killed, buried under the ruins of his home. But the war has not killed his humanity. He comes across a hungry little orphan boy, adopts him and gradually comes back to life. The story is extraordinarily powerful. Short though it is, I know of no other story in which the tragedy suffered by millions of people in the last war has been revealed with such stark simplicity and psychological depth.

Sholokhov may write slowly, but he is going to be read for a long time to come. And the 1965 Nobel Prize came as a just reward.

Chapter 21

The New in Soviet Literature

Following the Twentieth Congress of the Communist Party of the Soviet Union in February 1956, serious changes took place in the ideological life of Soviet society and in Soviet literature too. These changes meant greater democratisation, in the Leninist sense of the term, and an upsurge in the development of the people's creative powers.

As we have seen from the foregoing, literature as a whole successfully weathered the difficult years of inhibited spiritual activity. To prove this point, there was Leonid Leonov's novel *The Russian Forest (1953)* with the odious character of Professor Gratsiansky, the stories of Valentin Ovechkin *On a Collective Farm, Difficult Spring* (1952-1956), and others. Ovechkin describes Borzov, a village official whose bureaucratic methods of work and indifference to people ran counter to the principles of communism.

Even before the Twentieth Party Congress stories of a satirical or critical nature had been appearing in the literary magazines. For instance, G. Troyepolsky's *From the Notes of an Agronomist* in which prominence was given to the exposure of characters who were alien to the entire pattern of Soviet life.

An element of criticism also characterises the works of the young writer Vladimir Tendryakov whose main theme is modern Soviet village life. In his story *The Fall of Ivan Chuprov* he shows how this energetic collective-farm chairman changes in character as he becomes more and more addicted to money-making in shady deals. Or take his story *Rainy Weather* which criticises the secretary of a district Party committee who, by giving unreasonable orders with an utter disregard for the actual situation, causes the collective farm serious material and moral damage. Vladimir Tendryakov, who entered the literary scene after the Second World War, bases all his stories (*Ruts, A Tight Knot* and others) on sharp psychological conflicts.

The same is true of Pavel Nilin whose story *Cruelty* is well known. He is another writer who became popular in the post-war years. More often than not the principal characters in his stories are criminals and those engaged in fighting crime, of which he has a first-hand knowledge, having worked in the criminal investigation department in his youth. Nilin's exciting stories have nothing in common with those murder stories, so current in the West, full of horror and gory killings. With Nilin, the important thing is not so much the crime itself as those psychological and philosophical problems which arise from instances of law-breaking by different types of people.

Vasily Azhayev's novel *Far From Moscow* gives a panoramic view of a construction project in the Far East where an oil pipe-line is being built. Against this background, people stand out in their true colours. For instance, Batmanov, who is in charge of the project, proves to be a strong-willed man who likes to give the orders and who believes in keeping a distance between himself and others. Engineer Grubsky, for all his training, turns out to be a man of backward views and because of him construction is held up. Azhayev's novel throbs with the tension of those years. The plot also follows a pattern typical for that time: the pivot is the construction project, and all the happenings are determined by it. The "hero" is the collective of workers with whom the construction project comes first, mattering more to them than individual desires or ambitions. It is remarkable that Azhayev managed to give a dramatic rendering of such things as a Party conference, discussions of purely technical matters, and so forth, which one would imagine could hardly be described artistically and even less so entertainingly.

Galina Nikolayeva's novel *The Battle* (published in 1954, although it was written much earlier) is also about people working at a large plant. It is a story of conflicts in the staff's business and personal relations. The central theme is the battle fought by Bakhirev, the chief engineer, against the director Valgan for the reconstruction of the plant on more progressive lines, and his battle for happiness with the woman he loves. He wins the first battle but loses the second.

Thus, there are numerous examples to prove that shortly before the Twentieth Party Congress Soviet writers were already dealing with these historical contradictions in their novels, presenting them from the viewpoint of the Party's and the people's struggle for communism.

Still, the main tendency in those years was to pile up the eulogies and further romanticise the "positive" characters and situations. Some writers really "wallowed in ode-singing" to use Belinsky's expression. What is more, this eulogising reduced the informative merits of the books. Critics then evolved a theory of "art without conflict", although a conflict between the excellent and the more excellent was considered quite all right. Thus, for instance, in Alexander Korneichuk's play *In the Steppes of the Ukraine* the conflict is between Galushka, a good collective-farm chairman who says that "life is fine enough under socialism" and he is thus in no hurry to attain communism, and Chesnok, a better collective-farm chairman who is anxious to change life on communist principles as soon as possible.

It would be wrong to attribute all the tendencies to embellish reality which originated during the Stalin personality cult to that cult alone, or to put them down to the spread of a dogmatic and unrealistic approach to life.

The Soviet people themselves having shown such heroism and self-sacrifice in realising the ideals set before them by the Party, radiated romantic fervour and enthusiasm. And this naturally left its imprint on literature.

However, an unhealthy tendency attached itself to this healthy and understandable one, namely an evasion of historical contradictions, a shirking of the subject even from progressive ideological positions, and a proneness to round off all the corners. This came from an erroneous understanding of the purpose of literature. Some writers imagined that their books would have a greater effect on the readers if they only described achievements and happy occasions. This faulty tendency appeared in many books published soon after the war about the life of collective farmers, industrial workers and intellectuals.

The new course set by the Twentieth Party Congress was naturally very important for the development of socialist realism, an artistic method based on truth to life and inviting the writer to state this truth without any embellishments or pure eyewash.

Clearly, this reappraisal of values must apply to everything that was connected with the Stalin personality cult and its manifestations, to questions of dogmatism, embellishment, etc. However, there can be no reappraisal of values in the main thing, which in Soviet literature is to present the people as the guiding force in history, and to show how all people become spiritually renovated through creative endeavour and the struggle for communism, resulting in the emergence of a new type of man. Thus the main thing in the aesthetic code of the new society's literature is the Leninist principle of partisanship, which requires that all artistic, descriptive and stylistic means be subordinated to the idea promulgated by a literary work.

The view that the aesthetic means of literature and the writer's skill must meet the ideological aims of a given book is the underlying theme of Fedin's treatise *The Writer, Art and Time* (1961). Together with Maxim Gorky and Alexei Tolstoi, Konstantin Fedin is one of those writers who have given a most complete and profound exposition of the principles of Soviet literature. Fedin writes: "... writing is worthwhile only if it is an activity that serves society and the people. History has confirmed that longevity and immortality come only to those works of art which are rooted in the same soil as their authors' thinking and which embody this thinking in images." Gorky, Alexei Tolstoi, Fedin, Sholokhov, Fadeyev and Leonov–all these leading Soviet writers held that the main purpose of Soviet literature was to embody in artistic images the heroism of the people in its struggle for communism.

What then were the new features which appeared in literature after the elimination of the Stalin personality cult? What were the consequences of the new policy?

The consequences were manifold. The first problem which loomed before the writers was how to interpret the capabilities of the method of socialist realism in view of this reappraisal of the aims of literature. It was obvious that writers had more right and opportunity to present reality in a critical light. But the question was: what measure of criticism and what methods of criticising events and people were appropriate in Soviet literature? What new artistic means were demanded by the new tasks, by the new tendencies in the country?

Different solutions were found, and several distinct trends gradually took shape. One was characterised by a heightened interest in all that was until then taboo. The writers who adhered to this trend (let us call it a "critical trend" as a convenient term of reference) focussed their attention mainly on the contradictions and the negative aspects of Soviet life. They described scenes of mental cruelty, indifference, bureaucracy and violations of the law as if they wanted to say to the reader: "Look at this. It is all foreign to man whom we want to defend. It is contradictory to communism."

Writers adhering to the second trend (which we shall call "heroico-publicistic") on the other hand, gave prominence to the figures of Communists and workers.

Writers who followed the third, lyrico-romantic, trend sought living images through which they might unburden their hearts of their infatuation with life and their gladness that there were, after all, good people in the world whom they called "daylight stars". (*Daylight Stars* is the title of a book by the poetess Olga Bergolts). The element of the tragic, in which, alas, our life still abounded at the time, is present in the books of these writers as well. But the tragic is wrapped, as it were, in the happiness of the authors' knowledge that they are living in this world and participating in the great events of the age. As the nineteenth-century poet Tyutchev once said:

> *How fortunate the man who visited this world at fateful*
> *hour!*
> *The gods have summoned him to converse with them*
> *at their feast.*

Naturally, my division of the Soviet literature of that period into several trends is quite arbitrary. They cannot in fact be delineated exactly. Elements of all of them will be encountered in different works. Besides, all these distinctions, shades and trends are embraced by the general concept of socialist realism.

The new and even more widespread trend in literature was the general interest in moral problems. I do not simply mean the appearance of a whole series of books raising questions of ethics and conscience—as, for instance, Vladimir Tendryakov's story *Jugdment* which tells how the accidental killing of a man on a hunting trip aroused the conscience of all the people involved in it, or Pavlova's novel and play *Conscience*. There can hardly be a modern work of literature which does not touch in some way upon the subject of conscience—that control mechanism of human behaviour.

The liquidation of the consequences of the Stalin personality cult took a weight off the people's hearts. Alexander Tvardovsky wrote about this in his poem *Space Beyond Space*:

> *While on the subject, I have noticed*
> *Throughout the country, south and north,*
> *That men are growing kinder, less self-wronging,*
> *And smiles appear more often than before....*

It is thus quite natural that the new Party programme, adopted by the 22nd C.P.S.U. Congress in October 1961, should have devoted a special section to the moral code of people building communism. The code is based on principles of socialist humanism and mutual respect between people, and not simply on the idea of serving society. "Man is to man a friend, a comrade and a brother." These words make one ponder on the diametrically opposite thesis of private-property society, expressed in the well-known Latin saying and proclaimed in the 17th century by Thomas Hobbes: *"Homo homini lupus est."*

The idea of good as a creative force awakening in men a desire to work for the good of society, serving it honestly and conscientiously, are themes which have been embodied in hundreds of books published in the last few years.

In this connection I should like to mention *Meet Baluyev*, a novel by Vadim Kozhevnikov, a prominent figure in the Union of Soviet Writers, editor of the literary magazine *Znamya*, and author of several collections of short stories and an autobiographical novel. The hero of Kozhevnikov's last novel *Meet Baluyev* typifies a Soviet official and a Communist who directs the building of a gas pipe-line, an important construction project. He is not a young man, and his character as a person and an official was shaped in another time. It is obvious that an overweening, bureaucratic manner was common to him in the past. But he has become a different man. The new demands made on everyone, and communist leaders in the first place, after the 20th Party Congress, are expressed most accurately by Baluyev, when he says: "It's hard to be a man nowadays. So much is expected of one in the line of unwritten moral duties, apart from one's work and professional competence.... We have so overstated the norms of human behaviour that nowadays everyone demands the heights of virtue from his fellow men."

Baluyev tries to meet these new moral demands in his work. He takes a personal interest in the people working for him, and teaches the beautiful radio-telegraph operator to be more congenial and less self-conscious of her looks. " 'Smile at a man! Well, as a sign of friendship, or something. Let him like you and trust you.' And then he added angrily, in the tone of an order: 'Stop being afraid of yourself because you're beautiful. The sight of a beautiful thing makes men want to do something noble. He'll look at you, then at the seam (he is talking of welders here.—K.Z.), and he'll see the glaring discrepancy and want to do a more beautiful job.' "

True, Olga Dmitriyevna Terekhova, one of the characters in the book, says this to Baluyev: "You are kind not because you're like that, but because you believe it's most important and right to be kind just now."

A curious remark. Men like Baluyev were probably different in the past. But is it a bad thing that they have grown kinder? Baluyev's story, as told by Vadim Kozhevnikov, testifies to the all-embracing educational importance of the Leninist policy pursued by the Party.

How must we classify this novel if we regard it in its purely artistic aspect? The question is a valid one because every work of literature is judged not merely for its content but also for its form, not just for its philosophising or its descriptions but also for its emotional content, imagery, expressiveness, style and language. Nor must a novel be classed with publicistic writings, and it would be wrong to treat it as embodying stylistic aims alone. "The novel is omnipotent" as Boris Rurikov, editor of the literary magazine

Inostrannaya Literatura (Foreign Literature), said at the symposium of the European Writers' Association held in Leningrad in August 1963. The novel is capable of embracing the whole stream of life and it is free to use any of the aesthetic means evolved during the entire history of world literature.

I remember the meeting of Italian and Soviet writers held after the Rome congress in 1961. The Italian novelist Pasolini appraised the books of Soviet authors from Croce's angle of "stylistic criticism" as it is called. Roughly, he said the following: take Aksyonov who wrote *A Ticket to the Stars,* take Yevtushenko. Stylistically, Aksyonov's novel maintains a good-humoured tone throughout, a tone which too often verges on sentimentality. Yevtushenko's poetry is also profoundly sentimental in colouring. The basic tone of his poems is a vague discontent, and irrational criticism of some "inessential aspects of Soviet reality" as Pasolini puts it. But by means of stylistic operation—of very dubious quality, according to Pasolini—this irrational discontent turns into rationalism which, on the contrary, defends the kindness of Soviet society.

Pasolini arrives at the conclusion that on the whole Soviet writers are trying to overcome the difficulties of this period by leaping over—quite rightly, too—what for the West is the experience of decadence. But, by leaping over the experience of decadence, they land in the romanticism, pure and innocent, which really went before it. This romantic, blissful, good-natured, good-humoured and, at best, classically naïve and chaste atmosphere can no longer satisfy European readers.

This is the impression made on the Italian novelist by the more recent Soviet literature. I mention it here because this view is a very wide-spread one in the West. Pasolini was right about some of the faults common to Soviet literature, such as a certain tendency towards sentimentality. But his approach taken as a whole is wrong. For a start, as we have seen, there is no question of the impasse which allegedly Soviet literature came to at one time. There were shortcomings, to be sure, but never an impasse. Can Leonov's *The Russian Forest* or the second part of Sholokhov's *Virgin Soil Upturned* be called the products of an impasse? And then, why does a "classically naïve and chaste atmosphere" not satisfy the West-European reader?

This obviously speaks of an insufficient knowledge of Soviet literature and a lack of taste for those heroic and moral motifs which prevail in the books of Soviet authors.

The writers who adhere to the heroico-publicistic trend are not at all alike. All they have in common is their striving to express the main thing, that is the heroism which became part of the Russians' life after the October Revolution.

Take Boris Polevoi, for instance. He is, I think, one of the most consistently typical representatives of this trend. His is the selective principle. He chooses the most commendable examples from real life, trusting in their educational influence. In this sense, Boris Polevoi is a preacher of heroic conduct. You cannot criticise his characters on the grounds that "there aren't any such people". Boris Polevoi's plots are documentary, his stories are true. This being so, his characters are naturally bound hand and foot to the fact, to the documentary evidence. The method has its limitations, but then the "law of authenticity" comes into effect. The reader, in spite of himself, becomes spellbound by the beauty of heroism. Overwhelmed by the hero's deeds he is prepared to forgive or overlook the artistic weaknesses of such novels as Nikolai Ostrovsky's *How the Steel Was Tempered*. The hero of Polevoi's *The Story of a Real Man* is a flesh-and-blood person. His real name is Maresyev, changed in the book to Meresyev. During the Second World War his plane crashed on enemy territory. Wounded in both legs he crawled through the snow and managed to get across the front line. His legs had to be amputated. He had artificial limbs made for him, and by sheer effort of will and urged on by his impatience to go back and fight for his country, he learnt to use them amazingly well. And he did make a comeback. He was to fly again, and bring down more enemy planes. It is the living fire of his soul that Boris Polevoi communicated to his book *The Story of a Real Man*.

Dazzled by the victories of the Romans, Polybius wrote in his famous *Universal History* that it was enough for him to recount an event without the slightest bit of fabrication to arrest the attention of his readers. It is enough for some Soviet writers (Boris Polevoi, for one) to recount the events of the Revolution or the last war to captivate the reader with the example of its heroes.

This can be a successful method, but it is nevertheless a one-sided solution. Alexei Tolstoi voiced a passionate objection to it in one of his 1924 articles. He wrote: "So that's what it is! A modern novelist describes events, he collects material for his descendants. He has studied the styles excellently, he has jotted down some telling little words, taken an instance from real life and concocted a story. What for? So our grandchildren might know how we lived, talked and suffered. A splendid aim, I agree. But when our grandchildren come to read these chronicle stories they will not learn anything from them except particular facts, facts, facts; that and what words we, their grandfathers, used."

Alexei Tolstoi dreamed of creating literary types of the new man. He believed that every creative person should be alive to the grandeur of what was taking place, and then he would conceive the idea of a heroic novel. Let there be sweeping gestures, because life takes great swings and says piercing, cruel words. Cumbersome descriptions, prolixity and boring characterisations were nothing to be afraid of, he said. And indeed, features of epic monumentality are common in Soviet novels. The art of socialist realism is like a crystal reflecting a multitude of lights, of which heroism shines the brightest. It has an appealing, magnetic power. As the trend which I have called heroico-publicistic develops, we may still encounter books whose artistic merits will not quite satisfy us. We will go on complaining that their range of verbal colours is poor, that they lack Shakespearian characters and a feeling of grandeur equal to the epoch. But while placing these demands before ourselves we have no right to ignore those discoveries in Soviet literature which, for all the shortcomings that can be found in them, express the new features and feelings characteristic of Soviet life.

Take Vsevolod Kochetov, for example. Born in Novgorod in 1912, he started out in life as an agronomist at a state farm, and took up professional writing after the war. His novels *Under Native Skies* (1950), *Our Youth Is With Us* (1954) are in a sense a chronicle of the events of the last twenty years in this country. In the *Zhurbins* (1952), and *The Yershov Brothers* (1958) Kochetov portrays the people who make the bulwark and mainstay of Soviet power: skilled industrial workers. In *The Zhurbins* they are workers employed at a shipbuilding plant. The reader is taken into their homes. He is introduced to their way of life and their spiritual, political and cultural interests. The life of the industrial workers (especially in *The Yershov Brothers*) is shown in connection with (and sometimes in contrast to) the life of the white collar workers and the technologists. The author raises various topical problems of the theatre, the cinema and literature by making them the objects of debates between his characters.

Kochetov's latest novel *The Secretary of the Regional Party Committee* (1961) belongs to the moral-and-political genre. The author seems to be telling the reader: this is the way to think, and this is the way to act. The novel is unquestionably informative because it elucidates the alignment of the motive forces of Soviet society.

Pasolini says that he is not satisfied with literature which gives too straightforward an answer to the question: how must a man live in today's world. And we, for our part, are not satisfied with literature of the kind produced by the existentialists or the disciples of the French "new novel". The writers who adhere to these trends (Camus, Sarraute, Robbe-Grillet) are really competing with the tape-recorder in registering the movement of all the currents in the stream of consciousness. Art, after all, is not an electrocardiogram of the human soul.

People in the bourgeois countries may like or dislike the Soviet type of literature because its heroes are held up as models for emulation. But such heroes really do exist. Millions of Soviet people take the keenest interest in problems concerning the choice of a road in life, and this interest is naturally reflected by Soviet writers. Mayakovsky dealt with these problems too, and his advice to young men starting out in life was to model themselves on Felix Dzerzhinsky. In another poem dedicated to Comrade Nette, a diplomatic courier who was killed on the train near Riga in February 1926, heroically defending the diplomatic mail, Mayakovsky wrote:

> *I'd live on and on,*
> > *and let the years race,*
> *But I want at the end*
> > *—no other behests—*
> *My end on this earth I want to face*
> *Like Comrade Nette met his death.*

This was written 40 years ago. But to this day, in the nineteen-sixties, the question still remains unsolved for some whether to devote their lives to the "sheep pen"—meaning the petty joys and comforts of a Philistine existence—or to answer the call of history and join in the struggle for a new world.

Here is a novel, written in 1962, whose very title contains a socio-moral maxim: *The Roads We Choose.* The pronoun "we" is used in a broad meaning, and is pronounced on behalf of the whole post-war generation of Soviet intellectuals by the young engineer Arefyev and the other heroes of the novel ranging in age between 30 and 40. The author of the novel is Alexander Chakovsky (b. 1913), a board member of the Union of Soviet Writers, who was the first editor of the magazine *Inostrannaya Literatura* (Foreign Literature) and is now editor of *Literaturnaya Gazeta* (Literary Weekly).

The scene is set in the north of Russia where a railway tunnel is under construction. By a curious coincidence, one of the characters —the secretary of the Regional Party Committee—is called Baulin (which sounds a little like Baluyev from Vadim Kozhevnikov's novel), who also shows signs of mellowing and growing kinder to people. Arefyev notices that the manner of officials has changed— they have relaxed their sternness and no longer use their former peremptory tone. But in Arefyev himself this constraint, emotional rigidity and gloominess remain unrelieved. This young engineer, a Communist, has consciously chosen his difficult road in life. He lives in a bleak room with unadorned walls and furnished with nothing but a camp bed. Early every morning he puts on miner's overalls, tall rubber boots and a raincoat, and climbs down into the shaft, to work underground in the tunnel. The wet walls glimmer darkly in the glare of the solitary electric light bulb. And the tunnel itself, independently of the author's intention, grows into a symbol of the road into the radiant future. This road lies through darkness, dampness and stone, through the perplexities of workaday life. Arefyev is thinking: "What do the workmen care, give them machines and material, and the rest is not their headache. Let the bosses worry, they get paid for it."

The situation in the country has changed. But there will always be different people, of course. And they accept the change that has come into life in different ways too. In Baulin (like in Kozhevnikov's Baluyev) this change prompts him to take a personal interest in people. With Arefyev the construction project and fidelity to the ideological line come first. Perhaps this is why the novel breathes of rationalism, and the faces of the people in it seem to be covered with a film of graphite powder.

Daniil Granin's novel *Into the Storm* is about the life of physicists, one of the pet themes in West-European literature. Daniil Granin's book in a way belongs to this sort of literature, but it is difficult to "docket" him exactly. The heroic element is very strong in his novel, whose chief characters in their bold experimenting are prepared to brave the hazards of flying into a thundercloud to investigate the nature of its formation. But at the same time this novel, like Leonov's, has a philosophical aspect. The purely publicistic element (in the dialogues, for instance) is pushed into the background by the heroes' psychological characteristics. It is a realistic, intellectual novel, and in my opinion one of the achievements of Soviet literature. It might have been more impressive if the fabric of the novel had been linguistically richer and its whole pattern more strongly permeated with philosophical thought.

When it comes to criticism of the numerous books of the heroico-publicistic genre, like the novels of Kochetov, Chakovsky and others, I would say that what I personally miss in them is poetic charm. The positive heroes follow their straight road. The correctness of the road they have chosen is defended very well by Arefyev in his argument with a foreigner at a Moscow restaurant. But it is arrived at by common sense rather than feeling (when the heroic and lyrical elements are fused).

Let us now examine another trend in modern Soviet literature, the one we have termed lyrico-romantic. In the numerous novels of this type the problem of choosing one's road in life, moral problems, the eternal themes of love and death, are also raised. The publicistic element is present, but the rational is accompanied by the emotional. One senses a stronger infatuation with life, its pulse beats, its passions, its greatness and infiniteness reflected in a drop of dew at sunrise, in the stars and in the glimmer of people's eyes.

Young writers who emerged on the literary scene in the post-war years were especially keen on this lyrico-romantic style. There are so many examples that we cannot possibly even name them all (let alone examine them). It would mean mentioning at least a hundred authors who have one or two books of short stories or poems in print.

Vasily Aksyonov is one of the most sensational young prose writers and a strikingly gifted one. He began with a long-short story entitled *Colleagues* (1960). Here there are three young men starting out in life, this time after graduation from medical school. His idiom, his rhythmic patterns and emotional colours convey the freshness of the young men's sensations and attitudes to life. Two lines from Yesenin come to mind:

> *The first snow falls,*
> *I tramp upon it with my dragging feet,*
> *And strength like snowdrops bursts in flower in my heart.*

One of the three young doctors, Sasha Zelenin, a shy man who is helpless when faced with the trivial of everyday life but is brave and strong in spirit, says: "What about our generation? The question is: can we pass a test like that for courage and loyalty? We, city boys, who take everything in the world with a pinch of salt, who love jazz, sports, stylish rags, we who occasionally strike the most weird poses but never cheat, never worm our way into anyone's confidence, never toady, and, shying away from high-sounding words, try to keep our souls clean, are we capable of anything like that? Yes, we are."

In this, Aksyonov's first story, the lyrico-romantic element predominates (even though the author does overdo the naturalistic fidelity to the slang used by teddy boys). In his later works, *A Ticket to the Stars* (1961) and *Oranges from Morocco* (1963) his heroes grow out of their romantic dreaminess and moral idealism. They develop anarchic and bohemian moods (as a way of self-expression). The boys and girls become casually intimate. Their walk grows careless, and their conduct reckless. The meaning of lofty-sounding words is almost wholly dissipated. And the style itself shifts towards naturalism.

What happened? I shall give a more detailed answer to this question at the end of the chapter. It was as if a wind-borne infection had swept through a certain part of the literary youth, settling in dust on all that is lofty and romantic, and resulting in a game of defiance and indifference.

But still the lyrico-romantic trend is probably the most widespread in modern Soviet literature, uniting writers of different generations. Take *Summer Holiday Time* and *Young and Green* by Alexander Rekemchuk, a newcomer to literature. These stories also depict the modern scene–a construction project and an industrial enterprise somewhere far away from Moscow. There are enormous difficulties, and people, always people who do not know the meaning of self-interest, who live by the lofty poetry of Lenin's ideas. It has become natural to them. And that is why the heroine of *Summer Holiday Time* foregoes her holidays when the chief engineer goes away and stays behind to make sure that the rate of production does not drop and the pulse of the enterprise continues to beat as rhythmically as before.

In his story *A Drop of Dew* Vladimir Soloukhin paints a lyrical landscape of a small village in Central Russia. Olepino, as this village is called, is the author's birth-place, and to him it is a sort of magnifying glass of love through which he sees the world. "I love looking at my village with both an ordinary and an inner look, just as I love looking at the tiny, round drop of crystal water which has gathered in the green palm of a leaf in the midst of a huge, lush meadow, at the tiny sun, reflected in this drop, at the tiny surrounding objects and at tiny me reflected in the same drop."

What nourishes the lyrico-romantic strain in literature? The author's infatuation with life, his love for people, for his country, and the new in it, built in accordance with Lenin's plans. This lyrical mood may well coexist with criticism, satire, or a sense of bitterness engendered by the negative aspects of our life.

Many of the books written in this lyrico-romantic key have been very popular with Soviet readers. Among them, *Great Ore*, a novel by Georgy Vladimov, Vil Lipatov's long-short story *Mainstream*, Konstantin Paustovsky's autobiographical trilogy, Efim Dorosh's *Village Diary*, Vladimir Fomenko's *Memory of the Earth*, Sergei Antonov's novelettes, Vasily Smirnov's novel *Discovery of the World*, and Georgy Markov's two novels *Salt of the Earth* and *Father and Son*. All these books differ in subject matter and mood, but what they have in common is a lyrical approach to the working people.

The stylistic means used in the lyrico-romantic trend bring a subjective touch into the realistic portrayal of life. A stream of definitions (like in satire, except that there they mean the opposite) illustrates the author's attitude to the objects portrayed. The romantic element, just like the satirical, is rather one-sided. And so among the socialist realists we find writers of different generations who avoid using those stylistic means (publicist, romantic and any other) which immediately betray the author's position. There are writers who want to hide behind their heroes, who want life itself to speak for them, and the reader to draw his own conclusions. There are also writers inclined towards an objective style. Such, for instance, is Konstantin Simonov in his war novels.

This "cool" manner of a chronicler dispassionately recounting soul-scorching, tragic happenings lends his narrative a peculiar eloquence. A fine example is Simonov's *Days and Nights* (1942). It is an idiom which Lermontov, Stendhal and Prosper Mérimée charged with remarkable dramatic power. Simonov's *Comrades in Arms* (1957), *The Living and the Dead* (1960) and *Men Are Not Born Soldiers* (1964)—the last two especially—hark back to Tolstoi's *War and Peace*. With Fadeyev, for instance (in his novels about the Civil War—*The Rout* and *The Last of the Udeghes*) features of Tolstoi's style emerged in the course of his search for the right stylistic key in which to render the complexities and conflicts in the spiritual life of the fighters for Soviet power and communism. With Simonov it was quite different. He found himself best attuned to the great Russian writer where (as in *War and Peace*) he describes the course of human destinies in the general stream of millions of people who have risen in defence of their country.

Konstantin Simonov's novels make an enormous epic canvas depicting the Soviet people's great struggle against nazi Germany. The historical material is presented from different angles, from above and from below, as it were. Together with the heroes the reader visits all the fronts, from Murmansk to the Crimea, and from Moscow to Poland and Germany. The author's central observation post has been entrusted to Captain Sintsov, an "average" army officer. Sintsov—a Communist, a political officer in the army—goes through the same experience as the other soldiers and officers in their thousands and hundreds of thousands. He suffers all the hardships of those first months of defeat and retreat. Wounded, he falls into enemy encirclement, and when he regains consciousness he discovers that his Party card is gone. For this he is expelled from the Party. He has to surmount enormous difficulties and go through incredible moral tortures to rehabilitate himself. Gradually he grows into a hero in our eyes, even a judge, developing not simply as an individual but also as an observer of history. Tvardovsky's Vasily Terkin is a collective image of the people, or rather of the peasantry, in war. In Simonov's Sintsov we see the features of the new communist intelligentsia.

Simonov, if only because he is a poet, cannot restrict his writing to the "objective style", and many of the tragic and psychological episodes in his novels are coloured in lyrical tones.

Victor Nekrasov, who gained prominence in the post-war years, is probably the most consistent champion of literature "without bravura". Already in his first novel, *In the Trenches of Stalingrad* (1946)–the author was himself one of the defenders of that city–he made it clear that he believed in drawing his heroes from nature the way they are, without any bias. I do not think Nekrasov, any more than Stendhal, deserves blame for naturalism. In spite of what

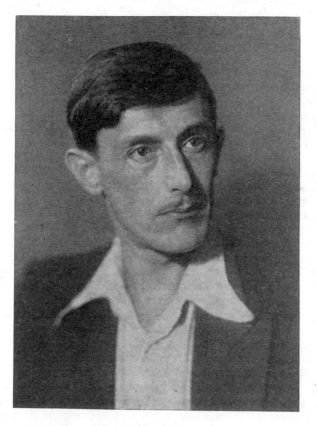

Victor Nekrasov. 1947.

Alexei Tolstoi said, extremely plastic characters (Julien Sorel, for instance) can also be created in the laconic manner of a chronicle. Nekrasov's consistent objectivism is of a different kind. It comes from the fear of falling prey to romantic exaggeration; hence his deliberate refusal to embellish his heroes or reality. He defended this position in one of his temperamentally written programme articles aimed against effusively hyperbolic and romantic techniques. The article met with protest from the critics, some of them countering Nekrasov's theory with the romanticism of Alexander Dovzhenko, the writer and outstanding film director. To Nekrasov the films produced by Dovzhenko (*Aerocity*, *Shchors*, *Tale of the Fiery Years* and others) are unacceptable because, he contends, this romanticised attitude to heroes produces an artificially formal, stilted impression.

Whereas Alexei Tolstoi in his article written more than forty years ago urged writers not to fight shy of grandeur because the epoch itself, the tremendous scale of events and the size of the characters was all full of grandeur, Victor Nekrasov preaches the exact opposite: beware of grandeur! His striving for complete, scientific objectivity, motivated by his aversion to varnish, pushes him willy-nilly to the other extreme. The cold and the dark begins to prevail over the warm and the light, although in real life the two continually clash and struggle.

In his last long-short story *Kira Georgiyevna*, Nekrasov begins the narrative with the return of this woman's first husband from prison camp where, an innocent man, he has done a term of many years, convicted on false charges. He was isolated from the world as a very young man, and in the meantime, Kira Georgiyevna has married an artist much older than herself. She also has a lover. All this is told in such a way that we find ourselves looking at everything with the eyes of the first husband who has suffered terribly and who, involuntarily, becomes the judge. This man from the "nether world" has preserved his moral purity, strictness of judgement and keenness of emotional perception, which have dulled so badly in the heyday of Stalin personality cult among the people surrounding Kira.

Vera Panova's works are also characterised by a lack of stress on heroism. The men and women workers in her novel *Kruzhilikha*, the doctors in *Fellow Travellers*, and the characters in her numerous stories perform no spectacular feats of heroism. It would be more correct to say that they make no claim to heroism, although in actual fact the things they do cannot fail to stir the reader. At the same time, her most typical stylistic feature is the presence of lyricism in all her writings. It is engendered by her affection for her fellow men, and her desire to surround them with kindness. Vera Panova's humaneness and lyricism are inseparable from her moral convictions.

She has a gift for drawing child characters as we know from her stories *Valya*, *Seryozha* and *Volodya*.

In the first story, set in wartime Leningrad, Valya's father is killed in battle and her mother is killed in an air raid. The little orphan finds a friend in Dusya, a factory worker, a lonely woman who becomes attached to Valya with all her heart and soul, the way Andrei Sokolov in Sholokhov's *The Fate of a Man* became attached to the homeless little boy he adopted.

Vera Panova's characters are guided in their actions by their natural moral impulses. And the fact that in her latest stories attention is focused on this aspect of Soviet life shows more convincingly, perhaps, than do any other examples the change in the moral attitudes of Soviet society.

Alexander Fadeyev always said that ours must be a "winged" literature, for such is Soviet reality itself with its ideas that stir the imagination and its ambitious plans for building up a new industry, a new culture, science, literature and art. Maxim Gorky once wrote that the old way of life was easier to portray, and that the unexampled new reality compelled Soviet writers to look for new expressive means, genres and styles, none of which the classics of the past had ever had to do.

But the magic spell of such great writers as Tolstoi, Dostoyevsky, Chekhov and Bunin, the aesthetic appeal of the masterpieces of West-European and American literature, old and modern, remains as strong as ever. And building a new pyramid from new stones when there are such edifices of human genius towering beside and behind it is not very easy to do. The temptation to simply assimilate what has already been achieved is there, of course. And after all talents differ. It is not given to all to blaze new trails, or venture out on an unchartered course. Mayakovsky once wrote:

> *Poetry–all of it,*
> *Is a ride into the unknown.*

In modern Soviet literature there are still writers who cling firmly to old traditions. In poetry, for instance, traditionalism is rather widespread. And indeed, when you come to think of it, there are certain limits to which one can go in attempting to change poetic form, to devise new rhythms, rhymes and intonations, because, after all, the real muse of poetry is thought. If a poem carries no thought, it becomes mere juggling with words. This applies to poetry in all languages. Mayakovsky's acute urge for innovation and his ardent temperament of a sculptor made him mould amazingly expressive rhythms, rhymes and neologisms. Only after an interval of thirty-odd years was another attempt made to change the verbal form of poetry. This was done by Andrei Voznesensky, a young poet whose talent was equal to his boldness. He undertook to remodel poetry according to the West-European pattern but, alas, he got carried away and was unable to avoid formalistic acrobatics.

Traditionalism in form is no great calamity. After all, the traditions of Pushkin and Nekrasov, assimilated so well by Tvardovsky, helped him rather than hindered him to express his truly revolutionary message and to speak in a language of humanism and love for the working people. It is too bad, however, when a writer who lives in the "midst of the revolutionary doings" (to quote Mayakovsky) fails to perceive these "doings" aesthetically and dwells in a world of past impressions. Books written in this key are usually translated with alacrity in Western Europe for the very reason that they bring back memories of something familiar. But it is the new, unfamiliar features that readers should look for in literature if they want to know and understand modern Russia.

Novels written in a critical vein, especially if they deal with formerly forbidden subjects, arouse a heightened interest in the West. Even if such a book has little artistic merit, anti-communist propaganda will build it up into a sensation, as was done with Pasternak's *Doctor Zhivago* and with Alexander Solzhenitsin's *Cancer Ward* and *Round One*. These three books are frankly directed against Soviet power and this being so were naturally not published in the U.S.S.R. But the enemies of Soviet power clutched at them and printed them abroad. In such cases there is no room for serious, aesthetic appraisal. Only political aims are pursued and the book is used as a means of denigrating communism and the Soviet system. Socialist realism is treated as a state-sponsored method of producing laudatory works of a sterile uniformity.

But there is no uniformity about the best Soviet novels. Furmanov's *Chapayev* (1923), Serafimovich's *The Iron Flood* (1924) and Fadeyev's *The Rout* (1927) which can be called the classics of socialist realism, have all stood the test of time precisely because they showed life and revolutionary struggle in all their contradictions. In "form", in outward appearance, the Red partisans are not attractive, but in content, in the purpose of their activity, they are much superior to Mechik, the immaculate intellectual. In his speech addressed to the First Congress of Soviet Writers in 1934, Fadeyev, it will be remembered, laid particular stress on the importance of the critical element in socialist realism.

Practices connected with the personality cult were criticised with particular sharpness by Yevgeny Yevtushenko, Yaroslav Smelyakov, Boris Slutsky, Vladimir Lugovskoi and a number of other poets.

Alexander Tvardovsky's *Space Beyond Space* (1950-1960) was the most serious attempt at a comprehensive and historically truthful assessment of the foregoing period. This poem reflects the life impressions of the poet—his childhood, his travels, his recollections of the Urals and Siberia. There are discourses on literature, and pictures of the people's endeavour in constructing the Siberian electric power stations, and in damming the Angara near Bratsk.

In the chapter entitled "Childhood Friend" the poet describes his meeting with this man who has just been released from prison camp. Walking about without a guard still feels strange to him, but he is free. Anguish grips the poet's heart, and he says:

> *He was a bit of my own soul,*
> *A pain and grief that was taboo.*
> *Between us to erect a wall*
> *The years were powerless to do. . . .*

His childhood friend has remained loyal to his country, so:

> *Whom shall I blame for my mute grief?*
> *The country? No.*
> *The country can't be blamed.*

and further on:

> *Or shall I blame it on the cruel people?*
> *The people?*
> *What had they to do with it?*

As the poem develops, flowing in admiration for the heroic deeds of the people (sketches of people encountered on the way follow one another), ironic remarks aimed at the critics are inserted into the fabric, then lyrical notes begin to prevail again, and finally, towards the end Stalin enters the scene. The chapter is called: "That's How It Was". The poet draws a life-size portrait of Stalin and ponders on his role in the life of the Soviet people during the last ten years before he died.

Andrei Platonov (1899-1951)—a trained engineer whose father was a locomotive driver, began to publish his stories at the end of the nineteen-twenties (the first collection was entitled *Origin of a Master*) and became especially well-known in the nineteen-thirties and in the war years. His popularity and fame grew, and young writers today have a great regard for him and learn whole pages by heart. Many of his stories have been translated into English and other foreign languages. Ernest Hemingway once said that Andrei Platonov had made an enormous impression on him, and that he had learnt a great deal from him. Although Platonov is one of those writers who followed the critical trend, he did not dwell on the darker sides of Soviet life for their own sake, but on human pain. Chekhov wrote about one of his heroes that he was exceptionally sensitive to pain "in general", and since Sergei Yesenin there has been no writer as generously endowed with this quality as Andrei Platonov. The anguish he feels for man, inhibited by all the circumstances of his existence, grows into a powerful symphony performed by thousands of instruments and voices. He has an inexhaustible resourcefulness in inventing situations in which grief and suffering merge with the sky, with youth and even with the sun itself. His style is an amazing combination of lyricism, satirical grotesquerie and intellectualism. By his very choice of words, his epithets and constructions he compels the reader to reconsider his old notions of every object and action. He compels the reader to think. He uses all the expressive means he knows and the power of his talent to put his reader in a state where the pain reflex keeps him remembering man. Maybe this was why Hemingway thought so much of Platonov. After all, Hemingway's heroes have a façade of manliness, behind which lurks disappointment in life, and even despair, because the net result is death.

In recent years, an especially rapid progress has been made in the literature of the non-Russian republics and the national areas. I cannot even name all the new writers and their books, which I am sure would fill a whole volume. A great many of these writers have earned renown in the East and the West. In the last twenty years more than 25,000 books by Soviet authors were published abroad in more than fifty foreign languages. In most countries people are able to read Soviet literature in their own language. In India, for instance, Soviet books are published not just in such more widespread languages as Hindi, Urdu and Bengali, but also in Kannada, Gujarati, Malayalam, Panjabi, Marathi, and Telugu. Sholokhov's *The Fate of a Man* came out in Oriya and Singhalese.

Abai (Abai Kunanbayev, 1845-1904, the founder of Kazakh literature), a two-volume novel by Mukhtar Auezov, a Kazakh writer, has been published in France and elsewhere. One cannot imagine anyone in a capitalist country writing of his recent, nomadic past in a manner that answers the standards of a European novel. Mukhtar Auezov gave modern readers a close-up of that life with the nomads' greatly involved relationships and psychology.

The years following the war witnessed the development of national literatures and also the emergence of many gifted Russian Siberian writers. In Soviet literature, Siberia had already been represented by such talented writers as Lydia Seifulina, author of the widely known play *Virineya*, and Vsevolod Ivanov, author of an equally popular play *Armoured Train 14-69* (both plays are about the Civil War) and a number of short stories. Since the war, and especially in the last ten or fifteen years, a large number of Siberian writers have entered the literary scene. Most of them are not very young people with a store of experience in different fields, and most of them begun writing rather late in life. Such is Konstantin Sedykh, author of *Dauria*, a novel about the Civil War; such is Georgi Markov, the author of *Salt of the Earth* and *Father and Son*; such is Sergei Sartakov, the author of the novel *Don't Sacrifice the Queen* and Frants Taurin. The novel by Frants Taurin which appeared in the 1950s was called *Towards a Common Goal* and told about people who in transforming nature became transformed themselves. The author worked for a number of years at industrial plants in the Urals, after that he worked for more than ten years in Yakutsk, and then in Irkutsk, and is naturally perfectly familiar with the life of industrial workers, to whom he has dedicated his trilogy *In Irkutsk Country* (1964).

Sergei Zalygin, a Novosibirsk agronomist, is a writer of talent with an idiom and narrational manner entirely his own. He, too, is over 50, and he, too, first took up the pen ten or maybe fifteen years ago. In his story *On the Irtysh* he describes the collectivisation of farming in Siberia. In *Virgin Soil Upturned* Sholokhov described the collectivisation of farming in the Don country from the point of view of Davydov, an industrial worker who had come to help achieve it; and in Zalygin's book the spokesman is Stepan Chauzov, a middle peasant. In this sense, *On the Irtysh* complements *Virgin Soil Upturned*.

Solyonaya Pad (1967-1968), Zalygin's major work, is based on historical material and tells how a partisan republic became formed in Kolchak's rear, in Siberia, in the years of Civil War. A remote little village was the centre of this Soviet peasant republic. Zalygin draws an impressive portrait of Yefim Meshcheryakov, a man of peasant stock who is devoted to his family, a strong character who is an indomitable commander in the revolutionary struggle.

The appearance of new books usually started debates and discussions in the literary press of the Ukraine, Minsk, Tbilisi, Yerevan, Baku, Novosibirsk, Alma Ata, and finally in Leningrad and Moscow.

An interesting discussion on tradition and innovation in modern literature was started in the magazine *Voprosy Literatury* (Problems of Literature) in November 1961, and went on for eighteen months. Thirty-two young writers took part in this discussion. Their declared literary "policies", however, must not be confused with their actual writings. It is curious that in their statements many of them showed a desire—a not very serious one for our times, and the more so for Soviet literature—to shock by using startling phrases and naming ill-assorted, mutually exclusive sets of writers as their teachers.

Andrei Voznesensky, speaking of assimilating the experience of predecessors and of past literary trends in general, said: "I doubt that closeness to his literary predecessors is good for a writer. . . . Incest results in degeneration. I learnt less from Byron than I did from Andrei Rublev, Jean Miro and the later de Carbusier." This, to say the least, is hardly serious. Another young prose writer named Dostoyevsky, Chekhov, Hemingway, Remarque and Bülle as his predecessors. Some called Boris Pasternak their principal teacher. Seeing that Pasternak had just been condemned for his *Doctor Zhivago*, this statement was probably made more from a spirit of defiance and opposition than from genuine regard for the poet's talent. One of these young prose writers when asked what he thought of form and style replied: "The most promising in the search for new forms, as I see it, is the search itself." The majority of the writers, of course, gave due credit to the truly revolutionary traditions of Soviet literature and the contribution it has made to world culture.

Ilya Ehrenburg wrote in his memoirs *People, Years, Life* that he would like to speak in defence of the remote past (the nineteen-twenties) when there were so many literary schools: imagism, Prolet-kults (Proletarian Culture), expressionism, subjectless art, and even the "nichevoki" trend (the nothing-nothing art). But this would mean recognising the coexistence of socialist realism and formalism.

The incompatibility of two different ideologies, the socialist and the bourgeois, and the impossibility of their peaceful coexistence is of decisive importance not only in our literary policy but in all the relations between the two camps.

The campaign against ideological distortions and, in particular, against certain departures from the method of socialist realism was concluded at the June 1963 Plenary Meeting of the Central Committee of the Communist Party of the Soviet Union, specially convened to discuss ideological problems. Speaking at this meeting, Konstantin Fedin, First Secretary of the Union of Soviet Writers (who was invited although he is not a Party member), admirably expressed the thoughts and feelings of all Soviet writers, whether members of the Party or not. He said: "The positions from which modern Western critics attack Soviet art—whether it is our views on the role of literary tradition, our themes, problems of form, and sometimes just idiom—are for the most part built on formalistic foundations. But whatever aspects of our art are discussed, nothing irritates and annoys the critics so much as the closeness of the Soviet writers to the Communist Party. The very thought that the Party might directly influence literature is considered inadmissible. By proclaiming indifference to politics as the artist's ideal, these Western critics apparently find their objections to the Party spirit in Soviet literature a good example of indifference to politics!

"This provides a free opportunity for cunning, but a misunder-standing might also occur.

"For instance, that recent case of proclaiming 'Soviet avantgardism' which created a sensation in the West, can be attributed to nothing else but cunning. The myth was exploded as too obvious a bait for popularity, but unfortunately two or three of our young poets fell for it. But myths are created and destroyed. Avantgardism remains in historical development of the West. And Soviet literature remains its own self."

Yes, Soviet literature remains its own self with its diversity of idioms and styles, with its humanism, and its discovery of a new world. In December 1920, with the approval of Vladimir Ilyich Lenin the Central Committee published a letter on the Proletkults. The letter, I remember, said that the Central Committee had no intention whatsoever of restricting the activity of the working intelligentsia in the field of artistic endeavour. On the contrary, the Central Committee wished to create healthier conditions for work.

The same aim was pursued by the above-mentioned 1963 Plenary Meeting of the Central Committee, and by the Party's criticism of certain faults and distortions in matters concerning aesthetics, literature and art.

Soviet literature remains its own self, and it draws its strength from those achievements of socialist realism which like Sholokhov's *And Quiet Flows the Don* and poetry of Mayakovsky and Yesenin, are undeniably a valuable contribution to the treasure house of world literature.

Chapter 22

Problems of National Literatures
The Literary Map
of the U.S.S.R.

The globe looks different to us today from what it did fifty years ago. Radio and modern aviation have brought the different parts of the world closer together somehow. The word "mankind" has acquired a peculiarly weighty, tangible meaning in this age of the atom and communism. Countries and peoples have become inter-communicating vessels, as it were. The days of regional self-consciousness are over. The time has come for global self-awareness.

In 1961, in the course of a conversation I had with an Australian author we came round to the subject of the staggering contrasts that characterise the world of today.

He gave me an illustrated booklet in which the life of the Australian aborigines is shown as it must have been thousands of years ago. Native tribes, he told me, live on a primitive level of development in their desert reservations. And nobody cares.

I told him about the book I had just read by Nicholas Guppy, a botanist and explorer, who managed to make his way into the unexplored jungles of British Guiana and Brazil along the Amazon. In this book *Wai-Wai* (the name of an Indian tribe) which was published in London in 1958, the facts adduced speak for themselves. The author, who is no Communist, writes that the methods of introducing the natives to modern civilisation are absolutely outrageous. Guppy, it must be said, has met Indians who had never seen a white man before. He was especially disgusted with the missionaries who garnish their trade in baubles and beads with the propaganda of Christianity. They intimidate the Indians with the notion of sin, instill in them a contempt for their native customs, and do everything to obliterate their national identity and belittle the proud sense of dignity which is so common to them.

Thousands of examples can be cited to prove that the colonialists in Africa, Asia and Latin America cared little for the interests of the peoples they ruled. Jawaharlal Nehru wrote in his *Autobiography*: "The British conception of ruling India was the police conception of the State. . . . The economic needs of the citizens were not looked after, and were sacrificed to British interests. The cultural and other needs of the people, except for a tiny handful, were entirely neglected."

Marx in his time had written about British rule in India with ruthless directness. It left the country's masses as illiterate as ever. Development of the national cultures of the numerous peoples and tribes inhabiting the earth is one of the most acute and urgent problems of our time. The urgency is caused by the mounting revolutionary protest against colonialism. The oppressed peoples and tribes refuse to live any longer in slavery, poverty and humiliation, to die out from epidemics and insupportable labour conditions, serving a "race of masters"–owners of the monopoly capital. People want to live like human beings whether they dwell in the jungles of Africa and Latin America, or in the deserts of Australia. All people throughout the world want to breathe the air of freedom, to benefit from the achievements of science and engineering, to send their children to school, to enjoy works of art and themselves write poems and stories in their native tongue. The colonial peoples will no longer stand for the looting of the land of their fathers, they refuse to be kept in ignorance and destitution any further.

The whip and the hunting gun are not the only weapons of the slaveowners today. They have all the most sophisticated means of mass killing at their disposal, but for all that the examples of the Congo, Angola, Algeria and other countries show that the ground is burning beneath their feet. The example of Cuba proves that a revolutionary people, inspired by the idea of national freedom, the idea of socialism and the prospect of creating their own national culture, can break free of the spider's web of imperialist exploitation.

The words "Moscow", "Lenin", and "Soviet Union" shine against the background of these events from thousands of miles away, through the haze of storms and sufferings. All the peoples inhabiting the U.S.S.R. are building up their national culture and literature. Kumar Goshal, the Indian writer, said in his book *People in the Colonies* (published in New York in 1948) that the leaders of colonial peoples were greatly impressed by the rapid economic and cultural development of Kazakhstan and the other Central Asian republics. This example, he went on to say, demonstrated to the still backward peoples with neither a written language nor a literature of their own that astonishing results could be achieved in a short, historically speaking, space of time.

Roughly two thousand five hundred languages are spoken in the world today. But a good half of the nations and tribes peopling the earth have no written language and, consequently, no means of recording their oral art.

The question arises: what course will world literature take if it develops in two and a half thousand languages? Will the number decrease or increase? Will the writers of the future address just their own "family circle"? This "family circle" will perhaps include tens of millions of people, but it will anyway remain a "family circle", a particle of mankind. The radio and modern aviation have removed the once insurmountable barrier of distance. People today have a different awareness of distance and of mankind in general. And so we naturally see literature against the background of and in connection with the growing contacts between the peoples of the world.

I believe that we shall find the answers to many of the questions the linguistic atlas and modern history pose before us in those processes of cultural development which took place in Russia after the Socialist Revolution of October 1917.

The development of national literatures in the U.S.S.R. was envisaged by and resulted from the nationalities policy adopted by the Government.

The national liberation movement will continue to give rise to hundreds of new national cultures and literatures. In the case of some peoples it will mean creating a written language to begin with, and the evolvement of a literary idiom. For most of the colonial peoples the process of shaping a national literature is complicated by the accumulated deposits of the colonialists', or the conqueror-nation's language and culture.

There are two ways of developing the world's national literatures. Nationalistic isolation is one way. In conditions of capitalism it is the inevitable way. The alternative is to develop the national identity and at the same time strive to overcome the language barrier by cultivating a community of human interests and an ideological closeness between the peoples. Such is the socialist way. And such has been the Soviet experience. From the example of the Soviet Union's multinational literature it is possible to picture the ways by which the world's incredible linguistic divergency is going to be overcome. Socialism ensures the efflorescence of national forms, their rapprochement and interaction. The new C.P.S.U. Programme contains the following: "The big scale of communist construction and the new victories of communist ideology are enriching the cultures of the peoples of the U.S.S.R., which are socialist in content and national in form. There is a growing ideological unity among the nations and nationalities and a greater rapprochement of their cultures. The historical experience of socialist nations shows that national forms do not ossify; they change, advance and draw closer together, shedding all outdated traits that contradict the new conditions of life. An international culture common to all the

Soviet nations is developing. The cultural treasures of each nation are increasingly augmented by works acquiring an international character."

National form (in the first place, language) is an historical development, an historical category. It is one of the manifestations of a people's historical community of interests resulting from generations of the same group of people living a communal life. National identity means the people's individuality, their personal "self".

In this epoch when dozens of nations are emerging on the historical scene in order to assert their identity, the method of socialist realism appears to suit the new literatures best. And indeed, is there a better way of declaring one's national "self" than this truthful artistic method in which the powers of the peoples fighting for the development and strengthening of socialism are fully revealed?

Pushkin brought into Russian literature the awareness of the fact that Russia is a multinational country. "And they will say of me in all the languages spoken here..." he wrote. And yet, a hundred years ago Taras Shevchenko said in his poem *The Caucasus* that in tsarist Russia: "From the Moldavian to the Finn, all silent are in all their tongues."

This country's literary map has changed beyond recognition. The once silent people have all "found their tongue"–those who had no written language of their own before the Revolution (there are over forty such nationalities in the Soviet Union), and those who had been literate since ancient times–like the peoples of Trans-Caucasia.

There were no blank spots any more on the literary map because all the nations, even the smallest tribes and national groups, took part in building up the new socialist economy and culture. There was no discrimination, they were all equals. The peoples living in what used to be called the fringelands of the Russian empire and who were retarded in their development because of the tsarist policy of oppression, received unlimited moral, material and political assistance from the Soviet Government in conformity with the nationalities policy proclaimed by Lenin. The implementation of this policy resulted in an amazingly rapid development of the formerly downtrodden peoples. A creative intelligentsia of their own emerged, gaining maturity in the post-war years. Books began to be published in the national languages, and since illiteracy has been eliminated in the Soviet Union and a compulsory eight-year education introduced, writers from all tribes and nations soon found their readers.

A bibliography of non-Russian books translated into Russian in the course of only twenty years (1934-1954) fills a volume of 750 pages.

However, the location of these literatures and the direction in which they develop is more illustrative than mere facts and figures.

All the fifty non-Russian literatures of the Soviet Union originated in different historical conditions and were rooted in different national traditions. A young writer faced with the task of rendering in words the new meaning of life and his own feelings, inspired by the revolutionary events, would naturally turn to the experience of his national literature for support. Even if it was only oral folk art he would anyway use it as a basis. Poetry was the prevalent genre almost everywhere—in Siberia, Central Asia and the Northern Caucasus.

I have an especially warm regard for those writers who responded so enthusiastically to the launching of the five-year plans from the remoteness of the Siberian and Far Eastern taiga and tundra. One of these writers is Djansi Kimonko, an Udeghe, the author of the charmingly poetic stories *Glow Over the Forest* and *Where the Sukpai Flows*. The Udeghes are a small hunting tribe who live in the Sikhote-Alin Mountains in the Soviet Far East. After finishing school in Khabarovsk, Kimonko was educated at the Institute for Northern Peoples in Leningrad. He came home after graduation and was elected chairman of the village Soviet and then chairman of a hunters' collective farm. He was killed on a hunting trip.

Or take Yuvan Shestalov, a young Mansi poet who has already published three books of verse. The Mansis (of whom there are less than seven thousand) live beyond the Urals in north-western Siberia in Khanti-Mansi National Area which covers a territory larger than, say, Finland. The Mansis and the Khantis have preserved their beautifully poetic folk traditions, but they remained illiterate and unknown until after the Revolution. Today, Yuvan Shestalov, moved by his sense of personal involvement in the world's revolutionary events, addresses the peoples of Africa: "Arise, arise, and take Lumumba's thorny path!"

Yuvan Shestalov's poetry combines the picturesqueness and lyricism of national Mansi oral art with the intelligence and breadth of vision of an educated Soviet person.

> *Where the lichen grows, and dwarf pines*
> *Hide their roots among the shadows*
> *Old wives' tales and superstitions*
> *Called us savages and wild men.*
> *Oh you, lying superstitions,*
> *Don't spread tales about my people!*
> *Would I sing this song of glory*
> *With the forest winds in chorus,*
> *Could I have become a poet*
> *If I'd grown up with the wild men?*

Akim Samar, a Nanai, is another example. He lived by hunting and fishing and wrote poetry. When the war broke out he volunteered for the front and died a hero's death in the battle for Stalingrad. His poetry was published posthumously. The Nanais are a small national group who live on the banks of forest rivers in the Far East. In translation the word Nanai means "man". This reminds me of a poem by Yanka Kupala, a Byelorussian poet, which Gorky liked very much and called a "Byelorussian hymn". I only know a few lines by heart, but I remember it said that the dream of a Byelorussian was "to be called Man".

These words were written in tsarist Russia, before the Revolution, but they are acquiring a new meaning today for those hundreds of peoples who are freeing themselves from colonial dependence. And it is not surprising, therefore, that the 2,500,000 copies of *The End of a Big House*, a novel by Grigori Khodzher, a Nanai, were sold out at once.

The destinies of the small national groups and tribes are proof of the correctness of the principles and creative character of our nationalities policy. No unbiassed person will deny the fact that this policy, proposed by Lenin, has fully justified itself. It is undisputed even by people who are far from being Communists.

Let us take Daghestan, a small republic in the Caucasus. The population numbers hardly more than a million, but they speak in more than thirty languages. There are villages where several different dialects are spoken. Daghestan is probably the most multinational spot on earth. I am not going to examine in detail the reasons for this here. What happened, apparently, was that the small tribes which settled along the shores of the Caspian Sea were compelled to go into hiding in the folds of the mountains so as not to be enslaved by the stronger peoples during their migrations, and as a result these small tribes perforce became isolated. They raised sheep and tilled the land, exerting themselves to cultivate tiny patches of arable land on mountain ledges. Many of these tribes were skilled in various crafts—especially silver chasing. Their work is displayed in some West-European museums, in London, for example. Especially famous for its silver chasing is Kubachi, a village perched like an eagle's nest on the top of a mountain. Kubachi has its own language in which it now publishes a local newspaper.

Daghestan is a veritable Babel. School instruction is in seven languages, among them Avar, Lezghin, Kumyk and Dargwa. Daghestan poets, in their Russian translations, have earned renown in the Soviet Union and in countries abroad as well. The best-known poets writing in Avar (the largest Daghestan national group of more than 200,000 people) are Gamzat Tsadasa and his son Rasul

Gamzatov. The pride of the Lezghins is Suleiman Stalsky, a folk bard or *ashug*, whom Gorky called the Homer of the 20th century.

It is a most curious fact that in this age of radio and printing plants the tradition of oral folk poetry has been revived. Some strikingly picturesque figures have emerged from the midst of those travelling folk bards who sang their ballads to the accompaniment of the simplest of string instruments like the Kazakh *dombra* or the Uzbek and Tajik *dutara*. One was the Kazakh *akyn* Djambul, known for the ballads he sang about Soviet achievements and for his denunciation of the feudal customs of the past.

Prose writing, however, especially the novel, is justly regarded as the most important form in the progressive evolution of literary genres. In the Soviet Union the modern socio-psychological novel is not the exclusive province of Russians, Ukrainians, Armenians, Georgians, Azerbaijanians, Latvians and Estonians, with whom the genre has long been developed. The names of the Latvian writers Vilis Lacis and Andrej Upit, the Estonians Rudolf Sirge and Aadu Hint, the Georgians Leo Kiacheli and Konstantin Gamsakhurdia, the Armenians Derenik Demirchyan and Stepan Zoryan, and Aksel Bakunts are sufficiently well known. The genre developed very quickly with the peoples of Central Asia where it was completely unknown before the Revolution. Prose writing appeared in Buryatia and Tuva, the latter only having acquired a written language of its own in the early nineteen-thirties.

The rapid development of prose among the once backward peoples can best be judged from the work of Chinghis Aitmatov, a Kirghiz writer. His *Jamila* has aroused interest both in the Soviet Union and abroad. It is a subtly psychological story of love written by an author who has complete command of all the modern literary means. Yet the Kirghizes had no written language of their own before the Revolution (if we discount the Arabic script in which the Turkic languages used to be written, which was totally unsuited for rendering the Kirghiz sound system, and which anyway was never a truly national medium, the little instruction there was being largely Moslem religious instruction). This totally illiterate small nation (numbering about a million people) led a nomadic existence, driving their herds from one mountain pasture to another, and maintaining vestiges of the tribal system in their way of life until well into the nineteen-twenties.

Colonial oppression was so hard under tsarism that many tribes and peoples (the Gilyaks, the Lamuts, the Udeghes, the Chukchees, and others) were brought to the verge of physical, let alone, cultural extinction. Scores of peoples led a patriarchal, nomadic way of life and their cultural level was so low that the thought of creating a written literature would never have occurred to anyone. In tsarist

Russia the persecution of national creativity and the ruthless bureaucratic Russification spared none of the peoples living in this "prison of peoples" whether illiterate or highly developed with millennial cultural traditions like the Georgians, Azerbaijanians and Armenians. Once their fetters were smashed they hastened to make up for lost time, fervently developing their literature and culture, setting up printing houses, libraries and theatres, re-discovering masterpieces of classical national art, creating their own dramaturgy and music, gaining in momentum with every year and continually increasing the social significance of what they were doing.

The themes prevailing in the national literatures and the manner in which these literatures developed will be easier to appreciate if one bears in mind that they were re-born and blossomed out for the second time after long years of silence and repression.

Hassem Lahuti, an Iranian revolutionary who became a Tajik poet, said at the Paris congress in defence of culture in 1935 that: "It is a legend, of course, a myth that people had been brought back to life by Mohammed and Christ. But parables were composed about them, they were talked about, and poets wrote verses about them. There are peoples who have been brought back to life by the October Revolution. It is a fact, reality. But no one talked about them. Even their names could not be found in the dictionaries. They lived in the steppes and the tundra, in the mountains and valleys, all those unknown and forgotten, small and large, nomadic and settled peoples like the Turkmenians, Karelians, Tajiks, Nenets, Uigurs, and Kara-Kalpaks."

Hundreds of examples illustrating this genuine revolution in the development of national cultures could be adduced. In the libraries of Kazan, the capital of Tataria, no more than a hundred books in Tatar were indexed in the course of fifty years, from 1845 to 1917. As many as 145 works of fiction were published in 1934 alone, and 2,057 books with a total printing of 24,000,000 copies came out in 1961. Even the works of Galimjan Ibragimov (the story *The Cossack's Daughter* and the novel *Our Days*), a prominent Tatar writer who was by no means a revolutionary and whose books were imbued with nationalistic motifs rather than any other, even his works were banned by the tsarist censorship and did not come out until after the Revolution. It was the same with other old writers, for instance the Bashkir author, Gafuri.

M. Djavakhshvili, a Georgian author, in an article on Georgian Soviet literature published in *Literaturnaya Gazeta* (No. 1) in 1937, wrote: "The scale on which our culture is developing may be judged from this one fact, if nothing else, that many times more Georgian books have been printed in the last fifteen years than in the preceding three hundred years of the Georgian people's history. There was hardly a professional writer among us before the Revolution. Writers lived on the salary they earned in some office or on a private income. . . . The Revolution has built up large cadres of professional writers, and literary output has increased many times over. . . . Our poets have reformed the technique of poetry writing, and our prose writers have achieved a florescence of the Georgian novel which was on the decline before the Revolution."

The same may be said of Armenian literature. Avetik Isaakian, the greatest Armenian lyric poet of the late 19th and early 20th centuries, gained new eminence in Soviet Armenia where he was awarded the title of People's Poet. He is indeed the favourite poet of the Armenians. His poems, translated into Russian by our best poets, have been included in Russian school readers.

The process of collecting Armenian, Georgian and other literatures followed the same course: the growth of the new generation of writers went hand in hand with the assimilation of the classical heritage which had been suppressed and belittled before. Sundukyan, Proshyan and Nabaldyan of Armenia, the Georgians Ilya Chavchavadze, Akaky Tsereteli, Nikoloz Baratashvili, Vazha Pshavela and Shota Rustaveli, the famous author of the magnificent epic poem *The Knight in the Tiger Skin*, the Ukrainians Ivan Franko, Lesya Ukrainka and Mikhail Kotsubinsky, and scores of other excellent writers of the past have regained their rightful positions in their respective national literatures and in Soviet literature as a whole.

When speaking of this cultural advance of Soviet nationalities one is tempted to quote Hafiz: "The child is only a day old but it has already traversed a road that would take another a hundred years to cover."

All these circumstances make the picture of literary development in the U.S.S.R. appear extremely involved and varied. The Soviet Union's national literatures may be divided into three groups. In the first we shall put those whose forms and traditions developed more or less similarly to Russian literature. These are Ukrainian, Byelorussian, Georgian, Armenian, Azerbaijan, Latvian, Estonian, Lithuanian, Tatar and Jewish literatures. They follow the general-European pattern in which the prose novel has become the predominant form of epic writing. They have their traditions, their pre-revolutionary intellectual background, and so on. The character of their development, the formation of groupings and their social struggle have much in common with what has been happening in Russian literature during the last twenty years, with certain national peculiarities and deviations, of course. They show a preference for prose and dramaturgy.

In the second group we shall put literature of a mixed or a marginal type with a prevalence of poetry and subjective forms. Here, prose originated only in the last few decades, and the influence of oral folk poetry and folklore is still very strong. These are the literatures of peoples who were least affected by urban capitalist culture, and consequently had not developed. In this group we may include the following: Turkmen, Uzbek, Tajik, Kazakh (in part), Kirghiz, Chuvash, Kara-Kalpak, Mari, Komi, Karelian, Buryato-Mongolian, Yakut, the majority of literatures of Daghestan, including Avar, Lak, Lezghin, and others. All of them developed as literatures, in our understanding of the term, mainly in Soviet times.

The third and last group comprises the literatures of the recently nomadic tribes and peoples, the vast majority of which had no written language before, and so by "literatures" we really mean oral art in most cases. Whereas the *ashug* or *akyn* was a figure who enjoyed equal rights with the authors in the literary development of peoples we have placed in the second, and even the first group, in the case of such tribes as the Nenets, Gulyaks, Ossetes, Gypsies and others, oral art (intertwined with ancient songs, tales, legends and so forth) was just a form of artistic expression. But with these tribes too, thanks to the establishment of a written language and the rapid development of the system of public education after the Revolution, we observe an astonishingly quick emergence of all the European forms of literature. Suffice it to recall the world's first Ossetian novel.

Our division of literatures into three groups, for the sake of convenience, is rather arbitrary. The affirmation of the new "positive" hero, a realistically truthful representation of life in all its contradictions, and the struggle against any distortions of the artistic truth with the help of historical analogies or by resorting to naturalistic or formalistic means—this makes the content of all Soviet literatures. The main characteristic of Soviet literature as a whole is that it is multinational in form, socialist in content and follows the method of socialist realism.

Let us examine this subject from another angle, by trying to define those common features which emerged as a result of the development of national literatures in their native languages. On the one hand, Soviet literature is multilingual, and on the other the language barrier is surmounted by its spiritual closeness.

The Programme of the C.P.S.U. states:

"The exchange of material and spiritual values between nations becomes more and more intensive, and the contribution of each republic to the common cause of communist construction increases. Obliteration of distinctions between classes and the development of communist social relations make for a greater social homogeneity of nations and contribute to the development of common communist traits in their culture, morals and way of living, to a further strengthening of their mutual trust and friendship."

The question we want to dwell on is how these principles are implemented in literature simultaneously with the development of national traditions and forms.

Themes of friendship between peoples, of socialist construction, and so on, naturally link all Soviet literatures. But they have also much in common in the changes which their national forms undergo, and in the development of genres and styles. In other words, the spiritual community of all Soviet nationalities and tribes influences the very nature of artistic creativity on the basis of socialist realism, engendering new aesthetic forms. It is important as a point of principle that this process of renovation and modification of national forms and traditions for the purpose of rendering the new communist content of life, involves in equal measure those literatures which have an ancient written language and those that had no written language at all.

The strongest similarity between Soviet literatures is to be found in their approach to the depiction and characterisation of life's phenomena. There is nothing dogmatic in this approach: it has been prompted by Soviet reality itself. Writers focus their attention on those social forces which are aimed at building communism, in other words the people and their new relations in socialist society, formed in conditions of a revolutionary break-up of the old way of life. One observes the same regularity in books about the past: attention is focused on the principal motive forces of history—the people and the class struggle.

The similarity of themes, observable in many national literatures which follow the method of socialist realism, results in a similarity of plot and pattern of construction. For instance, a popular theme is how an illiterate hunter from a primitive tribe develops into a Soviet intellectual: an engineer, a doctor, or a scientist. The reason for this similarity is that in the Soviet Union all nations and national groups participate in all the spheres of endeavour: economy, industry and culture.

The third common feature is the tendency of national Soviet literatures to develop narrative prose and, ultimately, the monumental epic novel as they gain greater and greater command of the method of socialist realism. The transition from capitalism or feudalism to the new socialist system usually forms the background in these novels. This tendency is clearly pronounced in many literatures—in Russian (Alexei Tolstoi, Sholokhov, Fadeyev and Fedin), in Ukrainian (Gonchar and Stelmakh), in Latvian (Upits and Lacis), in Azerbaijanian (Ragimov), in Kazakh (Auezov), to give but a few examples.

These literatures also have much in common in the development of style, idiom and imagery. One tendency was to experiment with style in order to discover a new vocabulary and new rhythms, in other words to create new forms that would be equal to the epoch and would adequately express the revolutionary transformation. In Russian literature one immediately associates these seekings with Mayakovsky. His experience—his example—was enthusiastically copied by all the national literatures, especially by those of the Soviet East where the obsoleteness of the feudal tradition made itself felt most acutely. The other tendency—most pronounced in prose—was to develop the stylistic traditions of the classics with their clear and expressive language. As they gained maturity, national literatures shed those traditional peculiarities which were already becoming an obstacle to their development as socialist realist literatures.

Thus we see that what unites Soviet national literatures is not just their ideological content but also some general tendencies in the development of form.

Such, in outline, is the dialectically complex process of formation of the communist society's new culture and literature. Under socialism there is no opposition between the national and the universal.

But not so in the camp of capitalism. Our ideological opponents in the capitalist camp present a distorted view of the development of Soviet multinational literature, and give it a bourgeois-nationalistic bias.

Their objections allege the same thing basically: that in the Soviet Union literatures are trimmed down to a pattern, and writers are deprived of individuality by being "forced" to write according to the method of socialist realism, in other words, to sing praises to everything that happens in the country. The national character of literature is allegedly becoming obliterated because the Russian language is being all but forcibly implanted in the usage of all the other nations peopling the U.S.S.R.

As for the writers being deprived of individuality, I shall name just a few examples (the size of this book will not, unfortunately, allow me to dwell on them in detail) which will serve to refute such allegations completely.

First of all, let us take the Ukrainian playwright Alexander Korneichuk. His plays, beginning with *The End of the Squadron*, have won the widest popularity and are enjoying long runs not just in the Soviet Union but in theatres abroad as well. They are always modern in impact and in the problems they raise. For instance, *Front*, which criticised the army leaders of the old Soviet school, was published in *Pravda* at the height of the Second World War. In his plays about the collective farms—*In the Steppes of Ukraine* and others—Korneichuk touched upon some rather acute problems connected with the further development of the collective-farm system in the U.S.S.R. All these plays carried a message of warning against resting on one's laurels, to put it bluntly.

Or take the Kazakh writer Mukhtar Auezov. His novel *Abai* which has for its central character the figure of Abai Kunanbayev, the 19th-century founder of Kazakh literature, can justly be called an epic poem of the Kazakh steppes. This powerful realistic novel shows the involved and, if you like, refined relations between the heads of the ancient clans. For depth of psychological analysis *Abai* may be ranked with the best works of Russian and world literature. I hesitate to name another modern novel where the author, who had himself leapt over several centuries, as it were, has used such a modern approach and such modern expressive means to describe events which must appear fantastic and exotic to the West European reader. The realistic power of *Abai* is especially evident when you compare it with many of the novels by modern Latin American and African writers who also describe "primitive life". In the latter books, alas, the exotic is more often than not played up to the detriment of artistic merits.

Vilis Lacis, the Latvian author, gives a highly entertaining plot to his novels *Storm* and *To New Shores*, which deal with the serious, modern theme of Latvia's transition to socialism.

Aadu Hint, the well-known Estonian author, on the contrary has a tendency for psychological probing.

It is a pity that some of the magazines published in the West which claim to be the research centres of modern Soviet culture distort the true picture of Soviet literature's development as a *multinational* literature. For example, there was an article in *Survey,* a London magazine, whose author George Lutsky (a Ukrainian émigré who settled in Canada) arrived at the conclusion that all the national literatures in the U.S.S.R. are made of Russian stuff. He is annoyed not only by the spread of the Russian language in the U.S.S.R. but also by the school law according to which parents in any national republic have the right to decide what language their children will be taught in—their own or Russian. The author of this article hates everything Russian so much that he is prepared to turn Gorky—of all people!—into a rabid Russifier and a persecutor of non-Russian literatures. Yes, even Maxim Gorky is presented as a great-power chauvinist and Russifier. Maxim Gorky, who, even before the Revolution, stood up in defence of nations oppressed by the tsarist government (Finns, Latvians and Jews), and who, after the establishment of Soviet power, became a living symbol of friendship between the Soviet literatures, and who rallied the non-Russian writers together! Gorky, who in his speech addressed to the First Congress of Writers spoke of the need to make a deeper study of the classical heritage and experience of Soviet national literatures! Gorky, who declared to the whole world that Soviet literature did not mean literature written in Russian alone!

Are any comments necessary? This one example should be enough. The Canadian Ukrainian nationalist professor's attitude to all things Russian must be explained by his class outlook. In the eyes of all the world today, the Russian language is the vehicle of the ideas of socialist revolution, the spokesman for the unquestionable gains of the Soviet Union, and therefore all things Russian are hateful to this émigré. Even in the remotest African jungles the word "Russian" sounds like "brother" today. Many Russian words —soviet, kolkhoz, sputnik, and others—have come to stay as new concepts in most of the world's languages. Paul Robeson, the American singer, has learnt Russian in order to sing Soviet songs which, performed by him in concert halls throughout the world, sound like a symbol of brotherhood between peoples. And here is George Lutsky urging non-Russian Soviet writers to run from all that is Russian!

There is another article in *Survey* by G. Morris, entitled "The Literature of Central Asia", which is also extremely anti-Russian. The author used to work at the Central Asian Research Centre and is now on the staff of the British Museum. But the quality of his work is in sharp contrast to his "academic" titles, as in the case of G. Lutsky. Their articles have the same basic thesis that Central Asian literatures are subordinated to Russian literature. But G. Morris goes even farther and declares that modern Central Asian literature is a spurious growth. He does not notice that by using the term "Central Asian literature" he dumps Kazakh, Uzbek, Kirghiz, Turkmen, Tajik, Kara-Kalpak, Uigur and the literatures of all the other peoples living in Central Asia into one heap.

His basic argument "proving" the spuriousness of Central Asian literature is that realism is not natural for Central Asia, whose native tradition, he believes, is a high-flown, rhetorical style. And so, he states flatly, the future holds little promise for Soviet literature in Central Asia. In his opinion, from the professional point of view, the literature of Soviet Central Asia is altogether inferior to the Soviet Union's other literatures.

When you read supercilious statements of this kind you involuntarily picture those British and other colonial officers described rather realistically and quite often spitefully in some modern American and English novels (like Graham Greene's *The Quiet*

American). G. Morris simply cannot imagine how any "natives" (by the way, he also looks down on the literatures of India, Iran and Turkey, for being little acquainted with the literary tradition of West Europe) and even less so Soviet ones (doubly barbaric, in other words) could be capable of creating a literature in their own native tongue, not inferior in artistic merits to books by Russian and English authors. G. Morris does mention the name of Mukhtar Auezov, but obviously he has not bothered to read his *Abai*, otherwise he would hardly have ventured to write off the literatures of Central Asia and Kazakhstan so lightly. Readers abroad can easily form their own opinion because quite a number of books by Central Asian writers have been translated into English.

People who write for the magazines like *Survey* and who are so obviously guided by the spirit of national exclusiveness and the sense of their race's or colonialist nation's superiority over other races and nations, depart from genuine science by letting themselves be thus guided. These people either ignore facts or distort them and fail to see the real problems advanced by modern history.

And yet it is precisely now, when a new mankind is being born and when the entire planet is seething with contradictions, that these problems—national, linguistic, and, above all, social—simply clamour for attention.

In his famous predictions for the 20th century, *The Shape of Things to Come* published in England in 1900, H. G. Wells believed—drawing his conclusions from the experience of England and France as colonial powers—that European languages (English and French, and then German) had a chance to play a leading role in the world as a means of uniting peoples. But he had the circumscribed bourgeois world outlook, and so he was unable to picture how the development of social revolutions would really go in the 20th century.

Our revolutions changed the whole picture. Owing to the Soviet Union's social, scientific and technical achievements, the role of the Russian language as a means of uniting peoples is visibly growing at an ever increasing pace. In Western Europe and the U.S.A. it is not just the scholars who are learning it now for reading special literature. Russian, apart from being the language of a great literature, is now esteemed as the language of revolution, of Lenin's ideas, and of the achievements of the Soviet people. At the same time those languages which, like English and French, had indeed assumed importance at the turn of the century and had become the languages used in international relations, have now encountered opposition to their further spread. This opposition comes from the former British and French colonies. During the two hundred years of British rule in India, English became the lingua franca for the intellectuals of the numerous nationalities and communities. True, in India to this day English is spoken at congresses and conferences, and English is the language in which scientific journals are published. But at the same time, the new intelligentsia is already being educated mainly in Hindi, Urdu or Bengali, the more widespread languages of India, spoken by more than 220,000,000 people.

Today, the peoples of Africa speak approximately 120 languages (not counting dialects) belonging to eleven language groups. The trend towards African unity will possibly lead to an advancement of languages capable of becoming the linguistic basis for the further development of the African peoples' cultures.

Thus, national liberation movements and social revolutions stimulate the shaping of national cultures and literary languages. At the same time they engender feelings of closeness and unity in the hearts of millions of people. And the writers in all the liberated countries are tremendously interested in the theory and practice of the Soviet experience, where a harmony has been achieved between the revival of national languages and the cultivation of common ideas and a common realistic approach to the interpretation of life, uniting writers of different nationalities under the banner of socialist realism.

The questions which invite the closest study of these writers and scholars are the conditions in which the literary intelligentsia is reared, the pace of literary development, the character and style of poetry and prose, the formation of genres, the emergence of plots and the metaphoric system, and the balance between national traditions—folklore in particular—and the demands of modern literature.

The experience of Soviet national literatures has, unquestionably, an international importance not only because of the ideological message it carries but also because of its wealth of artistic forms.

At the Third Congress of Soviet Writers in May 1959, I met Jacques Alexis, a Haitian author, who was later tortured to death by the ton-ton macoutes of Doc Duvalier. Jacques Alexis and his friends, Haiti's progressive writers, set up a national theatre wholly devoted to folklore subjects but at the same time adapted to modern demands. They wanted to withdraw from the imported modernistic literature which seeped in from the United States and Europe. And they managed to do it, winning extraordinary popularity for their theatre.

During a conversation I had with some Vietnamese writers at the Gorky Institute of World Literature I was struck by the keenness of their interest in the coming Soviet publication of folklore material and the principles of compiling epic songs and poems.

Survey asserts that association with the Russian language and

Russian literature threatens ruin to the cultures of the other peoples in the Soviet Union, leading to the destruction of the specific national character and the loss of national form. This is just not true. National form (local colour and all that is specific and particular) has no independent value if judged as a separate entity, divorced from content. Whether we render it in architecture, painting or films, national form is anyway a derivative of human activity, even though it does have a large reciprocal influence on the content. It is as senseless to cultivate "national form for the sake of national form" as it is to defend the existence of "art for art's sake" and "science for the sake of science". Because then national form (like "art for art's sake") will become a weapon of nationalism and a means of disuniting people.

We follow a different course. We develop national form and use it only in so far as it furthers the development of intellectual, beauty-conscious people, and helps to unite nations embarked on building a new communist world. But as soon as an outdated form becomes an obstacle in our way, holding us up, we stop cultivating it. For us, national form is not a fetish. It is one of the manifestations of human community which took shape during the long course of mankind's development. And mankind today, it must be borne in mind, numbers 2,500 nations and tribes.

The history of the Old World, going back several millennia, is responsible for the confusion of colours on the literary map which brings to mind the Biblical legend about the tower of Babel.

We are standing on the threshold of the new world, about to take the leap from the realm of necessity into the realm of freedom. We have now seen the map of the world with new eyes, just as the cosmonauts, looking down from a height of three hundred kilometres, have seen the earth in a completely new aspect. The new world of communism will also create its new literary atlas.

Chapter 23

What the Peoples
of the U.S.S.R. Are Giving
Russian Literature

In this chapter I want to show the contacts between Soviet Russian literature and the literatures of the other peoples of the U.S.S.R. A great deal has been written about the influence of Russian literature on the literatures of other Soviet peoples. As I have already said above, anti-communist propaganda is anxious to prove that the non-Russian Soviet literatures have become completely dissolved in Russian literature.

I want to speak about something else: What have we Russian writers adopted from other peoples? These creative links were not made today, of course. They can be traced back to the 17th century.

Pushkin was the first writer in whose works Russia was clearly recognised to be a multilingual and multitribal state. In his article about *The Prisoner of the Caucasus* Belinsky wrote that: "Pushkin's Muse has sanctified, as it were, Russia's kinship with this country, which has actually been in existence for a long time...." In Pushkin's poetry and then in Lermontov's (*Ismail Bey* and others) the reference to Russia as a multinational country has such a progressive and sometimes revolutionary sound because it expressed the protest of the oppressed nations against tsarism and their desire for liberation.

Pushkin's behest to us was to think of ourselves in creative association with all the peoples of Russia. This is our Russian tradition which has been developed so gloriously in Soviet literature after the Revolution of 1917. Dostoyevsky had brilliantly divined in Pushkin's capacity for world-embracing sympathy the "main aptitude of our nationality". He noted in Pushkin a talent for identifying himself with other peoples (scenes from *Faust*, *The Avaricious Knight*, *Don Juan*, *In Imitation of the Koran* and others) as a peculiarly plastic characteristic of his artistic genius. Why did Pushkin turn to the life and images of other peoples? Dostoyevsky explains it as the great historical striving of the Russian people towards a "world-embracing humanity". The Russians unite other peoples "on the field of peace and brotherhood". Dostoyevsky says: "Now it's divination, now it's prediction." He put a mystic meaning into the Russian's idea of "world-embracing humanity", and linked it with Christianity, the main disseminators of which, he held, were again the Russian people.

But the Russian people became the disseminators of another, more realistic and potent teaching of world-embracing humanity and unity. This teaching is communism which carries the idea of brotherhood of nations and the brotherhood of all working people. Traits of world-embracing sympathy, Pushkin's traits, have long been part of our national character, and in the liberation struggle against tsarism and the bourgeois landlords, we Russians became fused into one family with our country's other peoples. It was then that our curiosity in the life of other nations was kindled and our readiness to help them out was aroused. *The Third Autumn* by Valery Bryusov who, Gorky said, was always listening to the voices of Russia's different peoples, Armenians especially, may have been inspired by this feeling. The poet envisaged new, Soviet Russia as a country that "leads all the world's tribes".

How could anyone fail to notice that it was precisely these traits of our national character that became developed after the October Revolution in socialist construction which was a melting pot of nations, and then in the war with nazi Germany which bound them more strongly still by ties of blood in defence of their common motherland? How could anyone fail to notice that our Russian Soviet literature in its entirety, all our better- and lesser-known writers, had adopted the Pushkin tradition of world-embracing humanity, developed it and given it a new meaning? By failing to notice this essential trait of Russian Soviet literature we minimise its value and gain an incomplete idea of its character.

Take Sergei Yesenin. The most Russian of Russian poets. But perhaps it was precisely because he was so "completely Russian" (to quote Gorky) that he was able to express the poetic appeal of the East (in his *Persian Themes*) with such humaneness and such a subtle penetration into the spirit of another people. When you read this poetry you involuntarily remember Pushkin's *Songs of the Western Slavs* and *In Imitation of the Koran*. Yesenin wrote in 1915: "Russia is lost mid the Mordva and Chud, and she knows not the meaning of fear". Like Pushkin, Yesenin thought in terms of Russia, as one single entity, although the Mordva and Chud belong to the Finno-Ugrian family. Soon after the Revolution, in the December 1917 issue of *Svobodny Zhurnal* (Free Journal) published in Petrograd, Yesenin wrote:

> *I'm not lonely in my constant roaming,*
> *It's not me alone who tramps this soil,*

Over Russian fields and sprawling plainlands,
Over grass and snow and wilderness.
Were I a Chuvash or Lithuanian,
It's all one, my cross is like the rest's.

In these lines we find our truly Russian breadth, and that nation-embracing feeling which was so very much alive in Pushkin. Yesenin made a journey to the Caucasus and upon return wrote in his poem *To the Poets of Georgia* (1924):

The Russian tsars a stranglehold
On all the best kept hard and fast.
We finished that with action bold
And Freedom spread its wings at last.
And every tribe and every clan,
Each in his native tune and tongue,
We all give voice the way we can,
By human feelings overcome.

This is the very essence of our national character. We love all goodness and beauty, but different poets and writers express it differently, revealing their artistic individuality in their approach to this theme.

I must make three provisions which will help us to enlarge our knowledge of the subject dealt with in this chapter, and to clarify for ourselves the best method of approaching it.

Firstly, it would be wrong to use the method of survey and enumeration: that is, to record where and what writer or poet has described or mentioned people of Soviet nationalities other than his own. This method would leave us little the wiser. Nor would it be right to look in the works of Russian Soviet writers for evidence of literary influence or reminiscences stemming from other Soviet authors. That, too, would narrow our field of vision.

Admittedly, Shevchenko's lyrical notes and the influence of Ukrainian folklore are easily discernible in Bagritsky's poem *Ballad of Opanas,* and especially in the libretto for the opera based on it. But then this poem also sparkles with the reflected glory of *The Lay of Prince Igor's Host.* The poet's ties with the Ukrainian people and culture have much deeper roots than is indicated by outward signs. Numerous such examples could be adduced.

It is not simply the penetration of themes that we must speak about, but mainly of how Russian writers treat foreign material. In genuine art, thought and feeling are more important than theme or material. For what purpose does a writer absorb some images or motives from the life of a foreign people? What purpose and why? In the answer to these questions lies the key to the writer's personality. One writer will treat foreign material casually, as a passing interest. For another it will be the medium in which he can best express himself as an artist.

So much for the approach. But there are two other essential points of method that should be clarified.

It would be narrow-minded and wrong to reduce all that we are receiving from other peoples of the U.S.S.R. to literary influences alone. Every nation is a collective entity, an aggregate personality, as it were. And just hearing this man sing one of his little songs out in the field somewhere or up in the mountains at sunrise, may so fire the imagination of a poet that it will immediately take flight on wings of fancy. We do not know what gave Lev Tolstoi the idea of ineradicable vitality—whether the folklore of the mountain people, or simply the sight of a broken Caucasian thistle—but it inspired him to create in Khadji Murat an image of enormous vital strength.

If we pursue our theme in this direction it will bring us to yet a third important conclusion: real art makes no distinction between big and small nations, between peoples with an ancient or a young culture. All peoples are equal, all are equally interesting and important. Thirst can be quenched by drinking water from a large river or from a small spring. Our Russian Soviet literature has learnt the songs and absorbed the colours of all the peoples inhabiting our country—the large nationalities and the small, those who have settled down in our boundless steppes, those who have gone into the mountains and found shelter in the forests, those who lovingly tend their grapevines under the scorching sun, and those who herd reindeer in the tundra.

Let us look at the work of Nikolai Tikhonov. He typifies most impressively a writer whose art is imbued with a spirit of friendship and communion between the different peoples of the Soviet Union. This communion is second nature to him. In this sense Tikhonov is a characteristic figure for Soviet literature. The friendly lyres of peoples, resurrected by socialism, accompanied his growth as a writer. He is a poet with a romantic vision and an ennobling emotional perception whose imagination is fired by his numerous encounters with people and his travel impressions. That is probably why Eastern, and especially Georgian imagery comes so naturally to him.

Speaking in Leningrad at an evening devoted to the poetry of Titsian Tabidze, Nikolai Tikhonov said: "Georgia is a revelation as romantic as a poetic image. ... The concept of poetry, or what we call poetic feeling, lives in the very nature of this country, in the soul of its people."

There is no gainsaying that the view from the top of a mountain is always thrilling and the call of distances is very strong. But there is a peculiar poetry of its own in our gentle Russian lowlands—in Yesenin's village world, in the taiga of Yakutia, in the roar of the Angara's rapids, in the revolving hydroturbines at Bratsk, and in the silence of the tundra illumined by the northern lights. And the people themselves. Poetry has always been alive in the heart of every people.

But Georgia, the Caucasus and the East gave Tikhonov what he was seeking, what answered the essence of his poetic gift, and that was: the romance of the sublime.

I can understand why Tikhonov wanted to translate Georgian poets and why he wrote that book of poetry entitled *Georgian Spring*. One cannot remain unmoved by the enchantment of Georgian poetry. I, too, love Georgian verse, which has come to us in the excellent translations of the Russian poets Nikolai Tikhonov, Boris Pasternak, Pavel Antokolsky, Nikolai Zabolotsky, V. Derzhavin and A. Mezhirov. One splendid quality of modern Georgian poetry is that its civic character is rendered with a genuine warmth of feeling. Another is that it is addressed, without unnecessary rhetoric, directly to that delicate apparatus of human perception which we call the soul. Just as the taste of wine is enhanced for us by its fragrance even before we have sipped it, so is the message contained in poetry disclosed more revealingly by its colours and moods.

Irakly Abashidze wrote in one of his poems (*Inspiration*) that rationalism and loss of ingenuousness are the most deadening things for a poet. Boredom sets in when "his pen ceases to respond alertly to the murmur of the grass in spring and the rustling of the wheat in autumn. . . ." This feeling of the fullness of life is common to most Georgian poets. This feeling, combined with youthful candour and the awareness of our revolutionary times, is amazingly well expressed in Georgy Leonidze's poem *To a Poet* written in 1930 and published in Russian translation a few years later. This poem will have the lasting glory of being one of the masterpieces not only of Georgian but also of Russian poetry, thanks to Nikolai Tikhonov's brilliant translation.

> *We call the loveliest, the most divine,*
> *Only that which is ripe and strong:*
> *A river in spring, or a mighty vine,*
> *A woman, say, or a field of corn.*

Tikhonov's translation is a fusion of his own personal perception of life, Russian expansiveness and Georgian romanticism. In his own poetry about Georgia–*Verses About Kakhetia, Georgian Spring*, his poems about Tbilisi and Abkhazia and the cycles *Mountains* and *Rainbow Over Saguramo*–this fusion is there, and everywhere we can feel what Georgia has given the poet.

The "Eastern theme"–not Georgian alone–has come to play a large part in Tikhonov's work. In his book about Pakistan and Afghanistan called *Two Streams* (1951) he says:

> *I walked into a dusky shack*
> *When in this country, far from home*
> *(This not in dreams, but actual fact),*
> *A friend–who had the right to come.*

His poetry about Pakistan has been translated into Urdu and greatly admired in that country. Tikhonov first wrote about India forty years ago, in 1919, before he had ever been there. The poem is about Sami, an Indian boy, to whom the name of Lenin held promise of ultimate deliverance from poverty and exploitation. *Sami* was the first poem about Lenin in the history of Soviet literature. And it is significant that the poet was so Russian in his understanding of the soul and the plight of another nation.

I have dwelt at such length on Tikhonov's work because it is easiest to trace from his example just what was absorbed by Russian poetry from the literatures of other Soviet peoples and why, in the case of Tikhonov, his poetic gift was most fully revealed in the Caucasian theme which happened to be closest to him in spirit.

Tikhonov's short stories as well as his poetry reflect these Eastern themes in numerous variations. His most successful prose work was his collection of stories and essays published in 1921 under the general title of *Nomads*. I have already mentioned earlier in this book how a group of Soviet writers (Tikhonov, Leonov, Ivanov, Lugovskoi, Pavlenko and Sannikov) went to Turkmenia in 1930 and what they contributed to Soviet literature as a result. *Nomads* was Tikhonov's contribution. All these writers differ in manner and points of interest, and so what would appear to be the same material is presented in their works through the prism of their different artistic vision. Each borrowed from the foreign nation he was describing that which best answered his psychological and artistic aims.

Today, reviewing the books written at the time in their historical aspect, we see their shortcomings but we also see what Turkmenia and Kazakhstan have given Russian Soviet literature.

Take, for example, the picture they painted of the Turkmenian desert or the Kazakh steppe. In his *Nomads* Tikhonov painted the desert in elusive pinks and mauves behind a shimmering haze, as a background on which he drew scenes from the life of the Belludjas and Djemides, the Turkmen tribes who farm the mountain regions. Vsevolod Ivanov lavished a wealth of colours and emotions on the Kazakh steppe. His heroes are Kazakhs, Kirghizes, Altai, Chinese and Russians—a community of friends. In his *Coloured Winds* he writes: "He wept and laughed with every heart."

Alexander Blok defined romanticism as an avid desire to live ten lives in one. This is a conditional designation of the sixth sense in its untarnished and unalloyed form, so to speak. If we take it to mean not simply one of the categories of literary criticism but interpret it as an imaginary veil with which the artist covers up that which he correctly senses but finds difficult to put into words, then we shall see that this sixth sense, born in us by the Revolution, is expressed in Vsevolod Ivanov's romantic prose, especially in his *Partisan Stories* which exhale the poetry of the Kazakh steppe. He writes: "We welcome your re-birth, land, your re-birth! Embrace the rains and the fields, and rejoice! Here is a handful of my native soil—it is in flower!"

In Vsevolod Ivanov's earlier works this gladness of revolutionary rejuvenation is expressed in the beautiful riot of colours with which the Kazakh steppes sparkle under his pen. Even the winds are coloured, and the sand is blue. But on the other hand there is the merciless desert, turning on man with all the fierceness of its desperate poverty. Gladness and cruelty go hand in hand. Let us remember his story *Encounter* with its tender opening tune: "My springtime thawing...". The Kara-Korum desert.... The yellow-blue evening, moist with dew, is licking at the stirrups of the Russian horseman. A Kirghiz, whose wife has been killed by the Whites, steps out of a bush and says: "Hand over your rifle, Russian. I've carried Kyzymil for twenty versts." And the Russian hands his rifle over to Kyzymil's husband.

The end of this encounter: "The time of spring—my thawing, it's time to light the fires of wisdom." It is like a poem in prose. Another story *Temerbei, a Kirghiz* is all cruelty, and cruelty alone. Two Red Army men are shot by a squad of White Cossacks. The bodies of the two men are covered with earth, but the yellowish arm of one of them sticks out. Temerbei touched this arm as soon as the executioners had gone, and the feel of it sent him blindly into the merciless desert.

From his work we can trace what Vsevolod Ivanov sought and found in the Kazakh steppes and the foothills of the Altai Mountains among the peoples living there; how his concepts of the country and the inhabitants changed; how life's contrasts influenced his thinking and his choice of descriptive means; how these contrasts gradually lost their sharpness and also—regrettably—some of their vividness; and how the author arrived at his novel *We're*

Going to India. He also arrived at realism, both ideologically and artistically, but with certain losses to his talent. After all, experimenting was his life, he was forever seeking, "weeping and laughing with every heart".

Vladimir Lugovskoi took something entirely different from the Turkmens and Uzbeks. His first book *To the Bolsheviks of the Desert and the Spring* was an expression of the turning point in his own thinking. What he sought in the East was more than local colour—it was the embodiment of revolutionary ideas. He sought facts showing how the socialist system had transformed the son of a Kulyab beggar into the owner of the earth and a master of his own destiny. The poet's oratorial voice was addressed to the epoch itself, as it were. He chose an extremely apt epigraph for his *Uzbekistan Poems* (1930-1947):

> *Men, moving water, soil and sands,*
> *The weight you've lifted with your hands!*
> *What strength our one and only state*
> *Has lent you to heave up that weight!*
> *I'd give my life for every one of you,*
> *The toilers building life anew.*
> *From you we should be learning everything,*
> *The steppeland Bolsheviks of spring!*

Lugovskoi's poetry about the people of the Soviet East is a combination of a rousing call to action, a chronicle and philosophical reflections, fused together by the feeling of the Soviet peoples' steady advance along the road of communism. Every line of his poetry is a step on the staircase leading to the top of the philosophical edifice which the author has called *The Middle of the Century*, his latest work.

I have shown three or four kinds of approach to foreign material taken by a Russian writer. The example of Pavel Luknitsky is an instance where a Russian writer has found in the life of another fraternal people everything from which a literary work is compounded: material, theme, situations and images. Luknitsky's work is devoted wholly to Soviet Tajikistan. He lived there for years at a time and has travelled the country far and wide. His *Tajikistan* in English translation represents one of the main sources of information for readers abroad about this once backward country which, under Soviet power, has been wonderfully transformed both economically and culturally. I have heard praises of this book from Englishmen, and also from the English-writing Indian author Mulk Raj Anand.

Luknitsky's prose, especially his collections of stories and essays *Beyond the Blue Rock, Time Is on Our Side, A Journey to the*

Pamirs, and his novel *Nisso*, describe the life of the Tajik people in different aspects from the early nineteen-twenties (Luknitsky, then a budding writer, had himself taken part in the struggle against the *basmatch* bands) to our own day. The book I like best is *Nisso* which presents in impressively written scenes the establishment and consolidation of Soviet power in the frontier regions of mountainous Tajikistan. Nisso, a beautiful and courageous girl whom the Revolution released from the *parandjah* and all it implied, is a romantic, charming and psychologically convincing character.

I see in the work of Luknitsky and other writers of the same cast a literary expression of what the Russian people in general—doctors, teachers, engineers, geologists and Party officials—contribute to the cause of friendship with the other peoples of the U.S.S.R.

All that I have said above can also be applied to Pyotr Skosyrev, author of the novels *Your Humble Servant* (about Kemineh, the poet) and *Farkhad and Shirin*, whose writing was devoted entirely to Central Asia, Turkmenia in particular.

Take a look at the population map of the U.S.S.R. issued in 1963 by the Institute of Ethnography. More than a hundred nationalities are shown, and you will see for yourselves that throughout the country—in the east, north, south and west, in the deserts and forests, and along the great Siberian rivers Lena, Yenisei and Ob—Russians live in close proximity and association with all these peoples allied both economically and politically.

Tsarist Russia had its colonies within the country, but progressive Russian literature did not create the genre of "colonial novel" such as developed in England or France, for example. It would be wrong, of course, to reduce the traditional British attitude in relation to other peoples to Rudyard Kipling alone. There is another tradition stemming from Byron. And it may be that in India today people no longer remember Rudyard Kipling with his racial "iron curtain" between the East and West, a twain that never shall meet, but that they read instead, say, Jim Corbett, that hunter, nature lover and writer, author of *My India, Man-eaters of Kumaon* and others. In Africa, too, Albert Schweizer is more popular than all those English and French authors of exotic novels about Negroes.

Any chauvinistic writers there may have been in tsarist Russia were defeated by their own mediocrity. The great Russian writers were never inspired by the glamour of dominant-nation superiority, and so no Kiplings grew in this soil. Nor could anti-Semitism have ever become the object of poetry.

Our Russian tradition is entirely different: to love other peoples as ourselves and to approach all with an open heart.

Far be it from me to underrate the books of progressive Western writers about the life of peoples foreign to them. This is a large theme and it goes beyond the scope of my book. But we cannot overlook the experience of Russian, and especially of Soviet literature which is important in principle and has an international significance as regards both approach to the portrayal of the life of fraternal peoples and the very method of assimilating the fruit of this friendly association.

In this respect, the Russians have presented to the world a new attitude which is vividly embodied in Russian Soviet literature, the literature of socialist realism. Our inner need to understand the soul of other peoples and create their images, and the aesthetic pleasure we take in the language and national features of other peoples is reflected in our own novels, poems, plays, and in translations of foreign literature. Among the leading characters in the majority of Russian books we are certain to find people of other Soviet nationalities. And very many Russian writers are authors of either a novel or a story describing the life of non-Russian people.

In Konstantin Paustovsky's autobiographical trilogy the images of the Ukraine, her people and scenery, are very poetic. Was the Ukraine, perhaps, responsible for that gentle lyricism which is such a charming feature of Paustovsky's writing? This lyricism is blended in Paustovsky with his profound respect for man, his admiration and pain for this man. I would call it ethical lyricism. The moral and poetic principles are merged in his style as closely as are the different national currents in the mainstream of his art—Russian, Ukrainian, Kazakh, Turkmenian (in *Kara-Bugaz*) and Georgian (in *Colchis*). Paustovsky glows with humanity, and reading him you envy him the happiness of esteeming his fellow men so profoundly, and of feeling an equal among equals.

Take F. Knorre's *Forever*, a novel which describes Lithuania just before it became re-united with the U.S.S.R. and then during the war years. As in Luknitsky's *Nisso*, the central character, a Lithuanian girl, is in love with a Russian. Or take Y. Lebedinsky's novel *Batash and Batai* which is "built on" Kabardino-Balkarian material. Or P. Pavlenko's novel *A Caucasian Tale* about Shamil and Khadji Murat.

I also know a case where the author thought little of his book, or at any rate did not fully appreciate the artistic and social importance of his work for which he had drawn his facts and images from the life of a non-Russian people. And it turned out to be the greatest thing he had ever written. During the war I made a short stay in Ufa and there I met this writer, N. Krasheninnikov. Until then I had only thought of him in connection with his *Virginity*, a novel of rather dubious merits although it had caught the attention of critics at the time of publication. Krasheninnikov felt that his novel was a challenge to Artsibashev's *Sanin* whose hero championed the right of every healthy male to sexual anarchy.

To tell you the truth I was somewhat puzzled by the attention lavished on Krasheninnikov by the government of the Bashkir Autonomous Republic and the Regional Party Committee in Ufa. And then I learnt something I had not known until then, to my regret. It appears that in 1907 Krasheninnikov had published a collection of essays and stories under the general title *The Fade-Out of Bashkiria* in which (as in his earliest novel *Amelya*, an Academy of Sciences prize winner) he told quite boldly for that time about the persecution and shameless robbery of the "Bashkirs, a voiceless country". Now that the "voiceless Bashkirs" have found voice, lifted their heads and acquired their human rights and their autonomy, they gratefully remembered what that old Russian author had written about their country.

Now a few words about that gift of artistic self-identification which, according to Dostoyevsky, made Pushkin "a phenomenon the like of which had never been seen or heard of before". But Pushkin, Dostoyevsky goes on to say, embodied in this gift a virtue common to our nation. If we strip Dostoyevsky's statement of its Messianic apparel, we shall see that there is something in the life of the Russian people that might well give grounds for such conclusions. Belinsky has also written about the peculiar sensibility of the Russians. It must be ascribed to the historical conditions of our existence and the closeness with which the life of the Russians was bound up with the life of the other nationalities inhabiting the country, a closeness that prompted us, while retaining our own identity, to penetrate this foreign atmosphere and try to understand it. When after the October Revolution all the dividing barriers were shattered, the non-Russian peoples began to develop culturally and the "exchange of spiritual treasures" (Belinsky) developed at an ever-increasing pace, the gift of self-identification with other nations was called to action in the new socialist conditions.

There is no need to remind readers of what Gorky, Bryusov and Blok had done in their time for this brotherly exchange of spiritual treasures. All I shall say is that most of the Soviet poets are making translations from the languages of our brother nations, and that translations into Russian have acquired an unprecedented scale, incomparably greater than was ever the case in the United States, Britain, France or Germany.

Today, we have the perfect right to speak of our own Soviet school of translation.

The social duty of the Soviet poet-translator is to forge a link of friendship between nations. But as a poet and artist he must also possess the gift of self-identification. In reproducing the original in his own language, the Russian poet discloses his own personality, though in the guise of another, by his choice of poem for translation. Translating poetry is the first step to Pushkin's gift of self-identification. And so very often translations lead to original poetry on the same themes: remember the poems of Nikolai Tikhonov and Yevgeny Yevtushenko about Georgia. It is no accident that translators are most successful with poets who are closest to them in manner. For example, take Mikhail Isakovsky's translations of Byelorussian poets, and Sergei Vasilyev's translation of P. Voronko.

But in no Russian poet's work have we ever heard such a chorus of nationalities as in the poetry of Ilya Selvinsky. This polyphony comes from the wonderful vitality of his talent, from his love of colour, this acute alertness to languages, dialects and accents, from the wealth of his expressive means and techniques of reproducing the slightest nuances of speech. Selvinsky's breadth of vision is displayed in this kaleidoscope of foreign pictures, landscapes, countries, cities and people. He urges us to see beyond the visible horizon and tries to enlarge for us our world of emotions, concepts and thoughts. He gives us a truly panoramic view of life and a glimpse of men and women of many different nationalities: Americans, British, Frenchmen, Italians, Germans, Poles, Rumanians, Chinese, Japanese, Koreans, Vietnamese, Norwegians, Arabs, Persians, Spaniards and others.

It is well in keeping with the character of Selvinsky's work that he should present Russia and the Russians in the spirit of the Pushkin tradition as the medium of uniting nations. His Russia, like Valery Bryusov's, "leads the tribes of the world". But Selvinsky gives a modern interpretation to Russia's historical significance, and says: "You're more than just a country: you're the world! The planet's fate is in your hands. . . ." These words come from the Prologue to his trilogy *Russia* which comprises three plays: "The Livonian War" (during the reign of Ivan the Terrible), "The Rebel Tsar" (during the reign of Peter the Great), and "The Big Kirill" (during the period of the February and October revolutions).

The Russian people "made the Tatars and the Byelorussians sing again and gave them hope. . . ."

> *The trail to the all-planet congress*
> *The Bolsheviks have blazed.*
> > *That's why*
> *The Russians' course is of such great importance.*
> *To every nation, every tribe.*

It is with the sympathetic curiosity of a *Russian* poet that Selvinsky studies the foreign scene. His poetry in all its diversity of genres is an eloquent example from which one can see how Russian Soviet literature can be enriched by its contacts with the other Soviet peoples. In Selvinsky's books we meet big and small nations, peoples with an ancient culture and nomadic tribes, Ukrainians, Chukchis, Armenians, Kirghizes, Karaims, Evenks (or Lamuts), Jews, Estonians and many, many others.

The life of those small tribes that had settled down in the Far Eastern taiga, the tundra and on the shores of the Atlantic Ocean is rendered rather extensively in Russian literature. Before their national writers could tell about themselves in their native language, progressive Russian authors acquainted the world with many of Russia's nationalities and ethnic groups, always writing of these small oppressed peoples with sympathy, concern and the Russian all-embracing humanism. This tradition was further and more widely developed in Russian Soviet literature. Even the pre-revolutionary past has been described from positions of socialist realism: Soviet writers, alive to the prospects opening before these ethnic groups and nationalities under socialism, examined their national peculiarities, psychology and inter-tribal struggle with particular attention. This can be seen from Nikolai Zadornov's novels *Remote Country* and *The Old Amur* which give a true picture of the local scene with people of different nationalities living together—Nanais, Russians, Yakuts, Evenks, Chinese and others. This new approach is made even clearer in Zadornov's *Mogusyumk and Guryanich,* a story which tells how the Bashkirs get on with the Russian workers in the Urals.

Tikhon Semushkin found in the life of the Chukchis what Skosyrev found in Turkmenia and Luknitsky in Tajikistan—the material, the imagery and the inspiration for his work. He travelled all over the Chukotka Peninsula in the middle nineteen-twenties during the all-Union census, and rode in a dog-sleigh along the Atlantic seaboard explored by Nordenskjold's expedition. And then he returned to live among the Chukchis as a school-teacher. Semushkin entered the literary scene with his book *Chukotka*, and then came his novel *Alitet Departs for the Mountains*, which tells how the Chukchis embarked on their extraordinary road in the nineteen-twenties, leaping across whole centuries, straight from the tribal system to socialism. When the first Russian Bolsheviks came to the Chukotka Peninsula they began by persuasion and material aid to free the Chukchis from the tenacious hold of superstition, tribal chiefs like Alitet, and from the American and other smugglers and profiteers who had for years been robbing this strong and courageous people. The story told by Semushkin immediately attracted the attention of the world reading public. It has been translated into at least twenty foreign languages. Katharine Prichard, the well-known

Australian authoress, wrote to the Union of Soviet Writers that she would like Semushkin's book to be read by as many people abroad as possible.

The Fleet-Footed Reindeer by N. Shundik, another Russian writer, comes as a sort of sequel to Semushkin's novel and deals with a later period.

Now at last the Chukchis have been able to tell their own story through their spokesman Yuri Rytkheu in his collection entitled *People on Our Shore, The Chukot Saga*, the long-short story *The Season of Melting Snows* and his novel *The Valley of Little Hares* —books which have evoked a lively interest among readers abroad.

In Azhayev's *Far From Moscow* we are introduced to the Nanais and other Far Eastern nationalities in association with Russian Soviet people whose ancestors figure in Zadornov's *Remote Country*.

I may be asked: precisely how did these peoples influence the development of Russian Soviet literature? After all, do not all these peoples and ethnic groups play a passive role in Russian literature, merely serving as an object of description? After all, they had no literature of their own; so what could anyone learn from them?

If you study Russian fiction closely you will see what the authors sought and found in the life of these ethnic groups. The inverse influence was far from passive. Sometimes it implanted the seed of a story in the writer's mind, as in the case of Lev Tolstoi's *Khadji Murat*.

Take Fadeyev's *The Last of the Udeghes*. The title immediately brings to mind Fenimore Cooper's *The Last of the Mohicans*. But Fadeyev's novel has an entirely different meaning. Fenimore Cooper's story is about the fighting adventures of honourable, proud and courageous Red Indians. The Udeghes inspired the Russian writer with a different idea, the embodiment of which he sought in the image of this small, hunting tribe numbering no more than fifteen hundred people who, in those years, led a nomadic existence in the forests of the Sikhote-Alin. Incidentally, V. Arsenyev has devoted a special ethnographic essay to the Udeghes, a fascinatingly written work, it must be said. In the mode of this tribe's life and in the Udeghes themselves Fadeyev saw the noble traits of primitive communism. These were the traits of which Engels wrote so enthusiastically in his book *The Origin of Family, Private Property and State*. As readers of the older generation will probably remember, the first edition of *The Last of the Udeghes* had the following lines from Engels's book for an epigraph: "What an amazing organisation in all its infancy and simplicity is this tribal system. . . ."

Chapter 24

Literature of the Future

What kind of literature is the new world, the new communist society, creating? What will it be like? Who will it be intended for? What form will it take? What role will the literature of the past play in the aesthetic and intellectual life of future generations? Will literature be printed on paper or will it be microfilmed instead?

Dozens of questions arise the moment we approach this subject which, actually, was first raised long ago. Plato, as we all know, proposed banishing poets from a republic governed by philosophers, because poets, he believed, could cause nothing but trouble.

The Utopian socialists wrote about the future of literature and art. So did Marx, Engels and Lenin.

Revolution releases all the hitherto fettered forces and gives them an outlet. The Russian Socialist Revolution freed the artists from the brunt of such prosaically oppressive conditions as the need to peddle their pictures and sculptures. The Soviet Government has become both their patron and their customer.

Lenin said: "Art belongs to the people. Its roots should be deeply implanted in the very thick of the labouring masses. It should be understood and loved by these masses. It must unite and elevate their feelings, thoughts and will. It must stir to activity and the art instincts within them."[1]

In order to make literature more accessible to the people and the people more conscious of art, we naturally first had to raise our educational and cultural level. By achieving a cultural revolution, Soviet power prepared the soil in which a truly great communist art could be grown, the forms of which would suit the content. It was up to our intellectuals, Lenin said, to carry out this immensely important and noble task.

---

[1] Clara Zetkin, *My Recollections of Lenin*, Moscow, 1956, pp. 19-20.

And so Lenin (like Marx and Engels), pondering on the future of literature, mainly saw it in relation to the masses, to those millions and millions of people who, in his lifetime, were for the most part still ignorant or semiliterate.

Can Soviet literature be called the literature of the future? As more countries embark on the road to socialism they will obviously cultivate the ideas of communism and become imbued with its sentiments, and their literatures will also draw images of the makers of this new society.

I naturally do not think that those specific features which are common to Soviet literature alone will necessarily be repeated in the literatures of other countries. The emergence of a new literature is a very complex process, and there are many sides to it. But I do not think I will be far wrong if I say that some traits typical of Soviet literature will undoubtedly be developed in the future literature of different nations.

Two features, as I imagine it, will be assimilated in the next hundred years at any rate. One is the social directedness of Soviet literature, its desire to address millions of people and to portray life from the point of view of those ideals which appeal to the masses. It is a quality present in the trends of world historical development.

The second feature is the multinational nature of Soviet literature. There is no doubt that the world will go through a stage of development and emergence of literatures among a whole number of newly literate or totally illiterate peoples. We have before us the example of India and Africa.

What I imagine will obviously happen in literature in the near future should not be taken as an overestimation of the importance of Soviet literature or mere vanity. It is also the view of non-Marxists.

In Charles Letourneau's book *L'evolution littéraize dans les diverses races humaines* written in the eighteen-nineties, there is a chapter entitled "The Literature of the Future". This well-known French anthropologist is the author of a series of books on the evolution of morality, marriage and the family, property and political institutions. He tried to make a sort of summing up from his survey of the literatures of African Negroes, Polynesians, the literatures of America, Peru, Mongolia, China, Japan, the literatures of the Egyptians, the Berbers, the Arabs, the Jews, the Hindus, the Greeks, the Romans and the Persians, of Mediaeval and 19th-century literatures.

Comparing folk art with the refined writings produced in palaces and also with our modern literature, Letourneau arrives at the conclusion that ancient civilisations (Egyptian, Greek and Roman) decayed because these societies were based on the system of slavery and their social ideals could not feed real literature.

There are symptoms that European states have also reached a "critical age", so to speak. Letourneau wrote about this long before Spengler, Toynbee, Berdyayev and many other apocalyptically-minded philosophers of our day, and like H. G. Wells, in those same years, he regarded the prospects of contemporary bourgeois civilisation with a good deal of scepticism. But unlike the "apocalyptics", Letourneau looked to the future with confident optimism. He was certain that our descendants would see a genuine re-birth of literature which would not be a mere imitation of the Renaissance. Since aesthetics is always closely connected with the political and social organism which it reflects, it is obvious, Letourneau concludes, that some changes must first of all take place in the social sphere. The task facing society is to reconcile or establish some sort of balance between personal independence and the demands of society (or state, while it exists). In other words, it lies with the future to find how a "taste for anarchy" can combine with a "taste for aim".

It must be said that artists in general have always demanded and will probably always demand unconditional personal independence and the right to an individual expression of their inner world. But at the same time, whether we like it or not, we shall not be able to deny society the right to organise itself as a *society*, as an aggregate of individuals. The increase of the population which promises to grow in geometrical progression as more of our planet is developed and as the two thousand-odd nations and tribes that people it achieve their cultural renaissance, will certainly make the problem of social organisation more and more acute. And this means that the problem of the social ideal will also grow in importance.

Letourneau referred to Homer, who was understandable to all because it was the ideals of a slave-owning society, professed by the ruling section of the population, that he presented as social ideals. It was from Homer that Letourneau extrapolated the theses for the society of the future, proceeding from the inevitability of one or another social organisation and, above all, a social ideal that would influence the minds of the majority of the population. Marx, as we know, posed a more difficult problem for solution: how to explain the fact that much of what has been created in the slave-owning society (in sculpture and architecture) still appeals to us, modern men?

It must be admitted that Letourneau displays acumen in many of his statements, although at times he may be accused of a racist approach. He is wrong in his extreme condemnation of the literature of the past. True, there are not so many books in the world that are worth reading. But still there are enough to fill a man's life. In any case, besides Homer and Marcus Aurelius, there are Shakespeare, Goethe, Pushkin, Tolstoi, Dostoyevsky, Stendhal, Balzac and other writers whom we customarily think of as our life companions.

Letourneau, however, is right in criticising the decadent trends that appeared at the end of the last century amid the moral degeneration of capitalist culture. We can also understand the Utopian socialists, starting from Thomas More, who placed their hopes in the future when great aesthetic and philosophical values would be created.

Therefore, Sartre's words about the great world novel of the future and similar hopes voiced by many other writers in the West (Ralph Fox, the English writer, once summed them up in his book *The Novel and the People*) are not unfounded. They hope and expect that a more perfect organisation of society will beneficially influence art as well. There is, of course, no direct dependence between the economic and technical development of society and literature. But nevertheless, Engels once said that, in principle, such a dependence does exist. In any case it is self-evident that pessimistic predictions like that of Renan on the imminent death of art (Guyau devoted a whole book to the refutation of these forecasts) have been proved false by life itself. In spite of the fact that all sorts of decadent perversions in art (from Dadaism to modern abstractionism) have become a staple product of the entertainment industry (Charles Snow wrote about this in the *Times* literary supplement) and have caused a certain amount of damage to literature as a whole, also foiling our expectations of new aesthetic values, the role and significance of serious fiction have remained undefeated. We might recall here what Yevgeny Baratynsky, a Russian poet and contemporary of Pushkin, said:

> *Poetic visions, childish dreams,*
> *Have vanished in enlightenment's glare.*
> *Our generation misses not the loss, it seems,*
> *Engrossed in its industrial cares.*

No, the poets' "childish dreams" have not vanished, but have on the contrary become filled with epic and lyrical visions of a new world.

I am not going to speak of the other aspects of future literature—its relations with science, the role of the scientific theme, the development of literary genres and, last but not least, the problem of the artistic method. The thought of new technical means of popularising literature must engage more of our attention than the evolution of literary genres and the character of romantic or realistic literature. Genres are slow to change, even the sonnet still grows in the soil of socialist realism, although some literary genres of the East, it is true, like the *qasida*, are losing their ideological and aesthetic significance. I want to speak of something else—of the correlation between the assertive and critical techniques in portraying reality. I am inclined to think that with time literature will acquire a more and more informative and analytic character. Of course, literature of a different kind—light reading, detective stories, and so forth—will continue to come out. And, naturally, "serious" literature—from Homer and Shakespeare to Hemingway and Sholokhov—which is characterised by its penetration into the depths of existence, the depths of the human soul.

As I have already said, during the period of the Stalin personality cult the informative, truthful and analytic character of Soviet literature was somewhat jeopardised. But this was a passing phase and, it must be noted, it did not affect such important writers as Alexei Tolstoi (except for his *Bread*) or Sholokhov.

I believe that the desire to explore the world aesthetically, which is an essential feature of literature, will develop further rather than wane.

But might not the art of the future from some new curve of the spiral slide down to a sort of aesthetic syncretism, typical for infancy? In some foreign countries—Britain, France, Italy and the United States especially—where the technical means of spreading information are in the hands of private owners, there is the danger that information and light entertainment will elbow out literature. The question is raised at international literary congresses, and made the subject of polls and questionnaires.

At the Penclub Congress in London in 1956, the American author Elmer Rice made a speech, the gist of which was as follows:

In the U.S.A. a successful play or a good novel will be seen and read by 300,000–400,000 people at best, while a film or a television show will be viewed by millions and even scores of millions. The potential TV audience numbers approximately a hundred million people. The fact that a writer's words reached a hundred million people simultaneously radically changed the material and methods of his work. An industrialisation of the writer's work could be observed. Whereas before the writer first composed his poems, plays and novels, and then sought a publisher or a producer for them, the process has now been reversed: in the U.S.A. there is a large industry engaged in distributing the material, and the writer is no more than a tiny cog in this huge industrial machine whose position differs little from that of the camera-men and technicians, decorators and so on. With only a few exceptions, writers are compelled to do a given job of work. The monopolies are growing, and the means of production and communications are concentrated in the hands of a few. This is big business, and not a small private enterprise.

In the West today one can hear it said that the new barbarians had exchanged the club for the atom bomb, and that they *read* Dickens, Dostoyevsky and Shakespeare in the cinema. Read them, mind you. They read the classics in condensed form and wonder why these authors did not write like that in the first place to save the future generations the trouble of condensing them. Readers are going to become as rare as pedestrians.

It must be said that America is putting out the greatest number of condensed books. For a few dollars you can buy a volume in which almost 2,500 of the world's best works are told in brief. These condensed books are also assuming popularity in France and partly in England. All this shows that in the given case art is being substituted by simple information. Perhaps the French author Denis Sorat is really right in saying that the writer will be gradually relieved of all free communion with his readers. The experts, whoever they are, will take care of this. They will be the experts of cybernetics, which is in fact the science of communication.

Burns Singer wrote roughly the following in his article *Mass Solitude* which was published in the London *Times* literary supplement (August 15, 1958): Instead of conventional literary works, created by a few, a mass production has now been started of "languages" invented by psychologists, engineers, and mathematicians, and calculated to communicate with the public by means of special signals. Thus, some commercial television programmes are calculated to evoke a response among those sections of the population which American advertising specialists title the "average majority". This language will find no echo in those who have a different social standing either higher or lower. The inventors of the means of mass communication are attacking the very concept of form which has always been bound up with conventions.

I should like to paraphrase yet another article printed in that same *Times* supplement because it expresses most strongly the pessimism with which certain writers in the Western world view the future of literature.

In this article entitled *No Room for the Book* Christopher Logue, a young poet, says approximately the following: Let us face facts; the book is doomed. Some books, of course, will survive in museums visited by cranks. But as a product of the publishing industry, as a product of culture, the book will go out. And it will happen for technical and economic reasons, and not for aesthetic or social ones.

With the appearance of better technical means of communication than the printing press, a book of prose becomes a thing of antiquity. Who will inherit prose, then? The poets.... As for prose, it would be better to record it now by means other than a printing machine. The thing to do is build a comfortable villa where generals, diplomats, bishops and others could live and memorise books by heart. Instead of saying, "there goes the Right Rev. So and So," we will say, "there goes old *War and Peace*, or *Ulysses*...."

"Reading is becoming an unpopular pastime. Soon rich young ladies will be taught it the way they are now taught singing and playing the harp. The time is not far off when a person who can read will be invited to parties to amuse the guests.

"What books will remain? The telephone directory, guides and various timetables. The large combines of 'Sound and Television' will arrange annual hunts for the other books. A child who gathers and hands in more than six books in six days will receive a huge TV set for a prize."

There is, perhaps, more spite than logic in this reasoning, but still we cannot deny the young English poet a certain amount of vision in forecasting what may happen when books—born of the writer's heart and mind, the product of human genius in all its individual complexity—will stand in the way of money-making. It will be just hard luck on the books. Marx and Lenin, having discovered the laws of social development, looked at the future with the eyes of scientists and builders of a new world, and it is obvious that they were right in their predictions. In the new socialist world, which now embraces more than a thousand million people, literature has become an enormously important factor of spiritual education, and technical progress merely facilitates this process of spiritual rebirth. The fact that in Bombay and Calcutta today people can see *Anna Karenina*, a screen version of the great Russian novel made in the U.S.A. by a German director with a Swedish actress in the star role, and the fact that this film brings tears to the eyes of Indian women, is hardly incompatible with the nature of art. Roger Caillois (of France) recalls that once, in the very heart of the Andes, at a height of 3,500 metres, he went into a cinema where *Hamlet* was showing. The spectators—South American Indians—were fascinatedly watching the acting of Sir Lawrence Olivier who played a Danish madman from a poem by an English sixteenth-century writer. I remember another story in this connection. Once, in Riga, I saw a book of Shakespeare's sonnets in Samuel Marshak's Russian translation on the desk of the duty militia officer in the outer office of the Chairman of the Council of Ministers of the Latvian S.S.R. I asked the man to tell me why he was reading this book, and he replied: "I'm learning the sonnets by heart, because the girl I love wants to hear real poetry from me and not an account of how I caught a thief."

Speaking in terms of the whole globe, which has become a more tangible and visible thing after being orbited by cosmonauts in their spaceships, it will take a few centuries before it is confronted by those critical problems which are today so mournfully discussed in the British and American press and which André Maurois broods upon in his famous book "Dialogues des Vivants" (1959).

I recall a conversation I had with the late Angioletti, then the chairman of the European Association of Writers, at the First Constituent Congress which was held in Naples in the autumn of 1958. It worried Angioletti that even the large Italian publishers were retreating before the onslaught of the television companies which filled their programmes with entertaining material of little artistic merit. "Look at our newspaper kiosks," he told me. "What kind of literature is popular with customers? Detective stories, the adventures of gangsters, and stuff like that. The other day I picked up one of those books: the picture on the cover showed a half-naked woman killing another half-naked woman in bed. The curious thing was that among the obviously trashy stories which packed that volume there was one story by Edgar Allan Poe. Everything was mixed up. Before long readers will no longer be able to tell good from bad."

Angioletti regarded it one of the main tasks of the European Association of Writers, apart from rallying the progressive anti-fascist-minded writers of Western and Eastern Europe, to defend literature from the onslaught of commercial dealers who were adapting it to their own aims.

In the West-European capitalist states this problem is extremely urgent. It is less so if we take the world as a whole. Real literature is treated quite differently not only in the vast socialist camp but also in dozens of other countries (especially in Africa), the one-time colonies of old West European powers—Britain, France, Germany, Italy, Holland, Portugal and Spain. To begin with, writers in socialist and newly independent countries are ambitiously striving to build up a truly great, significant literature not below the level of such peaks as Shakespeare, Tolstoi and Dostoyevsky. This literature may also become the ideological and aesthetic ideal for peoples engaged in reconstructing their life on new principles. In other words, it will be a factor of social life, a vehicle for the shaping of minds. A number of aesthetic problems connected with the character of realism, the use to be made of the classical heritage and so forth will arise. But they are of secondary importance. The main thing is what literature itself will bring into the future, say in the next

273

two or three hundred years, and how essential a factor it will be in men's intellectual and emotional world.

Secondly, what I have said above about the development of technical communication and the triumph of information, in terms of the whole world will not be as visualised by some of the authors in the literary supplements of *Times* or by Penclub members.

After all, our main worry today is not that the masses are over-sated with literature but, on the contrary, that they should be given access to it. In this respect a great deal could be drawn from Soviet experience. The extraordinary keenness on amateur art activity-music, drama and literary circles—and the fact that the country's more than 400,000 public libraries have their hands full, are proof of the Soviet people's avid interest in both art and science. The radio and television do not make books redundant, but rather—as Soviet experience has shown once again—prompt listeners and viewers to reflect more deeply on the book they have heard excerpts from or seen a screen version of.

Television is a new form of art. There is no doubt that it will develop in the future in forms that would probably appear inconceivable to us today. There is also no doubt that TV will absorb a part of the writers who could only have expressed themselves in books before. But surely this does not mean, as Renan saw it, that there will be no room for literature—the most impressive product of a man's preoccupied reflection on the surrounding world in artistic images—in the future.

The Soviet experience shows that the masses are increasingly drawn to literature. There is no ebb. Someone may say, of course, that we are only at the initial stage of this process and that the people who read books so enthusiastically are the ones who were denied the chance before. That's true enough. Long before the Revolution Lenin wrote that Russia did not know her Lev Tolstoi and it took a revolution for the whole country to become acquainted with him. People are now discovering riches to which they had no access in tsarist Russia. This applies to the non-Russian republics especially. These people are really making their first discoveries of the classics the way to whom was barred for them before by mountains of illiteracy and oppression.

Speaking in London before the war Alexei Tolstoi said that being a writer was a hard job because he had hundreds of thousands of readers constantly assaulting him. At the conference of cinema producers in 1939 he said: "Take a look at the library records. See whose books are most widely read in the Soviet Union. Pushkin's. Does this not speak of excellent taste? A few years ago I saw *Oedipus* staged in the open-air for an audience of several thousand

Leningrad workers. What do they play in the provinces, the backwoods so to say, the collective-farm theatres and the drama circles? They play the classics and they are eagerly awaiting a truly popular Soviet play. . . . The land has been ploughed, the seeds have been sown, they have now sprouted and are ready to flower."

Yes indeed, Soviet experience shows that literature is going to flower on the soil upturned by the communist revolution.

PROGRESS PUBLISHERS HAVE RECENTLY PUT OUT
THE FOLLOWING BOOKS:

**LENIN PRIZE WINNERS—MASTERS OF SOVIET ART. STAGE
AND SCREEN** (Collection)

The whole world is familiar with these names:
Alexander Dovzhenko, Roman Karmen, Sergei Bon-
darchuk, Grigory Chukhrai, Georgi Tovstonogov,
Yuri Zavadsky, Grigory Kozintsev, Innokenty Smok-
tunovsky, Galina Ulanova and Maya Plisetskaya.

The recollections, articles and stories collected in
this volume will further the readers' acquaintance
with these celebrities, and tell them about the work
on the films **Land, The Ballad of a Soldier, War and
Peace, Hamlet,** and the stage productions of **The
Masquerade** and **An Optimistic Tragedy.** Actors
Maxim Shtraukh and Boris Smirnov, who have most
successfully rendered the image of Lenin on the
stage and the screen, speak of their work.

Cloth 14 × 17 cm 372 pp

LENIN PRIZE WINNERS—MASTERS OF SOVIET ART. SCULPTURE AND PAINTING (Collection)

This book will give the reader a general idea of the trends in Soviet sculpture and painting, and the creative careers of such well-known masters as V. Favorsky, A. Deineka, P. Korin, B. Prorokov and others. Their meetings with Sergei Konenkov and Martiros Saryan are described by writers Ilya Ehrenburg, Marietta Shaginyan and Natalya Konchalovskaya.

Readers will be interested to learn all about the creation of such famous monuments as the one to Pushkin in Leningrad (sculptor M. Anikushin), to Karl Marx in Moscow (sculptor L. Kerbel), to Mayakovsky, also in Moscow (sculptor A. Kibalnikov), and to the victims of fascism in the Lithuanian village Pirciupís (sculptor G. Jokubanis).

Cloth 14 × 17 cm 240 pp.

The books are lavishly illustrated.

REQUEST TO READERS

Progress Publishers would be glad to have your opinion of this book, its translation and design and any suggestions you may have for future publications.

Please send your comments to 21, Zubovsky Boulevard, Moscow, U.S.S.R.